AN ILLUSTRATED
CULTURAL HISTORY OF ENGLAND

AN ILLUSTRATED

CULTURAL HISTORY OF ENGLAND

F. E. HALLIDAY

with 374 plates

CRESCENT BOOKS · NEW YORK

TO PRIAULX RAINIER

This edition is published by Crescent Books, a division of Crown Publishers, Inc., by arrangement with Thames and Hudson Ltd.
a b c d e f g h
CRESCENT 1981 EDITION

Printed and bound in Great Britain

Library of Congress Catalog Card Number: 81-39

Contents

Anybody who attempts to write even a short account of such a vast subject as a Cultural History of England must be indebted to innumerable books. Among those that I have found most helpful are: *The Pelican History of Art*; *The Oxford History of English Art*; Eric Blom, *Music in England*, 1947; William Gaunt, *A Concise History of English Painting*, 1964; Peter Kidson and Peter Murray, *A History of English Architecture*, 1962; Herbert Read, *A Concise History of Modern Sculpture*, 1964; Stuart Piggott and Glyn E. Daniel, *A Picture Book of Ancient British Art*, 1951; O. E. Saunders, *English Art in the Middle Ages*, 1932; Percy A. Scholes, *The Oxford Companion to Music*, 1947; J. M. C. Toynbee, *Art in Britain under the Romans*, 1964; G. M. Trevelyan, *English Social History*, 1942.

Preface

Culture is a concept too elusive to be pinned down by the lexicographer, and has never been, perhaps never can be, definitively defined. For Matthew Arnold it was 'The acquainting ourselves with the best that has been known and said in the world', a characteristically English literary interpretation that ignores, apparently, the world of music and the visual arts. Arnold was an Oxford man, and the *Oxford English Dictionary* echoes him: 'The intellectual side of civilization.' My copy of the American *Webster* is more catholic: 'The characteristic attainments of a people', which suggests that a cultural history of England should include Parliamentary democracy, cricket, and fish and chips: that cultural history is much the same thing as social history.

There are three main branches of history. Best known, because the only one normally taught in schools, is political history, largely a record of man's destructive activities, or, as Gibbon put it, 'little more than the register of the crimes, follies and misfortunes of mankind'. Then, there is economic history, an account of man's constructive activities, his discoveries and inventions, and organization for the production of useful commodities. Social history is also much concerned with these things, and the constructive use of material goods, for social conditions are mainly determined by economic conditions.

In the Introduction to his *English Social History*, G.M. Trevelyan defined the scope of social history as 'the daily life of the inhabitants of the land in past ages: this includes the human as well as the economic relation of different classes to one another, the character of family and household life, the conditions of labour and of leisure, the attitude of man to nature'. All these, but in addition, 'the culture of each age as it arose out of these general conditions of life, and took ever changing forms in religion, literature and music, architecture, learning and thought'. Here are other and higher activities of man, more than merely constructive, the truly creative: for these are the self-begotten issue of his spirit, serving little or no material purpose, but ministering to his spiritual needs.

It is in this sense that I understand culture: as the most creative achievements of man, and the cultural history of a people is their social history with a difference, a quite different emphasis; for it is little concerned with their 'general conditions of life', but is almost a spiritual odyssey, a history of their art and thought, with some account of the forces, political, religious, economic, and social, that have determined or modified them.

This book, therefore, is both a variation on the theme of my *Five Arts*, and the complement of my *Concise History of England*, a political history in which I tried to emphasize the creative activities of man, and in the Preface wrote: '. . . man is essentially creative, or he would not be here, and his destructive follies are merely aberrations in the grand design of his evolution. His highest activities . . . are all a creation of order, and . . . by giving a proper emphasis to man's creative achievements and potentialities, history can help to hasten the process.' In this age of anxiety, violence, disorder, and threatened destruction, a history devoted to England's creative achievements, as opposed to its crimes and follies, is not irrelevant.

St Ives
Cornwall
1966

F.E.H.

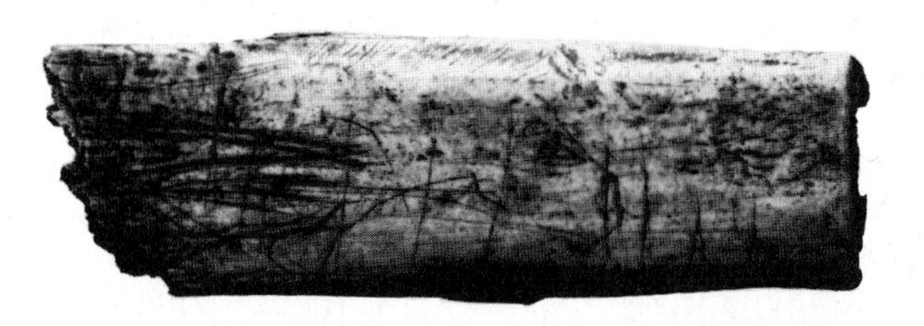

1 *Prehistoric Beginnings*

Some three-quarters of a million years ago primitive man reached north-west Europe, and for nearly three-quarters of a million years countless generations of these slow-witted, shambling creatures spent their lives, like the lower animals, gathering food and hunting, their greatest creative achievement being the stone tools and weapons that they made to help them in their struggle for existence. Then, about forty thousand years ago, during the last phase of the Ice Age, a new stock appeared, men not unlike ourselves, the big-brained nimble hunters of the final period of the Old Stone Age.

It is with these new men of Aurignacian and Magdalenian times that the history of art begins. The cold winds blowing off the ice-cap drove them to seek shelter in caves, and on their walls the hunters of southern France and northern Spain splendidly portrayed the animals they hoped to kill: the mammoth, bison, deer, and horses that roamed the steppeland to which Europe had been reduced. The primary purpose of their paintings was magical, as was that of the small figures that they carved and modelled, or engraved on stone and bone, but many of them are also records of an artist's spiritual experience.

Southern France was a favoured region in comparison with Britain, and it may be that the struggle for existence in its arctic climate exhausted the energies of these northern hunters and withered their artistic impulse. Although for innumerable centuries they inhabited caves, from Kent's Cavern in Devon to the north of Yorkshire, they left no graphic records on their walls, and the only remains of their art are a few engravings on bone, such as those of a horse's head and a masked man engaged in some magic ritual, found at Creswell Crags in Derbyshire. They are poor things compared to the work of the artists of Lascaux and Altamira, yet the line is sure and precise, and they are among the first works of art to be produced in Britain, some fifteen thousand years ago.

The story of man's early evolution as an artist is of necessity confined to the graphic arts and sculpture, for these were the only enduring forms of self-expression within his capacity. Moreover, they are basically the simplest, and the complexities of the other arts were beyond him. Dance and song of a sort there must have been, but it would be noise rather than music; he must have invented a mythology, but his tales of another world of gods and spirits, even if he had been able to record them, would be scarcely literature; so too, he must have had buildings of a sort, rude huts and shelters, but nothing that could be

Carving from the tomb at New Grange, Ireland, *c.* 1800 BC.

called architecture. And even this great age of painting, which for vigour and economy of execution has never been surpassed, came to an end twelve thousand years ago.

There followed the long barren centuries of Mesolithic times until, shortly before 2000 BC, men of the New Stone Age, bringing a Mediterranean tradition, arrived in Britain, and with them begins the real history of art in these islands. They were the builders of the great stone tombs which they covered with a mound of earth, long since washed away to reveal the huge uprights that form the walls of the chamber, and the great capstone that covers it. These tombs have some pretence to architecture, and some of the rather later chambered tombs in Ireland, of which the best known is New Grange, have elaborate designs carved on their stones, notably spirals and circles. But the noblest monument of the Neolithic and succeeding Early Bronze Age is Stonehenge.

Its construction covered four centuries, approximately 1800–1400 BC, for it was constantly altered and added to, and nowhere else is there anything like it: an outer circle of stones nearly fourteen feet high, pillars that support a continuous lintel, and within it a horseshoe of ten even huger stones, set in pairs, each pair with its separate lintel. An inner circle and inner horseshoe of smaller free-standing bluestones repeat the pattern of the major members. These great blocks of sandstone, or sarsens, some of them weighing fifty tons, were dragged more than twenty miles from the chalk downs, and the bluestones were somehow transported from the mountains of West Wales. They are not merely natural blocks of approximately the right size and shape, but each was carefully dressed to fit it for its function, and the ripples of the tooling, where they remain, are the most delicate detail of the building. Then, the uprights taper and curve towards the top, where tenons fit into the mortices of the lintels, which are carved to form an arc of the great circle. Moreover, the sides of the lintels of the horseshoe trilithons slope slightly outwards to correct the illusion of recession, the kind of refinement that makes the perfection of the Parthenon. These subtleties, indeed, suggest the influence of Greece of Mycenean times, as do the recently discovered carvings of bronze axeheads and a dagger on one of the stones.

Before it fell into ruin Stonehenge must have had much of the grandeur of an Egyptian temple, which, despite its circular shape, in some ways it resembles, and that it was a temple there can be little doubt. Surrounded by a ditch and bank, it stood, as it were, upon a plinth, complete, classical in its isolation, and Neolithic worshippers on its perimeter would watch the procession of priests about the ambulatory, and the celebration of mysteries within the sanctuary of the great trilithons. It would be not unlike watching the performance of a play, and perhaps Stonehenge is the prototype of the 'rounds' in which medieval miracle plays were presented, and ultimately of the 'wooden O' for which Shakespeare wrote.

Stonehenge, on Salisbury Plain. A unique temple of *c.* 1800–1400 BC. Unlike a fort, a 'henge' had a ditch inside, not outside, its surrounding bank.

◀ *(Left)* The first British pottery. Early Bronze Age beakers, *c.* 1700 BC.

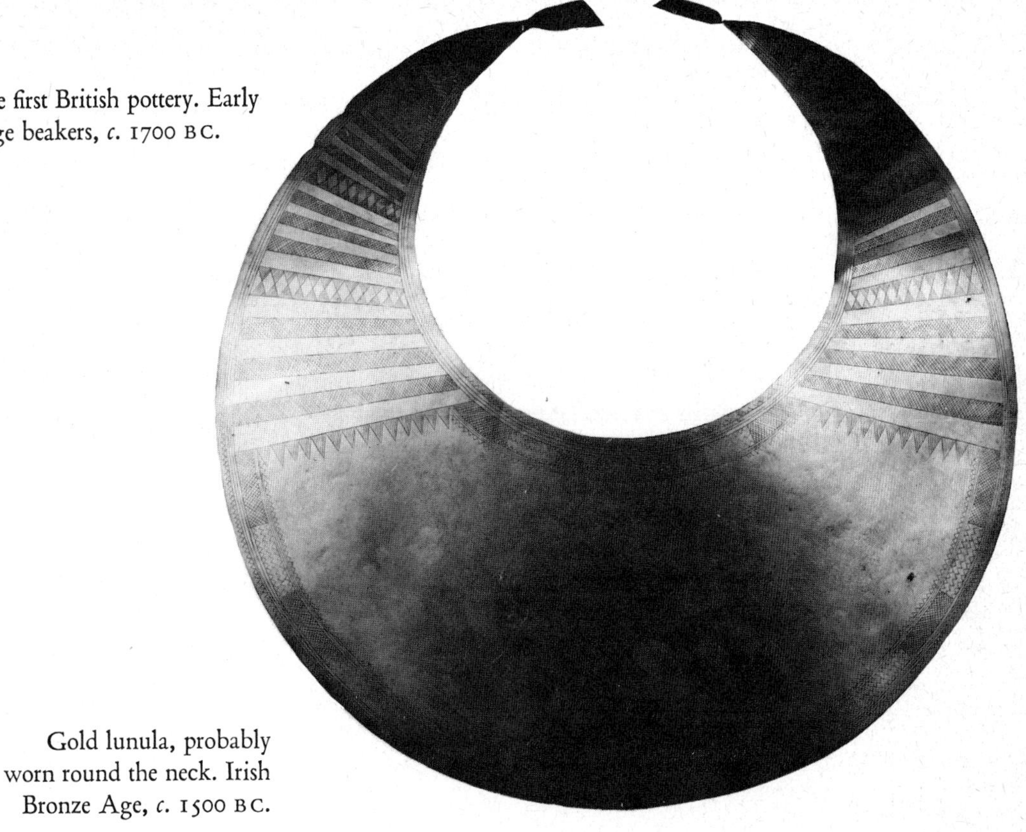

Gold lunula, probably worn round the neck. Irish Bronze Age, *c.* 1500 BC.

The Neolithic immigration involved a momentous agricultural and industrial revolution, for these new men were not nomadic hunters like the natives, but farmers who settled in villages and practised the crafts of pottery and metalworking. The period of the building of Stonehenge, therefore, is that of the making of the first British pots: bowls, drinking-mugs, beakers, the last characteristically decorated with bands of lozenges and chevrons. A similar design was engraved on the jet bead necklaces of the period, and on the delicate gold *lunulae*, or neck ornaments, beaten almost paper-fine to spread the precious metal into the same crescent-like shape, for gold was scarce and its source virtually confined to Ireland and Scotland. This rectilinear ornament seems to have come from Central Europe with the Beaker Folk, and is in strong contrast to the spiral designs brought from the Mediterranean by the megalith builders. A combination of the two traditions is found on the strange little chalk cylinders from Yorkshire, one of which has a concentric horseshoe pattern that resembles the round eyes and face of an owl. A few wooden figures of men, some of them four or five feet high and probably of the sixth century BC, have survived, but the art of the Bronze Age people was essentially abstract and ornamental, unlike the naturalistic painting and sculpture of their remote ancestors, the Palaeolithic hunters.

Top of small chalk cylinder, possibly an idol, *c.* 1500 BC.

A new era began when the La Tène Celts invaded Britain in the fifth century BC and, armed with iron swords against which the soft bronze weapons of the natives were useless, established themselves as a feudal aristocracy. Iron, however, although it revolutionized warfare and industry, is less beautiful than gold and bronze, and for ornaments these were the metals they mainly demanded of their craftsmen. It was an age of domestic squalor and barbaric splendour, for these Celtic warriors cared little for their homes and lavished their wealth on personal adornment: bronze scabbards, helmets, and shields, necklaces of twisted gold, bronze mirrors for their women, bronze masks and trappings for their horses. They enriched the geometric design of the Bronze Age with new motifs derived from Italy, in particular the tendril and anthemion, the formalized honeysuckle ornament of classical Greece, and developed a flowing curvilinear form that has the coiled energy of a spring.

There were two main schools of Celtic craftsmen. In north-east England their work was generally repoussé bronze, as in the splendid horse-masks with intricate design of plant-like forms, and more stylized and symmetrical shields, a fashion that was carried into Ireland, where it was magnificently applied to gold ornaments. The characteristic work of the south-west is best seen in the engraving of their bronze mirrors, the finest of which are those found at Desborough and Birdlip. Both are variations on the theme of three, a favourite motif, and the circular back of the Birdlip mirror is a series of circles within circles, three within one, and again three within one, each flowing into the others as the labyrinthine line expands into floral scrolls of hatched basket-work design.

Engraved back of Celtic bronze mirror, from Birdlip in the Cotswolds. The front was polished bronze. First century AD.

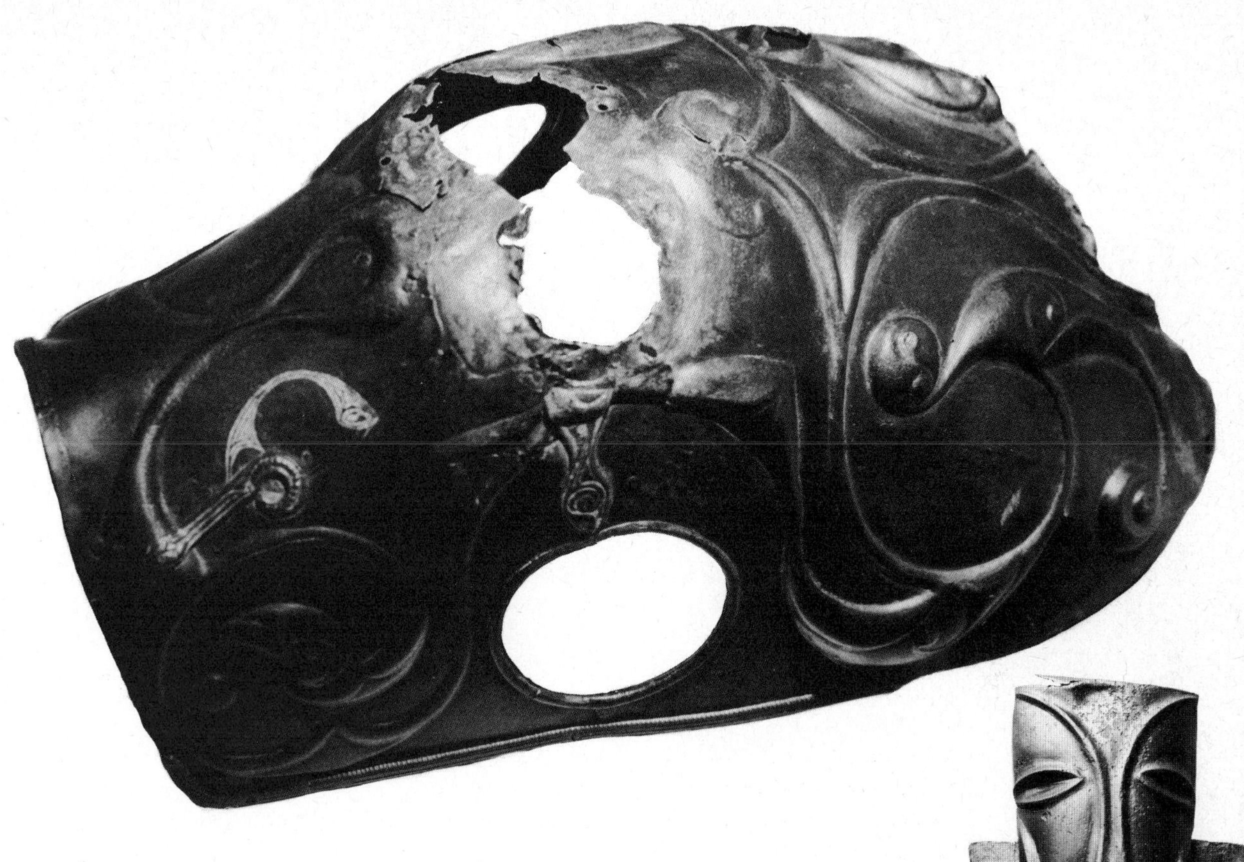

Repoussé bronze from northern Britain:
(*Above*) Celtic horse mask, *c.* 200 BC, found at Torrs in southern Scotland.
(*Right*) Stylized horse's head from north Yorkshire. First century AD.

These Celtic craftsmen were not interested in realism. Their art, like that of the Bronze Age, was essentially an abstract one, dependent on the beauty of its line, but with the Roman occupation of France in the first century BC, and the peaceful penetration of England by Roman merchants, classical naturalism inevitably had its effect, particularly on the newly arrived Belgic tribes of the south-east. Yet, although the Britons began to make small figures of animals, these were characteristically stylized to form a pattern: a horse's head was simplified into little more than a flowing linear design in repoussé bronze, while on a vastly larger scale the White Horse cut in the turf of the chalk downs at Uffington is an attenuated figure reduced to a few light springing lines. The human heads on their coins are more realistic, but even here the hair becomes a wave-like pattern that bears little resemblance to the naturalism of its Roman original.

Celtic gold coin.
First century BC.

Julius Caesar described the Britons as long-haired, woad-stained, blue-bodied barbarians, and this unflattering picture is still the popularly accepted one. But Caesar was in Britain for only a few days, and even if he saw any of its art probably dismissed it as equally barbaric, so very different from the realism and grandeur to which he was accustomed in Rome.

The White Horse of Uffington, Berkshire: possibly a British tribal emblem of the first century BC.

2 Roman Britain 50–450

It is difficult to realize, so little of its work remains, that from the middle of the first century for almost four hundred years, nearly a fifth of our recorded history, Britain was a province of the Roman Empire. England rather than Britain, however, for the Romans did not occupy Scotland or invade Ireland, while Wales and Cornwall were too remote and wild for civilian settlement, and in these northern and western parts the old Celtic way of life went on much as before.

The southern Celts were soon introduced to the civilization and art of Rome, and, if we exclude Stonehenge, Avebury, and the monuments of the megalith builders, architecture for the first time modified the appearance of England. The Britons had their wooden huts and villages, but now they saw the erection of stone and brick buildings that were designed not only for their function but also for their appearance. In the north the architecture was primarily military: Hadrian's Wall from Tyne to Solway was built to contain the Celts of Scotland, and York founded as a fortress and headquarters of a legion. Chester and Caerleon, commanding the north and south of the Welsh border, were also legionary fortresses, and it was mainly in the Midlands and south that towns were built as mercantile and residential centres.

London, owing to its position on the Thames, soon became the commercial capital and one of the biggest towns in western Europe, its walls enclosing an area of three hundred and twenty-five acres. Colchester, however, was chosen as the centre of Emperor worship, and within a few years a temple of Claudius was built, as well as a senate house and theatre. Verulamium (St Albans) also had its theatre, its market hall, and forum, and in its walls were four great gateways flanked by impressive semicircular towers. Bath was a small town, but architecturally one of the finest, for it contained the temple of the Celtic goddess, Sulis-Minerva, and curative baths with a European reputation, the largest of them, and no doubt the smaller ones as well, flanked by handsome colonnades. Cirencester and Wroxeter were large towns of some two hundred acres, but most of the others, Leicester, Silchester, and Winchester, for example, were only half the size, with a population, perhaps, of four or five thousand.

The towns were small because the Britons were countrymen and did not take easily to urban life, and, though landowners might also have their town-houses – there were twenty-five very big houses in Silchester – they generally preferred to live most of the year in their farmhouses, or villas as they came to be called. They soon adopted the Roman style of building, adding new rooms, above all a dining-room and bath-house, signs of social status, and a front corridor to connect them. This might then expand, as at Northleigh Villa in Oxfordshire, into a great house with four wings surrounding a courtyard, though, as little remains of these villas but foundations, it is easy to exaggerate their grandeur, for most of the rooms were on the ground floor, and superstructures might have been half-timber. The vast mansion at Fishbourne, near Chichester, is exceptional: begun about thirty years after the Roman occupation, it was five hundred feet square, and the four wings enclosing the courtyard had nearly a hundred rooms, almost all of them with mosaic floors.

And so Roman architecture came to Britain: country-house and town-house, senate house and forum, temples, theatres, amphitheatres, and public baths, and with them the classical form and detail of column and colonnade, architrave, pediment, and arch. Then, these new Romano-British public buildings and private houses were adorned with carvings and other works of art that were a strange contrast to native Celtic forms.

All art is a creation of harmony, of order out of confusion, the more or less conscious selection and co-ordination of the chaotic product of the imagination.

Classical architecture comes to Britain. The Great Roman Bath at Aquae Sulis (Bath). The colonnade is restored, but the floor of the bath is still covered with the original Roman lead from the Mendip Hills.

Roman realism: lifesize bronze head of the Emperor Claudius, first century AD. The eyes were probably made of enamel.

The degree to which the conscious mind, or reason, modifies the imagination may vary enormously, yet most works of art and periods of artistic production can be assigned with some confidence to one or other of the two great schools, classical or romantic, according to the extent of this modification. Thus, the ideals of classical art are order, restraint, symmetry, balance, simplicity, clarity, regularity, the parts subordinated to the whole; romantic art is less rational and more emotional, varied, irregular, mysterious, complex, restless, given to excess, impatient of rules and restraint, and as much interested in the parts as in the whole. Classical art tends to be that of a long-established and settled urban civilization, romantic of an age of transition; the one has the virtue of age, serenity, which, however, may decline into pedantry and senility; the other the vigour and elasticity of youth, which may become merely a silly eccentricity. Volume and horizontal form are characteristic of classical art; line and vertical form of romantic. One has the solidity of earth, the other the mercurial properties of air, fire, and water. The one is a record of the outer world, the other of the inner world of man; the one may be symbolized by the dome, the other by the spire.

The cave paintings of the Palaeolithic hunters were romantic, and so was the art of the Britons, most of whom were now confronted with a kind of art that was quite foreign to their tradition. Not only was Roman art classical, it was also representational, and one wonders what the Britons thought of the realistic bronze statue of Claudius set up, probably, in the Colchester forum, or the larger than life figure of Hadrian in London. But these at least were bronze, the favourite metal of the Celts, and even more foreign to their eyes would be the marble portrait busts that graced the public buildings and houses of the invaders, for to the Britons sculpture in stone was an unknown art.

It is all the more interesting, therefore, to see what they made of the new medium, and a fine example is the limestone head from Gloucester, carved by a British sculptor soon after the Roman occupation. The forehead might be Roman, but not the long melancholy face, all the features of which are seized upon to form a pattern: the shape of the prominent, serrated locks of hair is repeated in the great bulging eyes and narrow nose, the thin mouth repeats the line of the brows, their light and shade, and the ears make a characteristic curvilinear design. A more accomplished work of art is a stone head of the British god Antenociticus, found in his temple at Benwell, Northumberland. Here the features are less stylized, though the eyes are emphasized by the double scroll of the lids, and the hair is a snake-like pattern of locks, writhing symmetrically about the heavy fringe that falls over the forehead. The elusive, enigmatic smile is something very different from the standard expressionless portraits of Imperial Rome, and this is a splendid example of the fusion of romantic and classical, a lively Celtic variation on an uninspired Roman theme.

Most famous of all British carvings of the Roman period, however, is the stone relief of Medusa that formed the central feature of the pediment on the temple of Sulis-Minerva at Bath. Although Medusa was a woman, the head is that of a man with locks of hair intertwined with snakes that radiate wildly from the face like flames in a formalized picture of the sun. The huge glaring

British variations on a Roman theme, *c.* AD 200.
(*Left*) Stone head of a man, from Gloucester.
(*Below*) Stone head of a god, from Northumberland.

A British sculptor's interpretation of a classical legend. The head of Medusa on the pediment of the temple of Sulis-Minerva, Bath.

eyes, their pupils deeply drilled, have an almost hypnotic power beneath the inverted curves of the brows and patterned wrinkles of the forehead. The tips of the gigantic ears stand out like handles, and above them can be seen the delicately carved pattern of the wing feathers. Apparently the story of Medusa had deeply impressed the Celtic sculptor, and his carving is his interpretation of the Gorgon's petrifying ferocity.

As most of the walls of Romano-British buildings were long ago destroyed, little remains of their fresco-paintings, though sufficient to reveal something of the elegance of life in those times. Fragments of hundreds of square feet of painted wall plaster have recently been found at Fishbourne, and at Verulamium a few pieces of the paintings have survived. On one wall was a rather dull architectural design of a colonnade and marbled panels, on another a yellow frieze and floral scroll, within which were pheasants, a bird brought to Britain, apparently, by the Romans. There was another bird painting on one of the ceilings, of yellow doves on a purple ground, set in a complex geometrical design. These are all of the second century, and almost certainly the work of foreign artists.

So too were the mosaics with which the Romans and wealthier Britons covered their floors, for this to the native Celts was the strangest art of all. Greek in origin, it was developed by the Romans, who set small cubes of coloured stone in cement to form geometrical or more complex realistic designs.

These were the property of the firm that laid the pavement, though they might be modified to suit a client, and colours varied, for they normally used the stone of the region in which they worked, and as England is particularly rich in the variety of its stone they had a wide range of colours: white and black, and innumerable shades of grey, blue, red, yellow, and brown. As the Britons were unaccustomed to representational art, we should expect many of the early pavements to be abstract patterns, as were some of the very early ones at Fish-bourne, either black and white or polychrome geometrical designs. These abstract patterns, reminiscent of woven rugs, from which mosaics originally derived, were popular throughout the Roman occupation; the long pavement at Withington Villa near Cirencester, for example, a polychrome design of geometrical figures, is probably of the late fourth century. A simple form of figured design that also remained popular, partly because it was associated with bathrooms, was one of fishes and sea-gods, such as the shells and dolphins and head of Oceanus at Verulamium.

As the British gentry became more sophisticated and educated in Roman art and literature, they demanded more complex and vivid figured mosaics for their villas. One of the most ambitious of these is a brightly coloured pavement from Low Ham in Somerset, illustrating episodes from the *Aeneid*. In one panel is the arrival of the Trojan fleet at Carthage, represented by three ships, not unlike those in the Bayeux Tapestry. Then there are scenes depicting Venus, the match-maker, introducing the lovers, the famous hunt in Book IV, and finally Aeneas embracing a naked Dido in the cave. It does not follow that the British grandee who commissioned the pavement was a devotee of Virgil, for the design was probably a stock one from a North African pattern-book, but it is interesting as showing some acquaintance with classical mythology, and that by the fourth century (and even earlier) local craftsmen were trying their hand at mosaics, for the work is insufficiently accomplished to be that of a foreign specialist. How crude was some of the work of British craftsmen who imitated Roman models may be illustrated by the pavement at Rudston in the East Riding of Yorkshire. Yet, although Venus in the central medallion is a grotesquely distorted figure, her wildly waving hair and the obvious delight taken in the pattern of circles and semicircles show that the Celtic feeling for vigorous abstract design was by no means dead in the fourth century.

Virgil in a British villa: a mosaic pavement of *c.* AD 350.
(*Above left*) The Hunting Scene in the *Aeneid*.
(*Above right*) Dido and Aeneas.

A British vision of the Roman Venus. Part of a fourth-century Yorkshire mosaic pavement.

This was the century in which Constantine made Christianity the official religion of the Empire. At York in 306 he was proclaimed Augustus by the army, and at York was carved, though not by a Briton, the colossal stone head that was set up in one of the public buildings of the legionary fortress. A few years later came his conversion, when he adopted the sacred Chi-Rho monogram (☧) as his device. Some of the Britons accepted the new religion, and at Silchester are the remains of a fourth-century church. It was built in the form of a Roman basilica, or hall of justice, with a nave thirty feet long, flanked by aisles ending in rudimentary transepts, a porch across the east end, and at the west end of the nave an apse with a mosaic panel in white, black, and red. This is the earliest church to be found in Britain, but other relics of Romano-British Christianity are the recently discovered silver spoon with a Chi-Rho monogram near Canterbury, and the wall-paintings at the neighbouring Lullingstone Villa. These are fragmentary, but the head of a red-haired young man has been preserved, presumably a Celt and a Christian, for there are also remains of two large Chi-Rho monograms painted in red on a white background.

Christianity was also responsible for the first extant work to be written by a native of Britain, the Latin Commentary on St Paul's Epistles of the Irish monk and heretic, Pelagius. He wrote at the end of the fourth century, when the heathen English were raiding the east coast of Britain, and the Britons were burying their treasures, among them the hoard of silver at Mildenhall, Suffolk, with the great round dish, two feet across, and its head of Oceanus, sprouting flaming hair, dolphins, and seaweed, and reminiscent of the Bath Medusa. At the beginning of the fifth century the Roman garrisons withdrew, and the long interlude of classical art was over.

Silver spoon with the Christian Chi-Rho symbol.

Part of the buried Mildenhall Treasure of silver dishes, bowls and spoons. The work is probably Roman, not British.

3 The Anglo-Saxons 450–1066

By the beginning of the sixth century England must have looked very much as it did five hundred years before. The towns were down, temples and theatres in ruin, the statues fallen, columns broken, and the rubble of villas, pavements, frescoes, pottery, and glass lay under the roots of the returning forest. The heathen Angles and Saxons, the English, had destroyed Romano-British civilization, and little or nothing remained but the indestructible roads, the Latin language, and British Christianity.

It was one of these British Christians, St Patrick, who converted the Irish, whose monasteries, such as Kells and Durrow, became centres of light and learning in the European darkness that followed the eclipse of the Roman Empire. Their monks proved indefatigable missionaries: in 563 St Columba founded a monastery on the island of Iona, off the west coast of Scotland, and at the same time innumerable 'saints' crossed into the other Celtic countries of Wales and Cornwall. There the natives cherished the legends and sang the exploits of the heroic British leader who defended the Christian west against the pagan English. He is first mentioned briefly as Ambrosius Aurelianus by Gildas, a sixth-century monk and the first British historian, but two centuries later the Welsh historian Nennius called him Arthur, victor of twelve great battles against the Saxons.

These histories were written in Latin, a language unknown to the early English invaders, but they also had their heroes, and in their chieftains' halls minstrels celebrated the feats of warriors in the lands they had recently left, above all the adventures of Beowulf. There was adventure enough. Young Beowulf sails to Denmark to rid King Hrothgar of a monster, Grendel, who nightly enters his hall and slaughters his subjects. He wrestles with Grendel and tears off his arm, though the monster escapes to his den in a mere, where his blood makes the water boil as he dies. But the next night another noble is carried off, this time by Grendel's mother. Beowulf follows her to the mere, plunges in, and after a great fight cuts off her head, as well as Grendel's, before his sword melts in their venomous blood. Full of honour he returns to his native land, of which he becomes king, and reigns for fifty years. But the country is ravaged by a dragon, whose fiery breath consumes the wooden houses of his people. In a last great battle the old hero kills the dragon, but is himself mortally wounded:

Ne mæg ic her leng wesan.
Hatað heaðomære hlæw gewyrcean,
beorhtne æfter bæle æt brimes nosan;
se scel to gemyndum minum leodum
heah hlifian on Hrones næsse,
þaet hit sæliðend syððan hatan
Biowulfes biorh, ða ðe brentingas
ofer floda genipu feorran drifað.

'I can stay here no longer. Bid the warriors build a great barrow after burning my body on a cliff by the sea. As a memorial to my people it shall stand high on Hrones Ness, so that sailors who drive their tall ships from afar through the mists of the sea shall call it Beowulf's Barrow.' *Beowulf* is the poem of a primitive people, but it has the primitive virtues of vigour and simplicity, and is in every way on an epic scale. It is indeed the first great poem in the English language, or in any modern language, and with it English literature may be said to begin. The manuscript of *Beowulf* was written in about the year 1000, but in its first form, when recounted by bards some four centuries earlier, the language would be even more incomprehensible to modern ears. Unqualified by the music of long Latin vowels, Old English, harsh, guttural, costive with consonants, was by nature alliterative. Instead of rhyme or assonance, therefore, poets used the convention of alliteration and the repetition of consonants; the normal line of Saxon verse is one in which there are four stresses, two in the first half, on words beginning with the same consonant, and two in the second, with a repetition of the alliteration.

The consonant has the plucked quality of lute and virginal, the vowel, the long vowel at least, the orotundity of the organ; or in terms of graphic art, the consonant has the two-dimensional quality of line drawing, the vowel the three-dimensional quality of chiaroscuro; the one is essentially romantic, the other classical. As the English language has always been rich in consonants, it may be no accident that much of its greatest music has been written for stringed instruments, that most of its greatest poetry is romantic, that its painting is characteristically linear, and even its sculpture and architecture almost as much concerned with line as with volume.

At the end of the sixth century, after a severance of nearly two hundred years from Roman influence, England was once again linked to the classical civilization of the Mediterranean. In 597 St Augustine landed in Kent and began the conversion of the English to Roman Christianity, and with him architecture, as distinct from building in wood, returned to England. At Canterbury he found the remains of two Romano-British churches, and one of these he rebuilt as the first cathedral of Canterbury. Like the old church at

Silchester, it was basilican in plan, with a nave flanked by two aisles and ending in an apse. He also built a new church for his monastery, but, instead of aisles divided from the nave by arcades carried on columns, were blank walls with an opening leading to a series of chambers on either side. This was the normal plan of early Kentish churches, Reculver, for example, adopted perhaps because English craftsmen were insufficiently skilled to make cylindrical pillars.

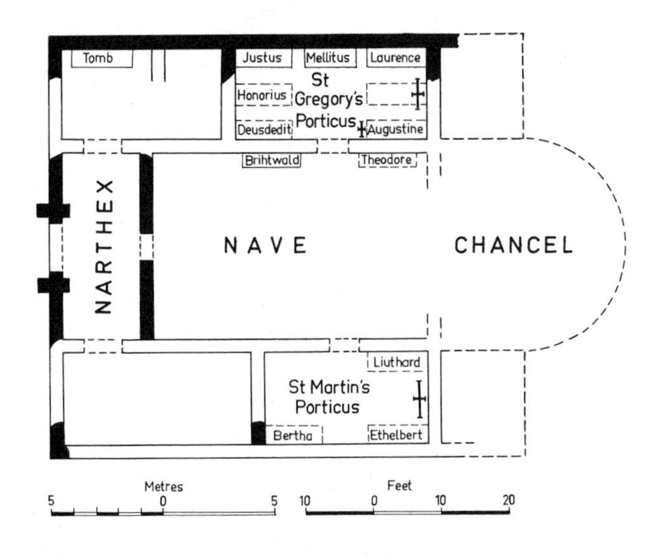

Two early Saxon churches with porticus and apse:
(*Left*) Plan of SS. Peter and Paul, Canterbury.
(*Below*) Foundations of Reculver, near Margate.

Roman Christianity was soon carried into the kingdom of Northumbria, but it was immediately followed by Celtic Christianity when, in 635, Aidan, a monk from Iona, established a monastery on Lindisfarne, or Holy Island, just south of the River Tweed. As Celtic Christianity had been for so long out of touch with Rome, it differed in detail from that recently reintroduced by Augustine, and when they met in Northumbria they inevitably came into conflict. This was given visual expression in their architecture, for instead of the modified Roman basilican form of Kent, the first Northumbrian churches, as at Escomb in County Durham, were built in the austere Irish style of an unaisled nave with a simple rectangular chancel. When, however, Northumbria adopted the Roman form of Christianity after the Synod of Whitby in 664, Bishop Wilfrid of York built churches at Hexham, Ripon, and York, which appear to have had nave arcades and aisles in the basilican manner. Yet the monastic churches of Monkwearmouth and Jarrow, founded by Benedict Biscop in 674 and 682, had high, narrow, unaisled naves leading into a small square-ended chancel.

Half-way between these southern and northern groups is Brixworth in Northamptonshire, the only Early Saxon church of any size to have survived. Nearly a hundred feet long, nave and choir were originally separated by an arcade, and at the east end an arch opened into a polygonal apse. The aisles have been destroyed, and the openings of the arcades walled in, but the four arches on each side remain, made of Roman tiles springing from stone piers. If the work is that of English masons, it was a remarkable achievement for so early a date.

The late seventh-century church at Brixworth, Northamptonshire: the finest example of Early Saxon architecture.

By this time, however, Northumbria could boast of even more remarkable achievements, for it was in this northern kingdom that English art first began to flourish. At the end of the seventh century Bede was a monk in the Monastery of Jarrow, collecting material for his great *History of the English Church and People*, which he finished in 731. As it was written in Latin, it cannot be claimed as a work of English literature, but it is the first English history, and one of the most valuable and delightful, for Bede generally managed to sift true history from legend, yet enlivened his story with anecdotes, preferably miraculous, and everywhere the goodness and compassion of the man shine through. To his book he also appended the first autobiography to be written by an Englishman: 'I was born on the lands of this monastery, and at the age of seven my family entrusted me to the reverend Abbot Benedict. . . . Since then I have spent all my life here, observing the discipline and singing the choir offices daily in church.' Here is the first, and tantalizingly brief, reference to English Church music.

Bede at work:
a twelfth-century miniature.

Although musical instruments of all kinds, stringed, wind, and percussion, are immemorially old, we know little about the music that was played and sung in Britain, or even in Europe, before the time of Bede. But dancing must be far older than musical instruments, performed to the rhythmical clapping of hands, and when dance came to be accompanied by music it too must have been rhythmical. Whether this early secular vocal and instrumental music had any form of harmony we do not know, though pictures of groups of people playing instruments of the same kind but different size, and therefore pitch, suggest that it had.

Early Church music, however, had neither harmony nor metrical beat, but was a measureless chanting by a number of voices in unison. This plainsong was introduced into England by St Augustine, but according to Bede it was nearly a hundred years before it spread to Northumbria, shortly before his own birth in 673, and it was Abbot John who taught him 'the chant for the liturgical year, as it was sung at St Peter's, Rome'.

One of the most charming of Bede's stories is that about Caedmon, at this time a cowherd in the Monastery of Whitby. He knew nothing of music or poetry, and when 'those present at a feast took it in turn to sing and entertain the company, he would get up from table and go home when he saw the harp approaching him'. On one of these occasions he went to the stable, where he fell asleep, and in a dream saw a man who said, 'Caedmon, sing me a song.' 'I cannot sing,' he replied. 'Nevertheless, you shall sing to me,' said the man: 'Sing about the Creation of all things.' So Caedmon, the ignorant cowherd, immediately began to sing about God and the creation of the world. It makes a good story, yet there is a poem *Genesis* of about this period, and it is just possible that this is Caedmon's. Bede added that 'others tried to compose religious poems in English, but none could compare with him, for he received his gift from God'. Yet so did Cynewulf, according to his own account in *Elene*, a poem that describes St Helena's finding of the Cross. Although we know nothing about Cynewulf, he is the only Saxon poet to whom we can confidently assign his work, for he signed his name in runic characters in three more religious poems, and may have been the author of others, perhaps of the dramatic and triumphant *Judith*.

Nearly all this Saxon art was inspired by Christianity, yet the most interesting and moving poetry is that of unknown writers who gave expression to their own feelings. Most of them have a similar philosophy, a common theme being regret for what time has taken away, yet, though life is hard, fatalism is tempered by courage and a determination to endure. Thus, when Deor is supplanted by a younger singer, he recalls the good times past, but also remembers how heroes like Weland endured affliction, and ends each verse with the refrain: 'Thæs ofereode, thisses swa mæg!': 'He overcame that, so may I this!' Then there is the love-song of the wife whose husband has been taken away from her, and she thinks of him in exile: 'My beloved endures much sorrow of heart, remembering too often a happier home.' The Wanderer, musing on the ruins of a great city, asks, 'Where is the horse gone? Where is the man?' yet knows that 'it is noble in a man to bind fast the casket of his soul, to hold firm his heart, whatever he may think'. The theme of *The Ruin* is similar: an unknown Saxon meditates on the Roman remains of Bath and its temple of Sulis-Minerva, long ago destroyed by his ancestors: 'There stood the stone courts, there the bath-halls, and the stream flowed in hot waves; but now the roof is broken, the walls are down, the towers fallen.' Nostalgia was to be the inspiration of much English poetry of later times, but there was no self-pity in these Saxons of the age of Bede.

The turn of the century, about the year 700, was the climax of this fine flowering of Northumbrian art, yet it was not entirely Saxon, for at Lindisfarne, an Irish foundation, the Celtic tradition still lingered. The greatest achievement of Irish Christian art was its illuminated manuscripts, religious books transcribed and painted by monks. Inspired by the curvilinear designs of Early Celtic metalwork, these monastic artists applied them to their pages, making

Abraham and Sarah in Lot's house. A tenth-century illustration of a verse paraphrase of Genesis, possibly Caedmon's. ▶

ƿam þe ƿurðiað þurh þe. lond buende. ealle on
fold. folc bearn freodo. 7 freond scipe. blisse min
ne. 7 bletsunge. on ƿoruldrice. ƿridende sceal. mæg
de ƿinne. monrim ƿeaxan. speda under swegle.
sunum 7 dohtrum. oð þæt from cyme. folde ƿeorðeð.
þeod lond monig. þine gefylled.

The Celtic love of pattern: St Matthew, from the Irish Book of Durrow (*left*) and Book of Kells (*centre*), seventh and eighth centuries. (*Right*) The beginning of St Matthew's Gospel in the Northumbrian Lindisfarne Gospels: 'Liber generationis . . .'

a coloured pattern of their texts and borders: a design composed of interwoven ribbons, spirals, knots, scrolls, trumpet shapes, and intricately entwined animals. These animals, however, are fantastic reptilian creatures of the imagination, details drawn to fit into the design, and when representing the human figure the Irish artists were again less interested in naturalism than in making a pattern.

The earliest of these Irish illuminated texts is the late-seventh-century Book of Durrow, the most famous the late-eighth-century Book of Kells, a copy of the Gospels from the monastery founded by St Columba, but equally famous is the earlier Northumbrian version of about the year 700, the Lindisfarne Gospels. The same Celtic motifs are here: spirals and scrolls, interlaced ribbons and letters strangely transforming themselves into lizards and birds, the same patterned background of red dots. The colours are soft and luminous, mainly red, blue, yellow, green, and purple, with here and there, though very rarely, a touch of gold. The Irish manuscripts have no gold, and its use at Lindisfarne shows a continental influence. Another is the drawing of the human figure.

It must be remembered that Roman art of the seventh century was very different from that of the period of the Roman occupation of Britain. The art that had then been brought to Britain was a development of that of classical and Hellenistic Greece, but after the removal of the Imperial capital to Constantinople (Byzantium) in the fourth century, it had been gradually orientalized, Western naturalism modified by Eastern conventions: all became more rigid and severe, more static and formal, and the young men of early Christian art were transformed into black-browed, black-bearded patriarchs. The influence of this classical-oriental Byzantine style, brought to Northumbria by supporters of Roman, as opposed to Celtic, Christianity, is apparent in the paintings of the Evangelists in the Lindisfarne Gospels. But although stylized, they are more natural, less concerned with pattern making than those in the Book of Kells, as can be seen by comparing the illustrations of St Matthew in the two manuscripts.

The Lindisfarne Gospels, however, are essentially Celtic, but the Northumbrian crosses set up at this time are the product of the Roman school encouraged by Bishop Wilfrid of York. The gracefully tapering shaft of one of these crosses still stands outside the church at Bewcastle, just north of the Roman Wall. Carved in relief on the front, one below the other, are the figures of St John the Baptist, Christ Triumphant, and St John the Evangelist. The other sides are carved with foliage designs, an adaptation of the Syrian vine-scroll motif, though these are separated by strips of Celtic interlacing ribbon ornament. The cross at Ruthwell, near Dumfries, is more purely continental in inspiration: both front and back are carved with scenes from the life of Christ, and down the sides runs the flowing vine-scroll, within which animals and birds are feeding on the grapes, Christian symbol of the source of life. There is a similar ornament in repoussé-work on the small silver bowl found at Ormside in Westmorland.

Little remains of this Northumbrian art, though enough to show that by the end of the seventh century the English were by no means the barbarians they had been before the coming of Christianity a hundred years before. The Danes were to this nascent English civilization what the English themselves had been to that of Roman Britain, heathen destroyers of what they did not understand. Their depredations covered most of the ninth century, and as a result we know little about the art of the Midland kingdom of Mercia, which wrested the supremacy from Northumbria, apart from the late-seventh-century treasure of the ship-burial at Sutton Hoo in Suffolk. Apparently this was a cenotaph celebrating some great noble or king, for there was no body buried in the long wooden ship, and the treasure was of regal splendour, among the objects being buckles of solid gold, golden clasps, and a purse-lid with cloisonné-work of garnets and glass, Byzantine silver bowls and spoons, an iron helmet and visor inlaid with bronze and silver wire, Frankish gold coins, a small harp, and a circular shield of Swedish pattern. Evidently these East Anglians had contacts with all Europe, from Scandinavia to the eastern Mediterranean.

Northumbrian art *c.* 700. The Ruthwell Cross.

Mercian art *c.* 700. Ornaments from the ship-burial at Sutton Hoo, Suffolk: gold clasps and a purse lid with cloisonné-work.

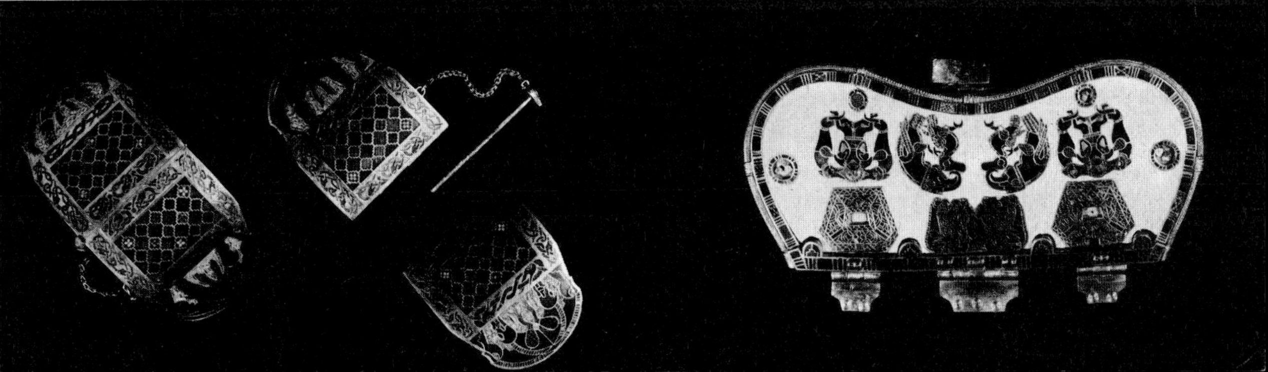

Wessex art: the ninth-century Alfred Jewel, found in Somerset.

The century from about 750 to 850 is one of the darkest periods of the Dark Ages in Britain, when the Danes put an end to the great age of Celtic art in Ireland, and only with the accession of Alfred as King of Wessex, the southern kingdom that succeeded Mercia in the leadership of England, does light begin to return. On the Continent, however, the early ninth century was the age of the Carolingian renaissance, the revival of art under Charlemagne, and it was only natural that the art of Wessex should draw inspiration from this source. This is shown in the Alfred Jewel, the inscription on which, 'Aelfred mec heht gewyrcan': 'Alfred had me made', suggests that it may be a portrait of the king himself, at least it is a miniature portrait of a man carrying what appear to be two sceptres. The jewel is made of gold and cloisonné enamel, an art that Byzantine craftsmen had brought to the Frankish Court: narrow strips of gold form the outlines of the design, and between these *cloisons* are the coloured glass pastes of the enamel, a light brown face and a green robe against a blue background.

According to Bishop Asser, who wrote a contemporary life of the great king, Alfred ordered the making of much gold- and silver-work, but of this little has survived, and the most important memorial of his reign is its literature; not so much original work, however, as translation, for it was a period of recovery and consolidation after the Danish destruction, and it is owing to its rendering into the West Saxon dialect that so much Northumbrian poetry has been preserved: the single precious manuscript of *Beowulf*, for example. Alfred gathered round him a number of scholars, some of them from the Continent, and with their help translated the Latin of Bede's *History* and Boëthius' *Consolations of Philosophy*. One feels that the liberal opinions of the sixth-century Roman statesman appealed particularly to Alfred, although he was a king: 'Ac tha ryhtæthelo bith on tha mode, næs on tham flæsce:' 'But true nobility is in the mind, and was never in the flesh,' as presumably they did to Chaucer, who was to translate the book five hundred years later. To history and philosophy Alfred added geography, enlivening Orosius' catalogue of the world's catastrophes with an account of contemporary exploration beyond the Arctic Circle; but most valuable of all was the inception of the Anglo-Saxon Chronicle, a historical register that was to cover the next two hundred and fifty years.

Alfred died in 900, and although the tenth century was the golden age of Saxon England, the first half was artistically barren, or perhaps most of its artistic activity went into the making of perishable embroideries, for which England was famous, like the vestments presented by Queen Alfleda to the Bishop of Winchester. With the accession of King Edgar in 958, however, another great period of Saxon art began. This was largely due to the monastic reformation brought about by Dunstan, Archbishop of Canterbury, and his followers, Ethelwold and Oswald, who introduced the strict Benedictine rule from the Continent, and in the last half of the century more than thirty

Saxon interior and exterior:
(*Above*) Deerhurst church: the tenth-century west wall (the aisle arcades are medieval).
(*Right*) Earls Barton: the tower. The 'long and short work' at the quoins, or corners, is characteristic.

monasteries were founded or refounded, including Malmesbury, Ely, and Peterborough. Yet, what remains of their building is curiously unprogressive. Deerhurst, for example, the biggest of these monastic churches to survive, might almost have been built three hundred years before; it had a long, narrow, and very high nave, and as there were no aisles, and therefore no arcades, there can have been little to see inside but a vast expanse of wall. The Saxons had not yet learned to think in terms of the architectural organization of space, nor even in terms of volume, sculpturally. They were builders rather than architects, and for them a wall was little more than a flat surface that could be decorated. Perhaps they painted the interior of Deerhurst; they certainly stuck on the exterior of Earls Barton church tower strips of masonry which look like, and have no more structural relevance than, matchsticks.

The emergence of sculpture. The Saxon Rood at Romsey Abbey, Hampshire.

Perhaps it is not altogether fair to say that the Saxons had not learned to think in terms of volume, sculpturally, for the Church frowned on sculpture as savouring of idolatry. Yet the few remaining examples of their stone-carving are merely reliefs, not sculptures in the round, though in the finest of them, the crucifix on the outside wall of Romsey Abbey, the figure of Christ has almost emerged from the stone, and much of its beauty lies in the shadows cast by the horizontally stretched arms and great hands, and by the vertical line of the body. Again, the ivory crucifixes of the period, however beautiful, are little more than two-dimensional, and the figures on the famous ivory crosier-head in the Victoria and Albert Museum are essentially decorative reliefs, details of a brilliantly conceived and executed design.

Most of this work came from the region of Winchester, where a school of art, similar to the earlier one of Wilfrid at York, flourished during the century after the appointment of Ethelwold as bishop in 963. The picture of King Edgar presenting the charter of the reorganized cathedral to Christ in 966 is the earliest extant illuminated manuscript of this school, and illustrates the English passion and genius for line, derived no doubt partly from contact with the Celts. The characteristic Winchester border is the English version of those in the Lindisfarne Gospels, and although there is a Byzantine formality in the figure of Christ, it makes an admirable contrast to the swirling lines of the lower angels and folds of the robes, while as a design it is beyond praise, the three figures at the bottom forming the base of a triangle of which Christ is the apex on which all the leading lines converge. The beautiful blue and gold *Benedictional of St Ethelwold*, although influenced by Carolingian conventions, is another example of the vitality and lightness, gaiety almost, of tenth-century Saxon illumination, though these things are best seen in the ink drawings of the Winchester *Liber Vitae*. One of these shows St Peter thrusting an enormous

The tenth-century Winchester School of Illumination: (*Left*) The Charter of King Edgar, 966. (*Right*) The Annunciation, from the *Benedictional of St Ethelwold*.

key into the ugly face of a devil who is trying to carry off a young innocent, and another depicts a devil forcing the guilty dead down the jaws of Hell. It is one of the first English illustrations of this monstrous mouth, which was to prove the most popular scenic element in medieval drama. Perhaps it had already made its appearance.

As early as the ninth century a dramatic element was added to the service of the Mass at the chief festivals of the year. Thus, at Easter, priests playing the parts of the three Marys approached the altar where another priest, representing an angel, asked whom they were seeking in the tomb: 'Quem quaeritis in sepulchro?' 'Iesum Nazarenum crucifixum,' they replied, only to learn that he was no longer there, but had risen as had been foretold. Heaven was probably symbolized by the altar, near which an 'Easter sepulchre' was built, and, because 'evil appeareth out of the north', Hell was on the north side, even in Late Saxon times, perhaps, represented by the gaping jaws of a monstrous beast.

The beginning of the drama involved a development in Church music, for the dialogue inserted in the liturgy took the form of melodic ornamental passages, or tropes, and perhaps these tropes in turn encouraged the elaboration of plainsong. Until about the tenth century this had been sung invariably in unison, as it still generally continued to be, but an elementary harmony was sometimes produced when higher and lower voices sang at intervals of a fourth or fifth, a form known as 'organum' or 'diaphony'. Music was still very simple, though written in a number of scales, or modes, in which the relative position of the semitones varied, and it was only in the sixteenth century that our present major and minor scales were adopted.

(*Below left*) A masterpiece of tenth-century Saxon drawing, from the Ramsey Psalter, *c.* 980. (*Below right*) An eleventh-century troper, or book of tropes, showing notation. (*Far right*) The Last Judgment, from the Winchester *Liber Vitae*, 1020. ▶

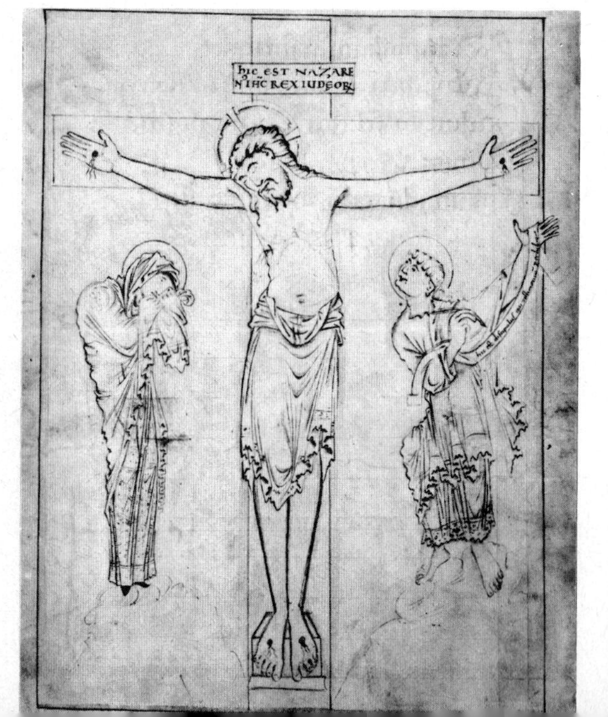

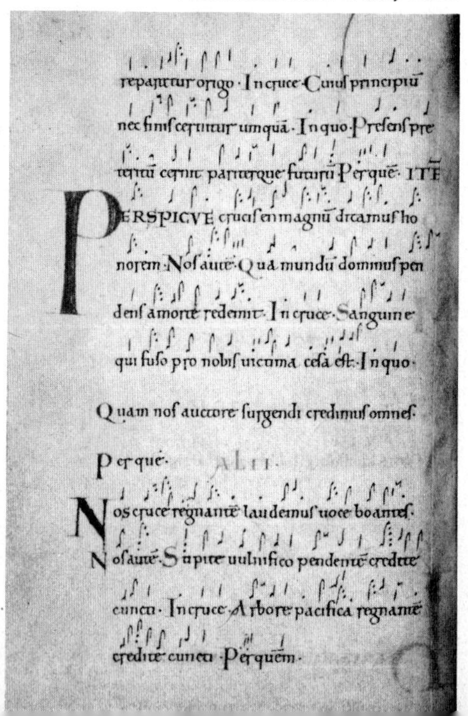
reparatur origo · In cruce · Cuius principium
nec finis cernitur umquã · In quo · Presens pre
teritum cernit pariterque futurum · Perque · ITE
PERSPICVE quas enim magnum dicamus ho
norem · Nos autẽ · Qua mundũ dominus per
dens amore redemit · In cruce · Sanguine
qui fuso pro nobis uictima cesa est · In quo ·
Quam nos auctore surgendi credimus omnes ·
Perque · ALII
Nos cruce regnantẽ laudemus uoce boantes ·
Nos autẽ · Si apice uulnifico pendentẽ credite
cuncti · In cruce · Arbore pacifica regnantẽ
credite cuncti · Perquẽ ·

The Bayeux Tapestry. William's army embarks for England. 'Here they drag the ships to the sea.'

The inspiration of this Wessex art was the heroic struggle against the invading Danes and Vikings, as when in 939 Athelstan routed an army of Danes and Scots at Brunanburh, a victory celebrated in a stirring poem inserted in the *Anglo-Saxon Chronicle*. But the century went out in failure, and *The Battle of Maldon* was a tale of defeat. Yet the poem ends on a note of stoicism and courage:

> Hige sceal the heardra, heorte the cenre,
> mod sceal the mare, the ure mægen lytlath.
>
> The mind must be firmer, keener the heart,
> the mood must be braver, as our strength fails.

Fortitude was not enough, however; English kings were replaced by Danes, and in alliterative prose Wulfstan, Archbishop of York, described the plight of his country: 'The Danes plunder and kill, shame and enslave us, and what is there in all this but the wrath of God, clear and plain, upon his people?'

Forty years after Wulfstan's death there was another visitation of God's wrath, the Norman Conquest, an event depicted in the unique, so-called Bayeux Tapestry. This is a band of linen two hundred and thirty feet long embroidered in coloured worsteds, the seventy-two scenes of which have the dramatic and lively linear quality that had made English drawing and illumination famous throughout Europe. It was a splendid ending to this last great period of Anglo-Saxon art.

'They carry arms to the ships: and here pull a cart loaded with wine and weapons. Here Duke William . . .'

4 *The Anglo-Normans 1066–1200*

The art of western Europe in the ninth and tenth centuries was that of the Holy Roman Empire, the attempt of the awakening peoples to recreate the art of the old Roman Empire that had been destroyed by their ancestors. Its ruins lay about them to serve as models and quarries, but inevitably the original classical style was modified by their own character and genius, and by the assimilation of other traditions, notably Byzantine and Celtic. Their architecture, however, was essentially Roman, one of massive walls, columns, round arches and, on a small scale, vaults, for the art of vaulting wide spaces had yet to be rediscovered, and most of their ceilings were wooden. Because the art of this period, from the ninth to the twelfth century, was derived from that of Rome, it has been given the name 'Romanesque'. Tenth-century Saxon was a provincial variation of Romanesque, and when Edward the Confessor became king in 1042 the influence of continental Romanesque was reinforced, for, educated in Normandy, he brought with him Norman architects and craftsmen who rebuilt the Saxon Abbey of Westminster.

It was not until the Norman Conquest, however, that the full impact of continental Romanesque art was felt in England. Great organizers and ruthlessly efficient, the Normans had a contempt for happy-go-lucky Saxon Church government and architecture, and it was not long before Saxon bishops and abbots were replaced by Normans, who began the rebuilding of their churches. This eleventh-century style was a severe one, but it was disciplined, and gave to English architecture a coherence that it had never had before.

As the flying buttress had not yet been invented, the upper part of these new cathedral and monastic churches had little outside support, and their walls had to be immensely thick to bear the weight of the roof, their windows small, though splayed inwards to admit as much light as possible. The interior was very different from that of a Saxon church, for instead of a bare wall, it was divided into three approximately equal horizontal bands of round-arched openings. The lowest was the arcade that separated choir and nave from windowed aisle: massive piers or pillars, or alternate pier and pillar, sometimes with attached shafts to support subsidiary orders of the arch. Above this was the triforium, another arcade that screened a windowless gallery above the aisle, and finally the clerestory which, being higher than the gallery roof, had windows. These three storeys were defined horizontally by string-courses or mouldings, and vertically the wall was divided into bays, each containing one unit of the

The development of Anglo-Norman, Romanesque, architecture:
(*Left*) Winchester Cathedral: west wall of north transept, eleventh century.
(*Right*) Durham Cathedral: vaulted nave and chancel, early twelfth century ▶

arcade of each storey, by shafts that ran from basic pillars to wooden ceiling, the main beams of which they supported. This early Romanesque, as at Winchester, for example, is very close to Roman, Norman interior to the exterior of the Colosseum, though whereas the capitals of the attached columns of the Colosseum are Doric, Ionic, and Corinthian, those at Winchester are merely functional stones that make the transition from cylindrical pillar below to cubical block above. These simple cushion capitals are almost the only ornament, if ornament they can be called, in this austere Early Norman style.

By the beginning of the twelfth century, however, this ascetic Romanesque had been transformed. At Durham, where the rebuilding of the cathedral began in 1093, the nave arcade opens up half the wall, the arches being supported by alternate piers and columns of enormous girth; up the piers triple wall-shafts soar to the clerestory, but instead of ending there, like the branches of a tree they fan into ribs that define the groins of the stone vault. The art of vaulting a wide space had been rediscovered, and for the first time a large Romanesque building was fully articulated, the ribs carrying the shafts of one wall overhead to meet those on the other side. Although the walls have to carry the weight of a stone vault instead of a wooden ceiling, the load appears to be lightened, and there is a feeling of tense and sinewy strength rather than brute bulk: inert Roman had given place to a more alert Romanesque.

Animal musicians. Capital in St Gabriel's Chapel, Canterbury Cathedral.

Norman solemnity was also qualified by Saxon delight in decoration. Chevron ornament enlivens arches and ribs, roll-mouldings the arcades, the great columns are covered with incised chevron, lozenges, and flute, and an interlaced arcade enriches the walls of the aisles. To the 'metrical system', the measured rhythm of bays further defined by the intersecting ribs of the vault, had been added the characteristic English linear quality imparted by innumerable springing shafts and undulating arches. It is significant that 'metre' and 'measure' are not architectural but literary and musical terms.

The essential elements of English Romanesque did not change very much during the twelfth century: the thick walls reinforced with flat exterior buttresses and pierced by small round-headed windows. The apse, however, was generally abandoned in favour of a square east end, pillars replaced piers, arcades were elaborated, and, as at Tewkesbury, a central tower defined the junction of nave and transepts. Unhappily, the early twelfth-century choir at Canterbury was destroyed by fire soon after its completion, but something of its splendour can be seen in the carved capitals of the crypt. The decoration at Durham was abstract, the capitals a variation of the plain cushion type, but here the capitals have foliage or even animal designs: a goat and a devil playing a duet, the one on a recorder, the other on a crowd.

Also in the Canterbury crypt are some of the earliest wall-paintings in England. Few of these have survived, partly because the English painted on dry plaster into which the colour did not sink, as it does in fresco-painting on wet plaster, and as a result it has faded and crumbled. Grey, black, red and yellow were the favourite colours, though blue and green were sometimes used, as in the best-preserved painting in the Canterbury crypt: *The Naming of John the Baptist*. It is an astonishing picture. In front of a domed and turreted Romanesque building sits Elizabeth with the rigid baby John in her lap; on the other side is Zacharias writing the child's name, and between them are five men wearing eight enormous buttoned boots that make a remarkable pattern overlapping the border. The faces are expressionless, eyes unseeing, gestures conventional; there is neither variety nor movement, either in the figures or in the drapery, the folds of which are sketched in with lines of different colours. It is, in fact, an amateurish version of a Byzantine mosaic, though not without an artless charm. More accomplished is the slightly later painting *St Paul and the Viper* in the chapel over the crypt. St Paul is leaning forward to shake the viper into the fire, and the bold line of his dark cloak sweeps hands, head, and feet into a rhythmical movement.

In the course of the twelfth century there was a great building of churches, and many of their walls must have been decorated with paintings, long since perished, though they have survived at Kempley church in Gloucestershire. The theme is the glorification of Christ, who is enthroned on a rainbow within a vesica, and below him on the chancel walls the Twelve Apostles are seated in identical attitudes, hands raised and heads tilted sideways and upwards in

Early Norman wall-painting in Kempley church, Gloucestershire. Adoring Apostles, with Bethlehem on the right.

Tewkesbury Abbey: the Norman tower. (The chancel and its *chevet* of chapels are fourteenth century.)

adoration. In these Byzantine figures there is nothing of the native English liveliness that asserts itself in the painting of the Last Judgment, a favourite subject, in Chaldon church, Surrey. At the bottom is Hell, where devils are boiling and frying the souls of the damned, some of whom are picked off the central ladder that leads up to more heavenly regions, where Christ is delivering Adam and Eve from Limbo, and the Archangel Michael, twice the size of a mere angel, is weighing souls in his scales.

The same subject is represented on a very much smaller scale on one of the few remaining pieces of twelfth-century enamel-work, a plaque only six inches high, probably from Winchester. The technique is champlevé, in which the powdered glass is put into hollows cut in the copper plate before being fused. Above Hell and its torments is Christ carrying souls into Heaven in a swirl of draperies. The emphasis on line is very English, though the ovals that represent folds in the dress are a Romanesque convention.

This, with other conventions, was probably derived from illuminated books of the period, more varied in kind and range of subject than those of Saxon times. There were Bestiaries, for example, moral fables about animals: how the lion sleeps with its eyes open, the snake is afraid of a naked man, the unicorn can be caught only by a virgin, and so on, fables that Sir Thomas Browne was later to expose as vulgar errors. As this unnatural history was the popular reading of the time, its illustration was correspondingly unsophisticated: the artist had certainly never seen a unicorn or phoenix, almost as certainly never an elephant or lion, and he drew and coloured these beasts according to his fancy, and rarely with any of the fashionable stylization.

In its extreme form this stylization was mainly the work of Cluniac monks, an order established in England soon after the Conquest, the classic example being the Shaftesbury Psalter of *c.* 1140. In this the figures have a forbidding Byzantine severity that is quite foreign to the native tradition: Christ, for example, is portrayed as a staring Oriental potentate rigidly seated on a rainbow, the arch of which is repeated, sometimes in reverse, to suggest the folds of his dress, a convention adopted by the painter of the walls in Kempley church.

Most English Romanesque illumination, however, is little more than a modification of the native linear style by these continental conventions. In the Lambeth and Winchester Bibles, for example, although gestures are theatrical and garments a complex of oval folds, though the figures are unnaturally attenuated and artfully grouped in line to face the spectator, they are by no means rigid, but sway bonelessly from the hips, something in the manner of those in the Bayeux Tapestry. They are, in fact, much more English than continental, and have more in common with the drawings of Blake than with the art of Cluny. Many of these Bible illuminations have plain gold backgrounds, against which the colours glow richly, and sometimes they are arranged in paired medallions, type with antitype, the New Testament as a fulfilment of the Old.

Byzantine conventions of Romanesque illumination:
(*Above left*) Lambeth Bible: the Death of Saul. Twelfth century.
(*Left*) Shaftesbury Psalter: St Michael raising souls to God. Twelfth century.
(*Above right*) Psalter: late Winchester School of about the time of the Conquest. Note the characteristic Winchester border (compare page 37).

Byzantine conventions of Romanesque sculpture, still only bas-relief: (*Left*) Apostles: Malmesbury Abbey. (*Right*) The Raising of Lazarus: Chichester Cathedral.

There is much the same range, from artless fantasy to sophisticated convention, in twelfth-century sculpture, still almost entirely confined to relief. The most extreme example of stylization is the two panels in Chichester Cathedral, particularly that of the Raising of Lazarus. The figures have a Byzantine formality, but the faces, with huge deeply cut eyes, resemble Greek tragic masks, and the pattern into which Christ's hair is carved is reminiscent of early Celtic art. More characteristically Romanesque are the Twelve Apostles in the porch of Malmesbury Abbey, six on either side, much more natural in posture than the painted Apostles of Kempley, looking almost as though they were posing for a photograph, though subtly grouped in pairs and unified by the hovering angel above. There is also more variety in the draping of their robes, for though the conventional ovals, and even inverted rainbow shapes, are there, they are only details in the overall rhythm of the design.

The unique contribution of the twelfth century to the arts was stained glass, which, like cloisonné enamel, the technique of which it resembles, was begun at Constantinople and developed in western Europe. It is important to realize that the glass was stained, dyed, in the making, that the colour permeates the glass, and that the only painting, at least in the twelfth and thirteenth centuries,

Noah and the Ark. A medallion in a twelfth-century aisle window of Canterbury Cathedral.

was with an opaque brown enamel, used for drawing faces, drapery folds, and other detail. As glass could be made only in small pieces, these were joined by strips of lead, a soft and heavy material that had to be supported by iron bars across the opening in which the window was to be inserted. Obviously these bars could not be ignored in the design, which had either to be made big enough to be independent of them, or small enough to fit into one unit of the frame. At Canterbury the first method was adopted in the majestic figures of the clerestory windows, the second in the aisles, where the detail could easily be seen: Noah in his Ark, for example, which served as a type for the Baptism of Jesus in a neighbouring medallion. Against a dark blue sky Noah is releasing the dove from a window at the top of the Ark, a multi-coloured, three-storied structure with Romanesque columns and arches, against the stability of which the writhing ridges of blue, green, and white-capped waves are powerless.

Romanesque art was not abstract, but because it was representational only within limits, partly because the artists were incapable of representing nature in depth, partly because they realized that nature was not art, stained glass was a magnificent medium for this formalizing genius, which made features of limitations; by emphasizing the black lines of the lead joints they increased the brilliance of their blues and rubies, and by bending their iron supports into medallions and outlines of borders they gave their glass a jewel-like quality that quite transformed the interior of their churches.

At the same time there was a transformation of Church music, the beginning of polyphony. The organum, the singing of the same melody in parallel fourths and fifths, inevitably developed into the conductus, the singing by two or more voices of different melodies that harmonized with the main one, or canto fermo. Moreover, unlike plainsong and organum, the conductus was metrical, for the words were those of metrical Latin hymns. Much as the nave and chancel of a church had become a progression of bays defined by wallshafts and intersecting ribs, so music became a measured progression of notes that could have been defined by bar-lines. It was still all very elementary, and in cathedrals, in Winchester Cathedral at least, the singing was led by a primitive organ, the great keys of which had to be thumped with fists, while seventy blowers, for each pipe had its own bellows, supplied wind for the two players.

Adam. A twelfth-century clerestory window in Canterbury Cathedral.

It is scarcely too much to say that the Norman Conquest transformed the English language, and therefore its literature. French became the language of the upper classes in their castles and fortified manor-houses, English the language of the hovel, where illiterate serfs modified or dropped the elaborate literary inflections, and the artificial poetic diction of the minstrels' 'word-hoards' was forgotten. As a result, though the twelfth century was a brilliant period of Anglo-Latin literature, English prose was written mainly for the edification of the masses, and poetry scarcely at all. When, therefore, at the turn of the twelfth century there was a poetic revival, it is not altogether surprising to read this:

Nu brotherr Walterr, brotherr min,
  Affterr the flæshess kinde,
And brotherr min i Crissenndom,
  Thurrh fulluht and thurrh trowwthe.

It is the beginning of the *Ormulum*, a series of homilies on the Gospels, written by a monk, probably from North Lincolnshire, called 'Orm'. It is not poetry, but it is verse: verse in the modern meaning of the word. Instead of the lax rhythm and alliteration of Old English poetry, here are twenty thousand unalliterated lines of alternate eight and seven syllables (the final *e*, as in French, being pronounced) each distich forming a single line of seven stresses. Moreover, although there are no French or Latin words in the lines quoted, and very few in the others, this Middle English is much easier to understand than the Old, *fulluht*, 'baptism', being the only word that needs a gloss. Incidentally, Orm invented a new method of spelling, by doubling the consonant after every short vowel, still the principle of English, though not American, spelling to this day. He carried his system to pedantic extremes, but it is invaluable as showing how his English was pronounced.

Again, it is perhaps not altogether surprising to read this:

Ich am eldre than ich wes, a winter and ek on lore;
Ich welde more than ich dude, my wyt auhte beo more.
Wel longe ich habbe child ibeo, a werke and eke on dede;
Thah ich beo of wynter old, to yong ich am on rede.

These are the opening lines of *A Moral Ode*, an anonymous poet's lament for the passing of time and a wasted life. The verse is the same as that of the *Ormulum*, a line of fifteen (or sometimes fourteen) syllables and seven stresses, but the rhyme is something new, a device that corresponds to the paired medallions of Romanesque illumination and stained glass, the correspondence of type and antitype.

Not only had the Normans disciplined the English people and welded them into a nation, they had also, directly or indirectly, given form and cohesion to their arts: a classical symmetry to their architecture, formal conventions to their painting and sculpture, measure to their music, and now metre and rhyme to their poetry. It was a beneficial discipline, but once it had been thoroughly learned, the time had come for variations on the conventions, for experiment, a greater naturalism, a freer, though still ordered, romanticism.

Malmesbury Abbey, south porch, twelfth century. The two inner bands of medallions depict scenes from the Old Testament, the outer band from the New: type and antitype.

5 *The Early Middle Ages* 1200–1350

The classical ideal was a harmonious balance in man, in nature, and in art, an integrated whole, serene and suggestive of permanence. The thick walls, time-defying columns, and round arches of Romanesque churches were essentially classical, and the conventions of Romanesque painting and sculpture emulated a Byzantine artifice of eternity. The men of the thirteenth century, however, had little sympathy with this static conception of life and art: it was a restless, thrusting, questing, experimental age, an age of intellectual ferment, of the scientific pursuit of knowledge, of the foundation of the universities of Paris, Oxford, and Cambridge, and this new spirit of aspiration and inquiry inevitably found expression in its art.

The ponderous and comparatively low Romanesque buildings, dark because of their necessarily small and deeply set windows, were quite at odds with the new ideals, the architectural symbols of which were height, vertical lines, and light. The problem was how to build higher and at the same time reduce the thickness of the vault-supporting walls and enlarge the windows that weakened them. It was solved in northern France about the middle of the twelfth century, and involved a new structural principle based on the pointed arch, which is stronger than a round one. Although it is relatively easy to vault a square bay with round arches, a rectangular bay is more difficult, as arches of three different diameters, and therefore heights, must be used; but this difficulty may be overcome by using pointed arches of three degrees of acuteness, with the additional advantage that the number of supports for the vault ribs can be increased. The weight of the roof is thus concentrated on the shafts from which the ribs spring, and if they are reinforced on the outside with flying buttresses, the wall between them becomes little more than a screen in which windows of almost any size may be set. This was the structural principle of the new Gothic architecture, by which the outward thrust of pointed rib-vaults was opposed by the counter-thrust of pinnacle-weighted buttresses, giving greater strength with thinner walls, greater height and, in every sense of the word, greater lightness. Inert classical balance had been superseded by an architecture of equilibrium, the downward pressure of superstructure converted into a soaring movement of a slender framework of intersecting pointed arches.

The pointed arch is the most obvious characteristic of the three centuries of medieval Gothic architecture, but it does not of itself make Gothic. The

Early English thirteenth century dog-tooth ornament.

Cistercians, who established themselves in England before the middle of the twelfth century and built the great Yorkshire monasteries of Rievaulx, Byland, and Fountains, were an ascetic order who favoured the austerity of the pointed arch, more suggestive of physical discomfort than the round one, but their buildings were Romanesque rather than Gothic. So were other churches of the period, though for a different reason, for at first the English failed to see that French Gothic was a revolutionary form of architecture, and adopted the pointed arch primarily as a new decorative motif to be applied to their Romanesque walls, as at Ripon. The first truly Gothic building in England was the choir of Canterbury Cathedral, reconstructed after the disastrous fire of 1174, but then that was the work of a Frenchman, William of Sens.

Canterbury was Anglo-French, but Lincoln, the rebuilding of which began in 1192, was Early English. Here, in addition to the essential features, are all the details that go to make the style: clustered columns of Purbeck marble, crisp and boldly carved foliage capitals, lancet windows, dog-tooth ornament, and pointed arcade arches with deeply channelled mouldings. The vaulting, too, is characteristically English, for the Gothic structural system, defined by the transverse and diagonal ribs of each bay, is confused by the addition of a central ridge-rib and a number of subordinate ribs that fan out from the supporting wall-shafts. French logic had been elaborated into English decoration. The west front was also peculiarly insular, a huge stone screen across the original Norman façade, but the west front of Peterborough, built at about the same time, was an extravagant version of the French manner, with three enormous

An architectural revolution: the pointed, Gothic style. (*Left*) Cistercian half-Gothic: the pointed arch applied to a Romanesque building at Fountains Abbey, twelfth century. (*Right*) True Gothic: the structural use of the pointed arch in Lincoln Cathedral, thirteenth century.

The west front of Wells Cathedral, a fine example of Early English Gothic; early thirteenth century, though the towers are later.

portals. But the English genius, like the climate and physical construction of their country which have moulded it, does not run to extremes; it is essentially moderate and distrustful of any form of excess, and the example of Peterborough was not repeated. Thus, the west doors of Wells Cathedral are insignificant, though this may have been partly because the façade, begun about 1220, was to be covered with sculpture.

English Romanesque sculpture had been virtually confined to carving in relief, and the ornamentation of small but prominent features, notably fonts and tympana, the semicircular space between the lintel and arch of a door, but Gothic architects took sculptors into partnership, and medieval carving in the round began. There were more than three hundred statues and reliefs on the west front of Wells Cathedral, and half of these remain, still showing traces of the colour with which they were enriched, red backgrounds in the niches, painted lips, eyes, and hair, and robes of red, green, blue, and black. The theme is no less than the Fall and Redemption of Man, and in one of the nine tiers are scenes from the Old and New Testaments, from the Creation of

Two kings from the west front of Wells Cathedral. The statues are among the first English sculpture in the round.

Adam and Eve to the Resurrection and Gift of Tongues. The sixth tier is a frieze portraying the Last Judgment, over which are the nine orders of Angels, the Twelve Apostles, and finally Christ enthroned between the Virgin and St John. The cult of the Virgin, which was to have such an influence on the arts, had begun, and at Wells the Virgin and Child are carved on the tympanum of the west door, and above is her Coronation. Like stained glass, sculpture was to be a visual record of the Bible story, and summary of Church doctrine: sermons in stone for the illiterate. The most noteworthy figures, however, are the large single statues in their niches. The vertical lines of their drapery, their restraint and simplicity, give them a certain dignity, but the old conventions have gone, and they are little more than dummies, lifeless attempts at a new realism, and not to be compared with the fluted, attenuated saints and martyrs of Chartres. The English are not a sculptural people. Yet, seven hundred years ago, the façade of Wells, when the afternoon sun began to light the western wall, throwing deep shadows and revealing the richness of the colour, must have been one of the most splendid sights in England.

The Saving of Bobby. A thirteenth-century stained-glass medallion illustrating the return to English naturalism after the Romanesque period of the Normans. From an aisle window in Canterbury Cathedral.

Salisbury Cathedral, however, is the most perfect example of the first phase of Early English architecture, for, apart from the fourteenth-century upper tower and spire, it was completely rebuilt on a new site between 1220 and 1258. It is interesting to compare it with Bourges, built at about the same time. Salisbury is long and narrow, with boldly projecting main and secondary transepts, square-ended like the Lady Chapel (another consequence of the cult of the Virgin) at the east: a series of rectangles. Bourges is short and broad, without transepts, but with an apsidal east end. The one is linear, and almost dreamily romantic, the other plastic, intellectual, taut, built like a ship and braced by flying buttresses. Inside there is no comparison, for Bourges has some of the most beautiful stained glass in France, whereas Salisbury has lost almost all its original windows, replaced with white glass by 'Wyatt the Destroyer' in the eighteenth century, and its present appearance is a bleak reminder that colour was an integral part of the design of medieval churches.

Few early-thirteenth-century windows remain, apart from those in the Chapel of St Thomas at Canterbury. Like the slightly earlier ones in the choir, their colour, notably the blue, has a depth and richness which have only recently been recaptured in the windows of Coventry Cathedral, and the small leaded pieces of glass, marking every change of hue, give them the appearance of brilliant translucent mosaics, which indeed is what they really are. There are the same conventions: a stylized floral border defines the window, and flowing scroll-work fills the space between the medallions, which, however, are more varied and elaborate, the outlines of their shapes being followed by the supporting ironwork outside. In the numerous scenes depicted, sometimes more than thirty in one window, there is still no attempt to make a realistic background: water is a blue undulation, earth a striation of green and brown, sky a festoon of clouds, but the figure-drawing is more lively, more natural, and the scenes enacted are more homely. The Byzantine barrier between sacred and profane was breaking down. Thus, though the east window runs from the Crucifixion at the bottom to Christ in Majesty at the top, its neighbour depicts, among other stories, the adventures of eight-year-old Bobby, who fell into the Medway while stoning frogs, and by the intervention of the blissful martyr, St Thomas à Becket, was rescued alive from the mud.

◀ Salisbury Cathedral, 1220–58. 'The most perfect example of the first phase of Early English architecture.'

Censing Angel, c. 1260, showing the influence of France and the new Court school. Westminster Abbey.

The next window, which cannot be earlier than 1220, is an interesting one, as it contains the only extant representation of Becket's golden shrine, erected in that year, and foreshadows a development, if that is the right word, in the art of stained glass. Obviously these windows were the work of extremely skilful artists and craftsmen, and their making was slow and correspondingly expensive, but speed and economy could be achieved by substituting for the scroll-work between the medallions a standardized geometrical design that could be mass-produced by apprentices; and this Canterbury window contains the first example of this mosaic diaper, a dark lattice with red rosettes on a blue background. A similar diaper pattern was a favourite form of decoration for walls and the background of illuminations.

Another kind of window, even more economical, and with the additional advantage of giving more light, was developed about the middle of the century. This was made of plain glass – not white, for the impurities in medieval glass give it a greenish tinge – the pieces being set in a pattern of leadwork, and lightly painted with a floral design. The finest example of this grisaille glass is the group of long lancet-windows at York, known as the 'Five Sisters', in which borders and medallions are outlined in strips of red and blue glass, though filled with the painted design that covers the rest of the window. Grisaille windows certainly give more light, a greyish, silvery light, but lack the profound beauty of the earlier glass, and are the beginning of the decline of the art.

The Five Sisters occupy the whole width of the north transept and, separated only by single shafts, look almost like one huge window. It was not long before lancets were thus combined, the narrow windows and their shafts being transformed into a series of lights and slender mullions from which sprang a delicate geometrical tracery within an embracing pointed arch that framed the whole, as in the Chapter House of Westminster Abbey. The wall had become merely a glass screen, and it is worth pausing to consider the difference between these Gothic windows and the small, round-headed windows so deeply set in the thick walls of Norman churches.

The rebuilding of Westminster Abbey in the middle of the thirteenth century was the work of Henry III, and marks the beginning of a new epoch in English art. Up till this time the principal patron of the arts had been the Church, but Henry gathered about him a Court school of architects, sculptors, painters, and craftsmen, and for the next three centuries, until the Reformation, patronage lay largely with the Court. As a result, art became more and more secularized, its subject-matter no longer confined to religious themes, and palace, college, inn of court, came within its scope. Moreover, whereas prelates had employed mainly local talent, Henry drew to Court not only the best artists in the country but also many from abroad, particularly from France, so that Westminster Abbey is the most French of great English churches. The influence of France and the Court school was to make itself felt in other fields as well.

Grisaille: a new form of stained glass giving more light. The lancets of the Five Sisters, York Minster, *c.* 1250.

Early English tracery. Salisbury Cathedral Chapter House, 1250.

'Ici gist Alianor jadis Reyne de Engletere.' The effigy, made by William Torel, *c.* 1290, one of the first, and most beautiful, life-size bronze figures in English art.

In the north transept of the abbey, under the great rose-window in the new French manner, were three traceried windows in the diapered spandrels of which censing angels were carved. Unlike the statues at Wells, these figures are full of life and movement, particularly the two end ones, their heads half encircled by their curving wings, and perfectly related to their hands and feet and flying drapery: Court school work that inspired the carving of the angels in the choir at Lincoln a few years later. Also at Westminster are the splendid bronze effigies of Henry III and his daughter-in-law, Eleanor of Castile, made about 1290 by the London goldsmith William Torel, the first life-size bronze figures in English art. There is still no attempt at portraiture, and the idealized faces with regular features might equally well have served for those of Christ and the Virgin. They are certainly regal, and bronze became the accepted medium for royal monuments.

The finest examples of early-thirteenth-century wall-painting are those in the Chapel of the Holy Sepulchre in Winchester Cathedral. This appears to have been an Easter Sepulchre in which the Cross, representing the Body of Christ, was laid on Good Friday, and removed on Easter Day to symbolize the Resurrection, when the three Marys of the liturgical drama visited the tomb. The paintings, therefore, are scenes from the Passion, and though most of

Early Gothic wall-painting, still influenced by Romanesque conventions. The Descent from the Cross in the Chapel of the Holy Sepulchre of Winchester Cathedral.

them are faint, their red, blue, green, and purple colours faded, the Descent from the Cross is clearly visible. As we should expect at this early date, Byzantine influence is still very strong: in the big dark eyes, pedimental eyebrows, extravagant gestures, and conventional folds of drapery, but there is more than a trace of the new naturalism in the figure of the Virgin, who is pressing Christ's hand to her cheek, and in that of the workmanlike Nicodemus, drawing the nails from Christ's feet with enormous pincers.

By the middle of the century Gothic grace had superseded Romanesque rigidity, and the figures, often in medallions like those in stained glass of the period, have a simplicity and economy of line that accentuate their human qualities: the Infant Jesus, for example, instead of being a mystical object of adoration, throws his arms round His mother's neck like any ordinary child. Illumination followed a similar course, towards a greater simplicity and naturalism. There were important schools of illumination at Canterbury, Peterborough, and Salisbury, but most famous was that of the Benedictine Abbey of St Albans, which Matthew Paris, an Englishman in spite of his name, entered as a monk at the beginning of Henry III's reign. Besides attacking the rival organization of friars, and drawing a remarkably accurate map of Britain, he wrote two histories in Latin, which he illustrated with line drawings to which he sometimes added a coloured wash. The best known is a Virgin and Child, remarkable for its ease, though not great subtlety, of line, and for the semi-humorous self-portrait below. The Evesham Psalter of *c.* 1250, the finest example of Early Gothic illumination, probably derives from St Albans, as do the Apocalypses that were so popular at this time, and some of these tinted outline drawings have a spring-like, lyrical quality that is the visual counterpart of the poem:

> Sumer is icumen in,
>   Lhude sing cuccu!
> Groweth sed and bloweth med,
>   And springth the wude nu:
>   Sing cuccu!

This is one of the earliest English lyrics, written probably *c.* 1250, and shortly afterwards set to music as a round for six voices in canon, four tenors entering at intervals of four bars, and two basses singing a perpetual ground, also in canon. It is the sole surviving example of such a form of composition, but it shows that by the middle of the thirteenth century English polyphonic music had attained an extraordinary complexity.

The *Cuckoo Song* itself, however, is by no means the only thirteenth-century English lyric, and by no means the best. The French influence introduced by

The English linear tradition reasserts itself: (*Left*) Tinted drawing *c.* 1250. The artist, Matthew Paris, depicts himself below. (*Right*) The Evesham Psalter, *c.* 1250. The background is gold.

Henry III affected not only the visual arts, but poetry as well, and it was the love-songs of the troubadours, with their elaborate stanza-forms, that inspired English poets. Perhaps the most beautiful of these early lyrics, prologue to the centuries to come, is *Alison*:

> Between March and April
>   When spray beginneth to spring,
> The little fowl hath her will
>   In her tongue to sing.
> I live in love-longing
> For the seemliest of all thing
> Who may me blisse bring,
>   And I to her am bound.
> A heavenly hap I have been lent,
> I wot from heaven it is me sent,
> For other women my love is spent
>   And lights on Alisoun.

Of course, in this century of faith, much religious poetry was still written, though this, too, was sometimes affected by the fashionable love-lyric. Thus, when a novice asked Friar Thomas of Hales to confirm her in the love of Christ, he wrote a courtly *Love Rune* in praise of one richer than King Henry

(*Left*) Apocalypse, St Albans, *c.* 1265. St John is shown by an angel a woman drunk with the blood of saints. (*Right*) 'Sumer is icumen in.' A round in the key of F, *c.* 1250.

and fairer than Absalom. The Virgin Mary, purest, most gracious and beautiful of all women, was a favourite theme, and the loveliest of all medieval lyrics is addressed to her:

I sing of a maiden
  That is makeles;
King of all kings
  To her son she ches . . .

He came al so still
  There his mother lay,
As dew in April
  That falleth on the spray.

Mother and maiden
  Was never none but she;
Well may such a lady
  Goddes mother be.

It is easy to see how the cult of the Virgin contributed to the romantic conception of women, or rather ladies, as superior beings to be revered and served by knights with absolute devotion in an attempt to win their favour; in short, every knight should love a lady, whether she were married or not.

Another contributory factor was the revival of interest in the legends of King Arthur. These had been recorded in English for the first time at the beginning of the century in the *Brut*, or British History, of Layamon, a long poem, remarkable not so much for its poetry as for its account of other Celtic legends, among them that of King Lear and his three daughters, and the story of Cymbeline. Again, in the reign of Henry III heraldry came into favour and established itself almost as a science with a picturesque language of its own, mainly French – blazon, fesse, gules, panache, tabard – and heraldic devices, clearly cut and brightly coloured, began to appear in stained-glass windows. Romance was in the air and in the countryside, and it cannot have been difficult to imagine Arthur, Lancelot and Guinevere, Mark, Tristram and Isolde, like medieval knights and ladies, with emblazoned shields, pennons, oriflammes, and guidons, riding on caparisoned horses through the gates of castles even more fabulous than that built by Henry's brother, the Earl of Cornwall, on the bleak headland of Tintagel.

Romance and chivalry: (*Left*) The Building of Stonehenge. An illustration from *Brut*, a legendary British History. Early thirteenth century. (*Right*) Hunting and heraldry, from an early-fourteenth-century Book of Hours. ▶

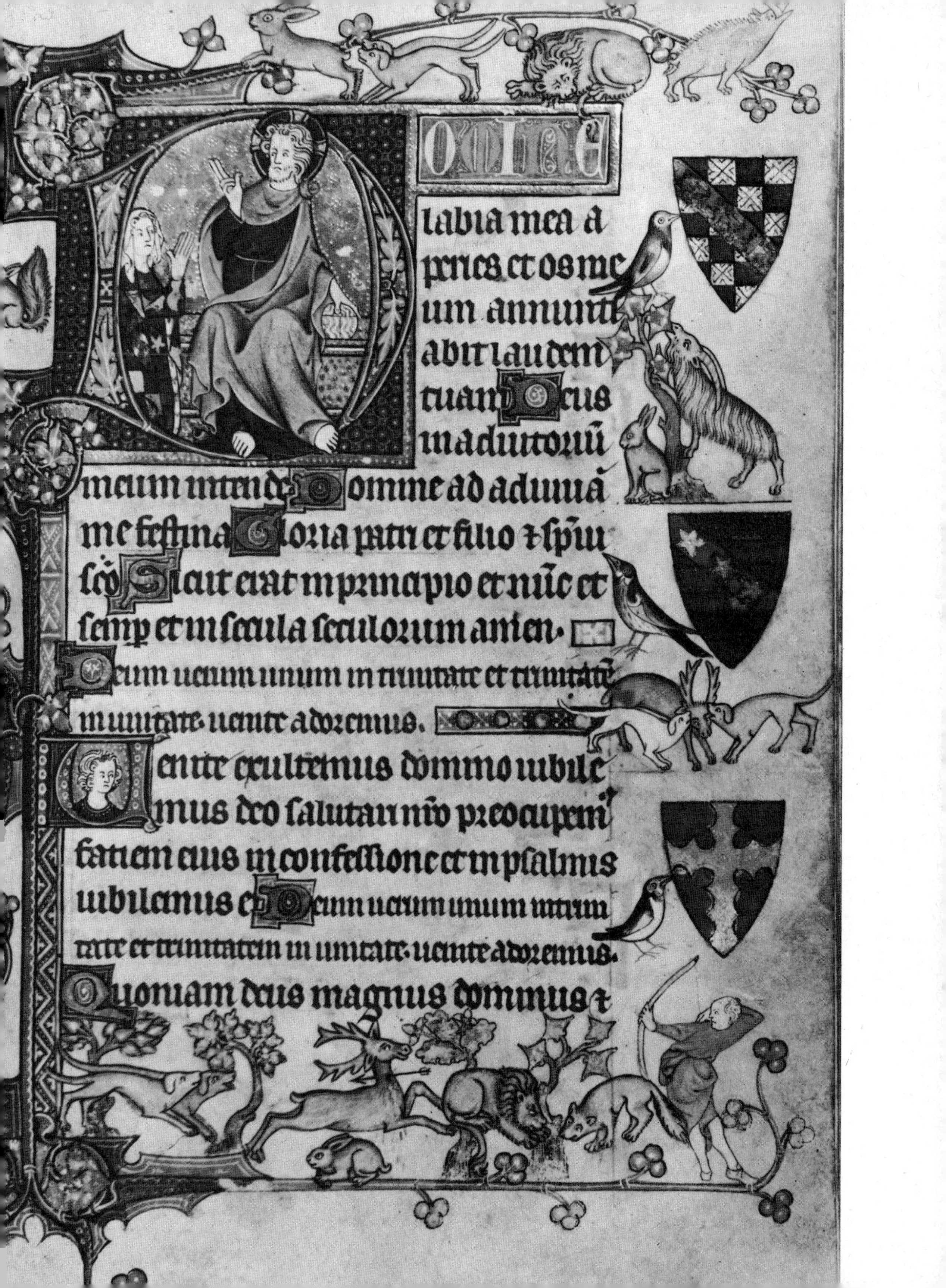

Domine
labia mea a
peries et os me
um annuncia
bit laudem
tuam. Deus
in adiutorium
meum intende. Domine ad adiuvandum
me festina. Gloria patri et filio et spiritui
sancto. Sicut erat in principio et nunc et
semper et in secula seculorum amen.
Deum verum unum in trinitate et trinitatem
in unitate venite adoremus.
Venite exultemus domino iubile
mus deo salutari nostro preoccupemus
faciem eius in confessione et in psalmis
iubilemus ei. Deum verum unum in trini
tate et trinitatem in unitate venite adoremus.
Quoniam deus magnus dominus et

Opus anglicanum. English ecclesiastical embroidery was recognized as the finest in medieval Europe. Detail from the Syon Cope, *c.* 1280.

No wonder the vogue of the verse romance began, and anonymous authors supplied sentimental ladies with the adventures of *Sir Tristram* and *Arthur and Merlin*, and of the beautiful boy, *King Horn*, while for knights with the ability and inclination to read there was the rather stronger matter of *Havelock the Dane*. Yet reading was not an essential accomplishment, for until the invention of printing the stories were sung by minstrels in courtly bower and hall; even monasteries had their minstrels, and the great Bishop Grosseteste of Lincoln his private harper, for music is a foretaste of Heaven: therefore,

> On harp, on tabor, in symphony glee
> Worship God: on trumpets and psaltery,
> On strings and organs, and bells ringing,
> On all these worship the heavenly King.

The lines come from the early-fourteenth-century poem, *Handlyng Synne*, by Robert Mannyng, who commended not only music in church, but also the acting of simple plays about the Resurrection, though he deplored the growing custom of other performances by laymen 'in ways or greens' and other public places.

When a great age of art has reached its culmination, its initial impulse spent and vigour exhausted, there follows a period when creativity declines into mere invention, inspiration into virtuosity, grandeur into prettiness, like the embroidered cadenza at the close of some fine piece of music. Thus, by the end of the thirteenth century, the freshness, simplicity, and economy of Early Gothic art was giving way to a sophisticated romanticism and elaboration. 'Decorated' is the word used to distinguish the architecture of this Middle Gothic period, from *c.* 1280 to 1350, and 'decorated' admirably describes its art as a whole, when the English delight in decoration had full rein, when structural logic was confused by ornament, and ornament reduced the significance of subject-matter in painting, sculpture, and stained glass. Even the embroidery for which England was famous throughout the Early Middle Ages, earning the name of *opus anglicanum*, suffered from over-elaboration, losing the simplicity of the famous Syon Cope of about 1280, with its red medallions on a green ground, and figures of gold and silver thread and coloured silks.

It is not to be expected that decoration should compete with structure in the castles built by Edward I to secure his conquest of Wales. These, however, belong to the end of the thirteenth century, the very beginning of the Decorated period, yet even in military architecture there was a development. A Norman castle, such as the Tower of London or Hedingham in Essex, was a high rectangular keep, the main stronghold, with a courtyard, or bailey, surrounded by an irregular wall and moat. Aesthetic considerations played little part in the planning of defences, but Edward's architects were as much concerned with design as were the builders of churches, and concentrated the strength of his

'Decorated' illumination at the beginning of the Hundred Years War. Sir Geoffrey Luttrell, from the Luttrell Psalter, *c.* 1340, important for its scenes of everyday life.

The development of Decorated vaulting in the fourteenth century: (*Left*) Exeter Cathedral, with intermediate ribs. (*Right*) Tewkesbury Abbey chancel, with liernes.

castles into symmetrical, concentric walls defended by round towers at the angles and along the sides. Harlech Castle, which seems to grow out of the rock it stands on, must have been as impregnable as it still remains splendidly monumental, a symbolic prelude to the aristocratic art of the next half-century.

The reign of Edward I was a short heroic age, and it was only after his death in 1307 that decoration became so characteristic of English art, mirror of the laxer standards in Church and State, and of the bogus chivalry of the Court of Edward III. This is most obvious in the development of tracery, when the simple geometrical forms of Early Gothic windows are fanned into a complex luxuriance of sinuous ogival curves that swirl upwards like flames towards the apex of the constricting arch, which may well be completely surrounded by the favourite ball-flower ornament. Vaulting underwent a corresponding elaboration: innumerable ribs, structurally irrelevant, spring from the wall-shafts to form inverted cones, so that the nave and chancel of Exeter Cathedral resemble a long colonnade of palms. Even more adventurous was the architect who reroofed the Norman nave of Tewkesbury Abbey, for parallel to the ridge-rib he added two more and a web of subordinate ribs, or liernes, making a traceried pattern emphasized by carved bosses at their crossings. It is very beautiful, though decoration has confused the simple Gothic structural system, and this was abandoned altogether at York, where carpenters vaulted the nave in timber, complete with imitation ribs, liernes, and bosses.

There is the same preoccupation with ornament in illumination. The Psalters of the East Anglian school of *c.* 1280–1340 are rich in colour and decorative detail, their pages crowded with small figures, their borders with birds and animals, peacocks and unicorns, angels and devils, jesters, tumblers, and heads in medallions, about which twine leaf-work patterns, no longer conventional, but naturalistic: vine, oak, sycamore, and ivy. Few paintings have survived, and the best are early work, the two life-size kings, probably Henry III and Edward II, on the sedilia of the sanctuary in Westminster Abbey. Although they retain much of the dignity and grace of Early Gothic work,

The canopied tomb of Edward II in Gloucester Cathedral, *c.* 1330. The canopy was a principal feature of the Decorated period.

Sedilia paintings, Westminster Abbey. Early fourteenth century.

there is a trace of affectation in the pose, the beginning of the S-bend or 'Gothic curve', which is so characteristic of the Decorated period. In wood and ivory carvings the Virgin often assumes this coy and languid attitude, and it is sometimes at its worst in the 'weepers' with which the Edwardians adorned their tombs, to express the grief they did not feel themselves. There can have been few who shed genuine tears for Edward II, who lies in alabaster in Gloucester Cathedral, not far from Berkeley Castle where he was murdered. One of the first effigies to be made in this translucent material, it is as dignified and simple as the bronze of Henry III, though dwarfed and half hidden by the architectural elaborations of the tiered and pinnacled canopy.

The growth of the canopy is perhaps the most obvious development in fourteenth-century stained glass, though by no means the only one. The division of a window into a number of narrow lights meant that the ornamental ironwork defining the medallions of early glass could be dispensed with. The medallions themselves, with their lively narrative detail, disappeared, and these brilliant mosaics were replaced by a single willowy figure under a gabled and crocketed canopy three times its height, a perfect example of ornamental detail crowding out the subject. Much of this detail was painted in silver stain, for it was found that clear glass painted with oxide of silver was stained an indelible yellow when fired. Instead of a different piece of glass for every colour and tone, therefore, relatively big areas could be decorated with silver stain, and grisaille painted in this way with a leaf or floral design was often extremely attractive. The vertical lines of the mullions demanded horizontals to balance them, so that a typical fourteenth-century window is divided into bands of colour and grisaille, a series of insignificant, almost identical single figures underneath fantastic canopies, sandwiched between grisaille of small diamond panes studded with rosettes or shields. The colour, when silver stain is not abused, is still very beautiful, but the designs are dull and repetitive; sometimes indeed, as at Tewkesbury, the same cartoon is used again and again, and they lack the spontaneity and vigour of Early Gothic glass. The windows in York Minster are exceptional, and retain something of the former liveliness, but they are not to be compared with their thirteenth-century predecessors at Canterbury.

The glaziers of York, as well as the bell-founders depicted in one of their most celebrated windows, were to play their part, literally, in the development of the drama. Early-fourteenth-century literature is composed mainly of verse romances, of Arthur, Charlemagne, and Alexander,

> Of Joneck and of Isombras,
> Of Idoyne and Amadas,
> Many songs of divers rhyme,
> English, Frenche and Latine.

These are four of the thirty thousand lines of *Cursor Mundi*, a Bible history of the world written in the northern dialect *c.* 1320. The unknown author attributes the evils of his age to this indulgence in a false chivalry, when no one is esteemed 'but he that loveth paramours', and he shows to whom true allegiance should be sworn by writing a love-song to the Virgin, 'Lady of ladies all'. He concludes with an apology for writing in English instead of the more courtly French; it is for love of the people 'of merry England', though he uses a number of newly incorporated French words, most of them abstract nouns – *chance*, *praise*, *language*, *outrage*:

> Frenche rhymes hear I read
> Commonly in every stead;
> Most is wrought for Frenche man,
> But what for him that no French can?
> Seldom was by any chance
> Praised the English tongue in France;
> Give we each his own language
> Methink we do them no outrage.

It is a fascinating glimpse of the literary scene, when English was struggling for recognition as a literary language. The poet then plunges into his history, which is a succession of stories as romantic in manner as the romances he deplores, the Harrowing of Hell, for example, being a contest between the King of Bliss and Sir Satan, Duke of Death and Prince of Hell. *Cursor Mundi* is an entertaining poem, written in lively octosyllabic couplets and, apart from its merit as literature, important as the storehouse from which the writers of miracle plays took much of their material.

By this time the artless Christmas and Easter plays performed in church had been extended and elaborated, and now, written in English instead of Latin, had become so popular that the clergy had handed them over to the laity, generally the craft guilds, who performed them in 'ways or greens'. Then, with the aid of *Cursor Mundi*, forty-eight short plays, ranging from the Creation to the Coronation of the Virgin, were written about 1340 for the guildsmen of York, and similar cycles for those of Chester, Wakefield, and Coventry. The medieval drama was a popular art in every sense of the word, and at midsummer, on the Feast of Corpus Christi, the guildsmen presented them. Each guild was assigned an appropriate play – thus at York the goldsmiths were the Magi of the Nativity, though the glaziers had to combine with the saddlers for the

A fourteenth-century coach, resembling the 'pageant', or movable stage, on which miracle plays were performed. From the Luttrell Psalter, *c.* 1340.

Harrowing of Hell – and this they performed on a large cart, or 'pageant', with a curtained dressing-room below the stage. Each play on its movable stage was performed at about twelve different places in the town, so that at each of these 'stations' the whole cycle could be seen between sunrise and sunset.

Of course the plays vary in quality, the best and most popular generally being those with a touch of broad comedy, like *Noah's Flood* at Chester, in which Noah's wife refuses to go into the Ark without her 'gossips'. Her sons carry her in:

> *Noye.* Welcome, wiffe, into this botte.
> *Wiffe.* Have thou that for thy note!
> *Noye.* Ha, ha! marye, this is hotte!
> It is good for to be still.

When we remember that men played women's parts, we can imagine the clowning and laughter of such incidents. Even better is the farcical interlude in the Wakefield *Nativity*, in which Mak steals a sheep and hides it in bed with his wife, pretending that it is a newborn baby:

> A pratty child is he
> As syttys on a woman's kne;
> A dyllydowne, perde,
> To gar a man laghe.

The shepherds discover the culprit and toss him in 'a canvas' before entering the stable to find Mary nursing the Child they were seeking. No wonder Shakespeare borrowed this native device of a sub-plot for his plays.

The pageant method of production was peculiar almost to England, but not all miracle plays were presented in this way. The three long plays of the Creation, Passion, and Resurrection, which constitute the Cornish cycle, were performed in round, open-air theatres, two of which still exist. The early conventions were observed: Heaven was at the east, Hell at the north, good characters on the south side and worldly ones on the west. Each main character had a tent, or 'house'; Heaven may have been a hut with a platform in front, and Hell was a pair of gaping jaws. The performance in the arena, or 'plain', was full of variety, from the lyrical love-making of David and Bathsheba, part of the Legend of the Rood taken from *Cursor Mundi*, to the brutal murder of Maximilla; and there was comic relief in plenty, as when God hurls Lucifer from Heaven, and he 'goeth down to Hell, apparelled foul, with fire about him burning, and every degree of devils of leather and spirits on cords running into the plain'. Similar plays, long since lost, were acted in similar theatres-in-the-round all over England. Although the art of the French-speaking upper classes was becoming effete, that of the people, the drama, was bursting with energy, and it was the English-speaking masses, particularly the rising middle class, who were to reinvigorate society and revitalize the arts.

6 The Later Middle Ages 1350–1500

After Edward II's burial under his elaborate canopy at Gloucester, his son, Edward III, ordered the rebuilding of the Norman choir in which he lay, and the original apse was replaced by a huge window that completely filled the east end. It was a revolutionary design, a sort of gridiron of vertical mullions and horizontal transoms, forming tiers of rectangular lights, each filled with a canopied figure. Even more revolutionary, this new tracery pattern was applied to the walls, to the openings of Norman arcade and triforium, and carried up into the new clerestory, so that everywhere this pattern of cusped panels was repeated – except in the vault, which was decorated with the most intricate of all lierne designs. The windows and mural veneer of Gloucester choir are the earliest Perpendicular Gothic, a style peculiarly English in its insistence on linear pattern, and peculiar to England, for in 1338 the Hundred Years War with France began, and continental Gothic developed in a different way. Yet the experiment was incomplete, and the new Perpendicular style reached its logical conclusion only with the building of the Gloucester cloisters, where the tracery panels were carried into the vault on the inverted concave cones, or fans, of which it was composed. This was soon after the middle of the

Enter Gloucester: seek the quoin
Where choir and transept interjoin . . .
Petrified lacework, lightly lined
On ancient massiveness behind.
The first Perpendicular Gothic, *c.* 1340.

fourteenth century, but meanwhile, in 1348–9, England, like the rest of Europe, had suffered the calamity of the Black Death.

This disastrous visitation of the Plague carried off almost half the people in England, inevitably disrupting the life and culture of the country, and there followed a period of discontent and demand for reform of social and religious abuses. John Wycliffe, or at least his followers, the Lollards, voiced both these demands, and like the later Puritans attacked the extravagance of religious art, its architecture, sculpture, stained glass, embroideries, and 'knacking of new songs', as they called its music. But more important than these negative activities was their translation of the Bible into English, the first complete version to be attempted. It was not great literature, but now that English was replacing French in law courts and schools, so that children 'conneth no more Frensche than can thir left heele', it was for the common man a gateway to great literature.

It came with the writing, *c.* 1370, of *Pearl*, an elegy of more than a thousand lines in the north-western dialect. The story is told by a father who, in a dream, is transported to a place where, across a river, he sees his dead daughter Margaret (Pearl) in Paradise. He wishes to join her, but wakes and resolves to submit to God's will. Considered merely as verse it is an astonishingly accomplished poem, for not only does the elaborate stanza combine the old convention of alliteration with the new convention of rhyme, but each stanza in each section of five has the same refrain, the last or principal word of which is repeated in the first line of its successor, and as the last line of all echoes the first the whole is bound into a mystical unity. Thus, the last line of stanza 5 is 'On that precious pearl withouten spot', and stanza 6 begins the next section:

From that spot my spirit sprang into space,
On that bank my body there bode in sweven,[1]
My ghost was gone in Goddes grace,
On aventure where marvels meven.[2]
I wist not where in this world it was,
But I knew myself cast where cliffes cleven:
Toward a forest I turned my face,
Where richest rocks were to discreven.[3]
The light of them might none believen,
The gleaming glory that from them glent,
For were never webs that wightes weaven
Of half so dear adornement.

Apart from its technical virtuosity, *Pearl* is the first great elegy in our language, at once passionate and as pure as the girl it celebrates.

The author of *Pearl* is unknown, but he probably wrote the other three alliterative poems in the same manuscript, discovered only last century: *Cleanness*, *Patience* and *Sir Gawain and the Green Knight*. The last is a romance of the Round Table, and of the temptation of Sir Gawain by the lady of the Knight, whose head, 'green as the grass', he had cut off. Again the stanza is a

1. dream. 2. move. 3. be descried. (*Very little has been changed, save the spelling, in this modernized version.*)

Late-fourteenth-century verse romances: (*Left*) *Pearl: A mayden of menske, ful debonere.* (*Right*) The headless Green Knight in Arthur's hall.

complex one, consisting of a varying number of alliterative lines clinched with a final 'bob and wheel': a single iambic foot and a quatrain. Thus, the Green Knight taunts Arthur and his Court:

> With this he laughed so loud that the lord grieved,
> The blood shot for shame into his fair face
> And lere;
> He waxed as wroth as wind,
> So did all that there were;
> The king as keen by kind
> Then stood that stiff man near.

It is a fantastic story, full of symbolism, myth, and moral, yet never tiresome, and written, one feels, primarily for entertainment. In any event, it is the best of medieval verse romances.

Most famous of the poems of this late-fourteenth-century alliterative revival, however, is *The Vision of Piers the Plowman*, written in the West Midland dialect, probably by William Langland. In the medieval manner, the poet falls asleep 'on Malvern Hills', and in a kaleidoscopic series of visions describes the abuses of his age. 'Pardon and penance and prayer' may well save souls on the Last Day, he concludes, but the best passport of all is 'Do-Well'.

In somer seson whan softe was the sunne
I shoop me in to shrowdes as y sheep were
& wente wyde i. þis world wondres to here
Vpon a May morwe on malverne hillis
By fel me a ferly as fayrye me thoughte
I was wery of wandrynge & wente me to reste
Vpon a brood banke be a bourne syde
& as y lay & lenede & lokede on þe wateres
I slumbrede in to slepyng it swyʒede so merye
Þan gan y to meten a merveylous swevene
Þat y was i a wyldernesse wiste y neuere where
I beheld in to the est an heyʒ to þe sunne
I seyʒ a tour on a tuft trielich y tymbred
A deep dale be nethe a dongon þer inne
With depe dyches & derke & dredful to syghte
& a fayr feeld ful of folk y fond þer be twene
Of alle manere of men þe mene & þe ryche
Wyrkynge & wandrynge as this world asketh
Summe putte hem selue to plowh & pleyede seldyn
& in settynge & sowynge þey swonken ful harde
& summe putte hem to pride & aparayled hem þer after
In contenaunce of clothynge komen fele dysgysyd
& wommen þat weren wastoures with glotenye dystroyen
In preyers & i penaunces putte hem selue manye
For þe love of oure lord þey lyvedyn ful streyte
In hope to have to hyre heuen ryche blysse
As ankrys & heremytes þat holde hem selue i sellys
& coveyte nought in cuntrey to kayren aboute
For no likerous lyflode here lykame to plese
& summe chesen chaffare to cheven þe bettre
As it semeþ to oure syght þat swiche men thryvyn
& summe merthis to make synneles y leve
But japeris & jangeleris ben judas children
þey feynen hem fantasyes & folis hem maken
& welden wit at wille to worche what þei sholde
What poul precheþ of hem y wil not preve it heere
For bidderis & beggeris faste a boute wentyn
& fele faytede for here fode & foughtyn at þe ale

Although the poem is an allegory and the characters are abstractions, it is at the same time dramatic, with frequent flashes of realism, as when a friar hears the confession of Meed the Maid, and whispers:

> We have a window in working will cost us well high,
> Wouldst thou glaze the gable and grave there thy name,
> Sure should thy soul be heaven to have.

And in the vision of the Seven Deadly Sins, 'Came Sloth all beslobbered, with two slimy eyen.'

By this time, however, a greater poet than Langland had appeared, and about 1390, in his *Legend of Good Women*, was writing humorously of himself:

> He made the book that hight The Hous of Fame,
> And eek the Death of Blanche the Duchesse,
> And the Parliament of Fowles, as I guesse . . .
> And for to speak of other businesse,
> He hath in prose translated Boece.

Yet, good as are these early works of Chaucer, fresh as the month of May, which he really loved, not merely as a convention, they are mainly translations from, or variations on, French and Italian originals, visions in the medieval manner. Even *Troilus and Criseyde* was taken largely from Boccaccio, though he added his own incomparable genius, a genius that was to be fully revealed only in his last and greatest work, *The Canterbury Tales.*

Chaucer was a new phenomenon, a writer acquainted with all classes of society, with a passionate interest in people, individual men and women, as opposed to medieval abstractions, and with a Shakespearean understanding of human nature, compassion and, therefore, tolerance. Although he wrote lines of extreme beauty, he was not remarkable as a lyric poet, but he was a supremely great dramatic and narrative poet; had he lived in the sixteenth century he would have rivalled Shakespeare, at least in comedy, and in the nineteenth he would have out-ranged Dickens. All the essential gifts of the dramatist and novelist were his, save perhaps that of real tragedy, his nearest approach to which is pathos, as in the dying words of Arcite in *The Knight's Tale*:

> What is this world? what asketh men to have?
> Now with his love, now in the colde grave
> Alone, withouten any company.

As a master of comedy, from the broadest and bawdiest to the subtlest irony, he has rarely been equalled, and the Wife of Bath is one of the greatest comic creations in any literature. But the important thing is that she is English, as are all the other pilgrims whom Harry Bailey conducted to Canterbury (where they would find the nave being rebuilt in the new Perpendicular style), and because of this Chaucer may well be called the father of English literature. In another sense also he was its father, for he established his own dialect, the East

◀ *In summer seson whan softe was the sunne.*
Piers Plowman falls asleep on Malvern Hills, and dreams of the abuses of the late fourteenth century.

Midland, as the standard speech of England, the iambic pentameter as the standard line of its poetry, and rhyme rather than alliteration as its characteristic convention. The contribution of his contemporary and friend, John Gower, was no mean one, but Gower still dealt with medieval shadows, and it was Chaucer who brought real, or apparently real, people, and realism, apparent reality, into our literature.

Thomas Hoccleve was another of Chaucer's admirers, and tried, somewhat feebly, to emulate his 'master dear, flower of eloquence', and in his 'Lament' for 'the first finder of our fair langage' he wrote – in the seven-line stanza, or rhyme royal, that Chaucer introduced:

> Although his life be quenched, the resemblance
> Of him hath in me so fresh livelinesse,
> That, to put other men in remembrance
> Of his person, I have here his likeness
> Do make,

and in the margin of his manuscript is Chaucer's portrait. It must have been drawn from memory, and though it may not be a good likeness, it certainly is an attempted likeness, not merely a conventional sketch, and illustrates not only Chaucer but the new realism in the visual arts as well as in literature. Then, in an early-fifteenth-century manuscript of *The Canterbury Tales*, at the beginning of each story is a small picture of its narrator: the hunting Monk, white-bearded Franklin, Chaucer himself, and the Wife of Bath on her ambling horse:

> Y-wimpled well, and on her head an hat
> As broad as is a buckler or a targe.

Similar realistic figures may be seen in stained glass of the period, and donors themselves now appear as kneeling figures at the feet of some saint or other, perhaps because they believed, with Langland's friar, that by presenting a window they could make certain of Heaven, their portrait serving as a memorandum to the saint and as a passport for the immigration officer, St Peter. There is the same realism in the sleeping soldiers of the 'Resurrection panel' of a retable in Norwich Cathedral; it is characteristic of the fourteenth century that it was a standard design, and alabaster reliefs of the same scene are even more realistic.

Hoow he þi seruaunt was mayden marie
And lat his loue floure and fructifie

Al þogh his lyfe be queynt þe resemblaunce
Of him haþ in me so fressh lyflynesse
Þat to putte othir men in remembraunce
Of his persone I haue heere his lyknesse
Do make to þis ende in soþfastnesse
Þat þei þat haue of him lest þought & mynde
By þis peynture may ageyn him fynde

The ymages þat in þe chirche been
Maken folk þenke on god & on his seyntes
Whan þe ymages þei beholden & seen
Were oft unsyte of hem causiþ restreyntes
Of þoughtes gode whan a þing depeynt is
Or entailed if men take of it heede
Thoght of þe lyknesse it wil in hym brede

◀ The new realism: (*Left*) A donor in a fourteenth-century window. Note the canopies and grisaille below. (*Right*) Chaucer's portrait in Hoccleve's *De Regimine Principum*.

Studies from a fourteenth-century artist's sketchbook.

One of the best examples of the new interest in naturalism is an artist's sketch-book with remarkably lifelike drawings of birds and animals, from thrush to seagull, from cat to squirrel. The artist is unknown, but we know the illustrator of the Lovell Lectionary, with its animal and heraldic borders. This was John Siferwas, a monk of Sherborne Abbey, who drew a realistic portrait of himself presenting his book to Lord Lovell. Of about the same period, 1420, is the Bedford Hours and Psalter, a late example, and the finest, of this style known as International Gothic. But the great age of English illumination was almost over; the art became commercialized, foreign work was imported, and after 1450 and the beginning of the Wars of the Roses there was nothing of any great value.

The reign of Richard II (1377–99), when Chaucer was writing his later poetry, was perhaps the most ornate period in our history, and it is not surprising that the art of the Court school still persisted, the large portrait of Richard in Westminster Abbey being one of its finest works. There is no attempt at realism: the King sits bolt upright in a Gothic chair, his boneless medieval fingers holding orb and sceptre, and all is formally symmetrical except the folds of his long red robe, arranged to reveal the blue and gold of the dress beneath. Nor is there much attempt at realism in the most beautiful painting of this period, the *Wilton Diptych*. Here Richard kneels in front of three saints who are presenting him to the Virgin and Child, surrounded by angels whose blue-tipped wings make a heraldic pattern against the diapered gold background.

(*Far left*) Adam and Eve, from the Bedford Book of Hours, *c.* 1420.
(*Left*) John Siferwas presents his book to his patron, Lord Lovell, *c.* 1400.

(*Right*) Richard II: a late-fourteenth-century painting in the courtly style. Westminster Abbey.

The *Wilton Diptych*. St Edmund, St Edward the Confessor and St John the Baptist present Richard II to the Virgin.

Yet realism was creeping in, even into the courtly style. In one of the manuscripts of *Troilus and Criseyde* is a miniature of Chaucer reading his poetry in the open air to a company of lords and ladies. It resembles courtly French painting, with an idealized castle against a sky of patterned gold, and though the trees are medieval conventions of the mushroom type, some of the members of the audience might well have been among the Canterbury pilgrims, and are probably portraits of real people. Even the bronze effigy of Richard II in Westminster Abbey, with its cruel eyes and weak chin, is a portrait rather than an idealized representation.

Richard II: the bronze effigy in Westminster Abbey.

Chaucer reading his poetry, possibly *Troilus and Criseyde*, to a courtly audience, *c.* 1400.

(*Left*) Angels on the double hammer-beam roof of March Church, Cambridgeshire. (*Right*) The Resurrection. A late-fourteenth-century alabaster panel of standard design.

The fifteenth century was a century of war, of the second half of the Hundred Years War followed by the thirty-year Wars of the Roses, when there was comparatively little major ecclesiastical building, and there are no cathedrals built entirely in the Perpendicular style, though towers were added to a number of them, to York, for example, and Worcester. It was, however, a great century for the enlargement and building of parish churches, ventures often financed by the wealthy middle class, notably those connected with the lucrative wool trade: Blythburgh in Suffolk, for example, and in the Cotswolds Chipping Campden and Fairford, and in the far west St Neot in Cornwall. The last two are remarkable as the only parish churches that have retained virtually all their original windows.

It was an age of standardization and mass production as well as, perhaps because of, war. Perpendicular tracery and wall-panels were themselves merely variations on a standard pattern, and companies of craftsmen supplied churches with their accessories, London specializing in sculpture, Nottingham in alabaster carvings, and York in stained glass. The most obvious development of this last art was the greater use of clear glass, combined with delicate painting in silver stain, particularly in the canopies. This meant that larger pieces of glass could be used, and that leadwork need not always follow the forms of the

Fairford Church, Gloucestershire. The Last Judgment in the late Perpendicular west window, *c.* 1500. The earth burns beneath Christ's feet, below is St Michael weighing souls, and Hell is on the right.

design, but could cut across them quite arbitrarily. Again, as such windows let more light into the church, it was no longer necessary to retain the device of putting in bands of grisaille between the rows of coloured figures. These lost the willowy grace of the fourteenth century and became more homely, the scenes more lively, and a still greater realism was achieved by modelling the faces. This was done by covering the glass with a film of brown enamel and, when it was dry but before firing, brushing out the lighter tones. Stained glass, in fact, was approaching the art of the painter, and by the end of the century almost all the original conventions, and with them the mosaic character, had gone: borders, decorative ironwork, defining lead-strips, and, as at Fairford, even the mullions were ignored, and the painting, for such it virtually was, ran through all the lights, to be framed by the outer masonry of the window itself. Although stained glass had lost its thirteenth-century richness of blue and ruby, these silvery windows are often exceedingly beautiful, and seem to be the inevitable complement of Perpendicular churches, with their tall arcades, spacious clerestories, and high timber roofs.

St Christopher. This saint, who protected the traveller, was generally painted on the wall facing the south door, so that the worshipper could see him when entering or leaving. Poughill Church, Cornwall, *c.* 1500.

The walls of these churches are now bare stone, but many of them were once covered with paintings, as were the panels of their rood-screens. Like so many other forms of fifteenth-century art, church painting was commercialized, and associations of craftsmen supplied standard work which, though often crude, was generally a vigorous reflection of contemporary life. A favourite theme was that of St Christopher, reputed to have been a giant, carrying the Infant Christ across a river, and his huge figure was painted on the wall opposite the south door, as in the fifteenth-century granite church at Breage in Cornwall. An even more interesting painting in the same church is that of Christ Blessing the Trades: a tall figure naïvely dressed in a loincloth and crown, surrounded by all manner of workmen's tools.

What kind of music exactly was sung and played in these churches we do not know, but by the beginning of the century there had been a considerable development in polyphony, notably in the gymel. This was a form of composition in which the main tune was sung by a lower voice, while two upper voices, in thirds with one another, sang a different melody. The gymel appears

Title-page of *Everyman*, 1530, finest of all morality plays. Death summoning Everyman.

to have been of English origin, and counterpoint was still further developed in the first half of the century by the first great English composer whose name we know, John Dunstable, who acquired a prodigious reputation throughout Europe. Henry VI was a patron of music as well as of the other arts, and it was in his reign that Cambridge University began to give degrees in music, and that the first Master of the Children of the Chapel Royal was appointed, boys who were to play such an important part in the history of the drama.

The time was not yet, however. Despite the realism of the graphic arts, the fifteenth century was much given to allegory and prolix moralizing, partly the result, perhaps, of the homilies delivered by Wycliffe and the Lollards, for preaching has ever been a failing, or a necessary foible, of reformers. In any event, the Biblical characters of religious drama gave place to abstractions, personifications of virtues and vices such as Charity and Sloth, and the miracle play, a dramatic representation of a Bible story, developed into the didactic morality play, a dramatization of the sermon. There is mention of a morality play at York in the late fourteenth century, but the earliest extant example is *The Castle of Perseverance* of about 1450. Like the Cornish miracle plays, it was performed in a round, the scaffold of God at the east, Hell Mouth at the north, and the Castle in the middle, the theme being the struggle of the World, the Flesh, and the Devil for the soul of Mankind. It is long, and even a medieval audience cannot have found it very entertaining, though they would be moved, as we are today, by the finest of all moralities, *Everyman*, in which the worldly possessions of Everyman one by one desert him at the last:

Alas, whereto may I trust?
Beauty goeth fast away from me;
She promised with me to live and die.

Chaucer was the precursor of fifteenth-century realism, Langland of its allegory and moralities, and allegory was relentlessly pursued in narrative verse by Stephen Hawes in his *Pastime of Pleasure*, a poem singularly lacking in that quality, though had he not written, Spenser would not, or might not, have written the *Faerie Queene*. The fifteenth century produced no English poets approaching Chaucer's stature, but Scotland did, and Robert Henryson's *Testament of Cresseid* is a sequel to Chaucer's *Troilus and Criseyde*. Deserted by Diomed, Cressida is stricken with leprosy, and as she sits begging by the roadside Troilus rides past; something in the repulsive creature reminds him 'Of fair Cresseid, sumtyme his awin darling', so he throws her a purse of gold and rides unhappily on. The half-blind Cressida does not recognize her former lover, but another leper tells her who her benefactor is:

When Cresseid understude that it was he,
Stiffer than steill thair stert ane bitter stound
Throwout hir hart, and fell doun to the ground.

That at least is worthy of Chaucer. So too is the poetry of William Dunbar, a man of many moods and styles, racy and violent as Burns, whose literary ancestor he was, sometimes gracefully majestic as Spenser – 'London, thou art the flower of cities all' – sometimes afflicted with medieval terror, as in his *Lament for the Makers*, for the poets, above all for 'the noble Chaucer', whom Death has devoured, and now,

I that in health was and gladness
Am trublit now with great sickness
And feblit with infirmitie:
Timor Mortis conturbat me.

Although there were no great English poets in the fifteenth century, there was great poetry, the poetry of the ballads, the majority of which appear to have been composed, or to have received their final form, in the later Middle Ages. Their authors are unknown, for most of them were probably communal compositions, any member of a group of humble folk at work or play contributing a line to the story, the theme of which was often emphasized by a refrain. As a result they vary greatly in quality, but the best, many of them of Scottish or Border origin, have a dramatic intensity and lines that any poet might envy – 'The channerin' worm doth chide' – and a century later Sir Philip Sidney was to write, 'I never heard the old song of *Percy and Douglas*, that I found not my heart moved more than with a Trumpet.'

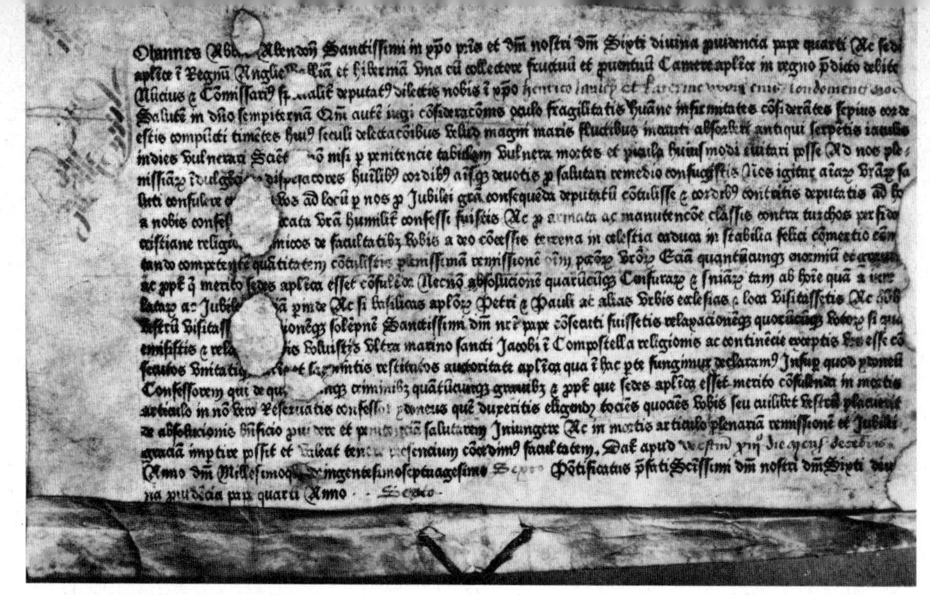

A cultural revolution. The earliest document printed by Caxton: an indulgence from the Abbot of Abingdon, 13 December 1476.

The most notable literary event of the century, however, was the publication of Malory's *Morte Darthur*, a version of the popular Arthurian romances, and the first great book of English prose. Sir Thomas Malory was an adventurer of the Wars of the Roses with an atrocious record of crime, yet, with apparent artlessness, he showed what could be done with simple English prose, from stark and vivid description to lyric grace: 'Therefore, all ye that be lovers call unto your remembrance the month of May, like as did Queen Guenever, for whom I make here a little mention, that while she lived she was a true lover, and therefore she had a good end.' But even more important than the writing of the book was its publication, its printing. In 1476 William Caxton set up a press in Westminster, and in the Preface to the first book printed in English, *The Historye of Troye*, wrote: 'It is not wreton with penne and ynke as other bokes ben . . . for all the bokes of this storye . . . were begonne in oon day, and also fynysshid in oon day.' Chaucer's Clerk of Oxford had dreamed of a library of twenty books, precious manuscript volumes that would take months and years to write 'with penne and ynke', but now as many copies could be printed in an hour. The Middle Ages were almost over.

Not quite, however. While Caxton was printing *The Canterbury Tales* and *Morte Darthur*, one of the finest of all medieval buildings was going up, the Chapel of King's College, Cambridge. Begun by Henry VI, it was completed by Henry VII, and for the first time a wide and high nave was roofed with fan-vaulting. It was the logical conclusion of Perpendicular Gothic, a linear style in which lierne ribs no longer competed for attention with window and wall tracery; all was now integrated and harmonized, walls, windows, and vault a contrapuntal composition of lace-like tracery. Perfection had been reached, after

King's College Chapel, Cambridge, *c.* 1450–1500. Fan vaulting, and the perfection of Perpendicular Gothic. ▶

Paintings on the north wall of Eton College Chapel. Although essentially monochrome, they have a few touches of colour. Commissioned by William of Waynflete, they were painted by

which there could only be decline, elaborated variations on the theme, as in the extravagant decoration of the interior of Henry VII's Chapel in Westminster Abbey. The sculpture varies in quality, the best being the half-life-size statues high up in niches, and the small bronze figures round Henry's tomb. This was the work of the Florentine sculptor Pietro Torrigiano – the man who broke Michelangelo's nose – and symptomatic of what was happening at the turn of the century, the decay of the native English tradition and infiltration of the new art of the Renaissance, not so much directly from Italy as indirectly from France

William Baker between 1479 and 1483. They represent the Miracles of the Virgin, each episode being defined by women saints standing in niches. A similar series dealing with men has perished.

and the Netherlands. Thus, the most remarkable of all fifteenth-century wall-paintings, the monochrome Miracles of the Virgin, executed during the 1480s in Eton College Chapel, though English in their feeling for line, appear to have been inspired by contemporary Flemish and Burgundian work, and it is possible that their painter, William Baker, was himself a Fleming. Certainly the King's Glazier, Barnard Flower, responsible for the stained glass – now perished – in Henry VII's Chapel, was a member of the prosperous Flemish colony of artists in Southwark.

Flower was both designer and glazier of one of the earlier windows in King's College Chapel, and on his death in 1517 was succeeded by Galyon Hone, another Netherlander, who glazed most of the windows after the designs of Dirick Vellert of Antwerp. They are splendid, but neither English nor medieval; Renaissance painting has overwhelmed the medieval art of stained glass: the old conventions have gone, the borders that defined each light as a separate work of translucent mosaic, and Romanesque repose has become a turmoil of figures that break through the mullions and other restraints, symbol of the restless energy of man's questing spirit in the new age.

Flemish influence. The five lower lights of a window in King's College Chapel, Cambridge, by Vellert and Hone, *c.* 1520. In the centre are 'Messengers' carrying scrolls that describe the scenes: on the left, Paul and Barnabas at Lystra; on the right, the stoning of Paul.

7 The Early Tudors 1485–1558

Although the Middle Ages in England did not end with the accession of Henry VII and the Tudors in 1485, they had not much longer to go. The old aristocracy had destroyed itself in the Wars of the Roses, and the medieval social and economic order was breaking down; a New World beyond the Atlantic had been discovered as well as a new world of the spirit, and printing presses disseminated the new learning and ideas of the Renaissance; the monasteries were dissolved and the vast estates of the Church passed into the hands of a new aristocracy and gentry, the Justices of the Peace who were to enforce the discipline imposed by King and Privy Council. It was a secular age, in which medieval unity and co-operation gave place to individualism and competition; no longer was the Church chief patron of the arts, ordering retables and stained-glass windows; cathedral workshops closed, and demand now came from moneyed laymen, not for Tudor churches and Elizabethan chancels but for houses, handsome chimneypieces, and family portraits, their ecclesiastical contribution becoming confined virtually to tombs and monumental effigies with which they encumbered the aisles of churches, hoping thereby to perpetuate their memory.

Court patronage of the arts was to prove capricious, but Henry VII, most parsimonious of princes, began magnificently by commissioning Torrigiano to make the tomb in his Westminster Abbey chapel for himself and Queen Elizabeth of York. It is a startling contrast to the screen of English workmanship that surrounds it, for this is Perpendicular tracery in bronze, medievally angular and linear, whereas the gilt-bronze ornament and figures on the black

Italian influence. Pietro Torrigiano's tomb of Henry VII in Westminster Abbey. A plump Renaissance cherub (*above*) looks down at the bronze effigy of the first Tudor king. 1512.

Italian terracotta reaches England. Medallion with bust of Julius Caesar by Giovanni da Maiano.

(*Right*) Hampton Court: hammer-beam roof of the great hall, built by Henry VIII, 1531–6, in the medieval style. ▶

marble tomb-chest are of the High Renaissance, classical in their plasticity and fullness of form. On each side are three large medallions enclosing Henry's patron saints; at each end the royal arms are supported by plump Italian cherubs, and above an ornate Corinthian pilaster an infant angel sits at each of the four corners. The effigies of the King and Queen, however, are more Gothic in spirit; though the faces are portraits, the robes, concealing the forms beneath, fall in long folds in the medieval manner. Torrigiano's other masterpiece in the same chapel, the tomb of Henry's mother Margaret Beaufort, is similar, though she lies, her wrinkled hands in prayer, within a horizontal Gothic niche, a traceried canopy at her head. A few years later this Renaissance type of tomb was imitated as far west as central Cornwall, when Prior Vyvyan of Bodmin died in 1533.

Tudor Gothic: red brick, flattened arches, square mullioned windows, towers and tall ornate chimneys. Wolsey's Palace of Hampton Court, begun 1514: the entrance gate from the courtyard.

Yet, although tombs might be Italianate and stained-glass windows Flemish, architecture remained insularly English, and foreign influence amounted to little more than the application of Renaissance ornament to buildings still essentially Gothic, though Gothic with a difference, a modification of the Perpendicular style for secular purposes. The Early English arch was a sharp pointed lancet, and its development through the Decorated and Perpendicular periods had been a gradual depression, until in Tudor times it became so blunt that the logical conclusion was the square-headed mullioned window. The splendid timber roofs of the period, spanning the halls of house and palace, followed much the same pattern: low pitched and concealed on the outside by parapets. The emphasis, as in costume – consider the portraits of Henry VIII – was on the broad and square. A further modification was the use of red brick instead of, or in conjunction with, grey stone.

Thus Hampton Court, begun by Wolsey in 1514 and completed by Henry VIII after the Cardinal's fall, was planned on the lines of the medieval colleges of Oxford and Cambridge. The entrance is characteristically Tudor: a great square gatehouse with an octagonal tower at each corner, and pierced by a depressed archway that leads into the base court, at the far end of which is another gatehouse and another court with its great hall, and beyond this the chapel. It is all very English; the magnificent hammer-beam roof of the hall was designed by the King's Master Carpenter, James Nedham, and its carving executed by Richard Rydge, who, however, introduced Renaissance detail such as scrolls and *putti*; but the terracotta roundels of Roman emperors on the gatehouses – perhaps the first terracotta ornament in England – were the work of Giovanni da Maiano, as probably was the terracotta panel of Wolsey's arms with *putti* as supporters: English architecture and Italian detail.

After Wolsey's fall in 1529 and the breach with Rome, however, the main foreign influence for the next thirty years was French. Henry VIII's great rival as a Renaissance prince was Francis I of France, and as the money from the dissolved monasteries flowed into his Treasury Henry began to build the grandiose Palace of Nonsuch in Surrey, probably in an attempt to surpass the

Château de Chambord. Nonsuch perished in the next century, but it is clear that much of the detail, fireplaces for example, was inspired by French models, and probably the work of French craftsmen. So too, in all probability, was the great carved screen that Henry presented to King's College Chapel in 1533–5. It has been called the finest piece of woodwork north of the Alps, but even in Italy there can be few masterpieces that excel the delicate carving of lunette and spandrel, cove, cornice, and pilaster. The carving, of about the same date, on the canopy above the marble and terracotta tomb of the first Lord Marney in Layer Marney church, Essex, though inferior in quality, is not unlike that on the King's screen, and even the black marble armoured effigy may be French, for instead of lying on a helmet in the ascetic English manner, the head rests more luxuriously on a cushion. The terracotta window-frames of Layer Marney Hall and its crestings with classical motifs are of about the same period as Wolsey's work at Hampton Court, and probably Italian.

The screen in King's College Chapel, Cambridge, *c.* 1531–5, with classical Renaissance carving.

After the Dissolution much monastic property came into the market, and a good example of what happened to it is Lacock Abbey in Wiltshire, acquired by Sir William Sharington, who in 1540 began its conversion into a house. Much of it has since been altered, but again some of the detail betrays French influence: a chimney, a fireplace, two stone pedestal tables, and a ceiling. Another of the new men to profit from the Dissolution was Sir Thomas Wriothesley, first Earl of Southampton, and grandfather of Shakespeare's patron. Henry rewarded him with Titchfield Abbey, which he converted into a house, building a great crenellated gatehouse with four octagonal towers at the corners. Like Hampton Court, it was medieval in plan, an imitation fortress when fortification was no longer necessary, and the houses of the new age were to be outward looking, not medievally introspective, looking into a courtyard.

One of the first of these houses, built about 1530, is Barrington Court in Somerset, which, though still medieval in its mullioned and transomed

windows and angle buttresses, is classical in its search for symmetry, not an easy quality to attain when the hall remained the most important feature. Built in the form of a capital 'E', the hall and buttery are accommodated in the long side, from the centre of which projects a porch, and at either end a wing. It is, in fact, a courtyard house opened up by the omission of its fourth side, and this was to become the characteristic plan of smaller Tudor country-houses. Another experiment was made, however, in about 1555 at Mount Edgcumbe, overlooking Plymouth. It was described by Richard Carew in his *Survey of Cornwall*, 1602: 'The house is builded square, with a round turret at each end, garreted on the top, and the hall rising in the midst above the rest, which yieldeth a stately sound as you enter the same.' It was an old-fashioned, crenellated ['garreted'] house, yet new-fashioned in that the hall usurped the place of the central courtyard, rising above the wings so that it could be lit by clerestory windows. It was warm – 'two closed doors exclude all offensive coldness' – and the experiment was repeated at Wollaton some twenty-five years later.

Much more important for the future of English architecture was Somerset House, designed about 1550 by Sir John Thynne for the Protector Somerset. In plan it was conservative, a courtyard house, but in elevation it was revolutionary, apparently the first attempt to build a house with a symmetrically classical façade, though it was to be another seventy years before the first truly classical building was erected. At one end of the courtyard was an open gallery, or loggia, a round-arched arcade surmounted by a cornice and divided by a central doorway flanked by pilasters. The Strand front was even more formal: a central gateway rising to three storeys, the windows again flanked by pilasters, the top two being crowned with pediments, as were those of the two-storied wings that ended in slight projections in which the windows were bracketed in pairs by a long pediment, in the French manner. Thynne was a great traveller, and evidently knew the châteaux that were going up in France, though he was no slavish imitator, and his next venture, Longleat – he had acquired the property at the Dissolution – was to be one of the first and most distinguished of great Elizabethan country-houses.

A Holbein painting: Sir George Cornwall.

Although innumerable foreign artists and craftsmen visited and settled in Tudor England, particularly after the accession of Elizabeth, there were only two of the very highest quality: Torrigiano and Holbein, and both at the beginning of the century. The explosive Torrigiano died in Spain in 1522, and four years later Hans Holbein, aged thirty, arrived in London with a letter of introduction from Erasmus to Sir Thomas More. He was acquainted with the work of the great Italian masters, and would almost certainly have been a painter of religious pictures had it not been for the Reformation, which put a Protestant end to such Catholic matter. It is not without irony that in Catholic southern Europe a pagan classical manner perpetuated medieval subject, while in the Protestant north secular subject perpetuated medieval manner. In all the arts the southern genius is for colour and volume, the northern genius for line, which

Barrington Court, Somerset. Tudor Gothic: stone-built, with high gables and chimneys, and without the fourth side of a medieval courtyard house, *c.* 1530.

Somerset House, London: the Strand front. Built by Sir John Thynne for the Protector Somerset *c.* 1550, it was probably the first English house to be built with a Renaissance façade.

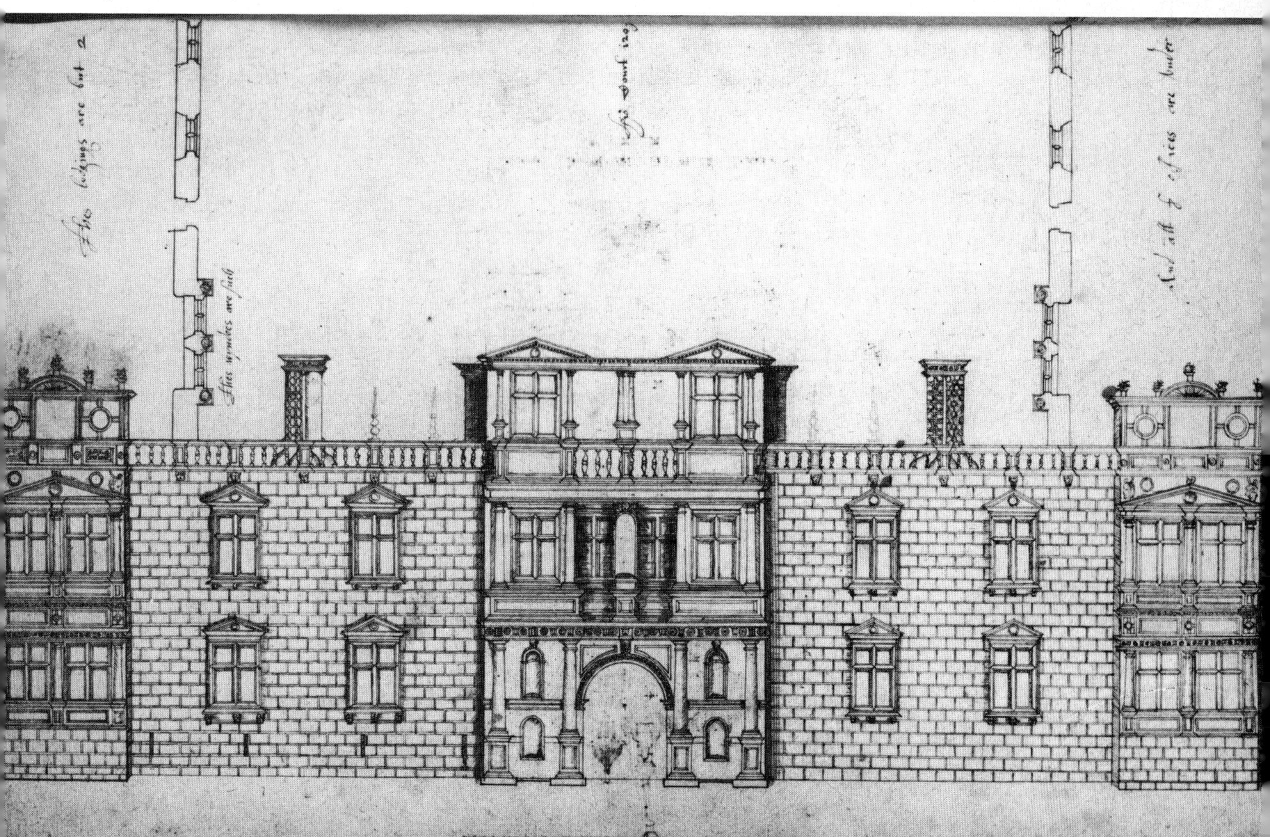

may be why the English have never been a sculptural people. It was, therefore, as a painter of portraits that Holbein arrived in England, and in his portraits of More and his circle he continued and confirmed the English linear tradition. This is best seen in the series of chalk drawings that he made in 1527 for the More family group, and the painting of Sir Thomas, despite the fullness of treatment, is a study in line as well as in character. It must be remembered that these are among the very first English portraits in the modern sense of the word, portraits for which the subject sat to the artist.

In 1528 Holbein went back to Basel, and when he returned to England in 1532 More was in disgrace, and he found his next patrons among the foreign merchants of London. Only in 1536 did Henry VIII take him under his patronage, primarily as a painter of potential brides, and it was in this year that he painted Jane Seymour, a portrait in which the emphasis is on line and pattern, the jewelled head-dress, necklace, and embroidery. The same is true of the portraits of the King himself, of what is perhaps his most beautiful painting, that of Sir George Cornwall, and of the splendid series of drawings preserved at Windsor Castle: Sir Thomas Wyatt, the Earl of Surrey, Sir Philip Hoby, and the rest.

A Holbein miniature: Mrs Pemberton.

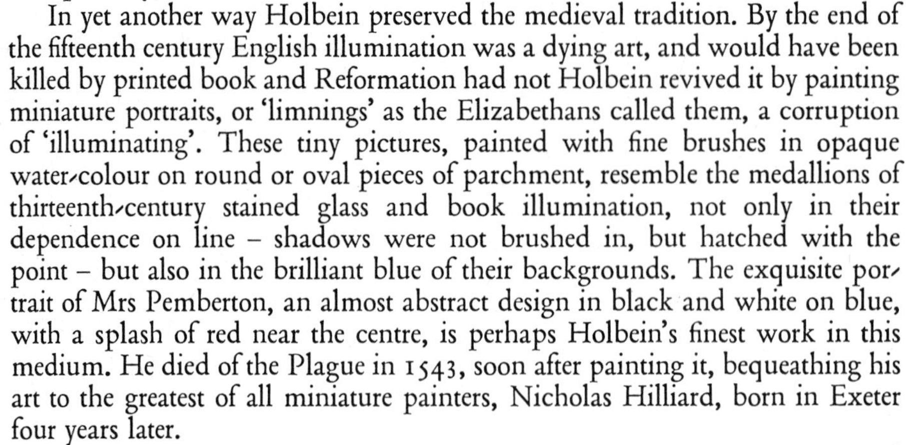

In yet another way Holbein preserved the medieval tradition. By the end of the fifteenth century English illumination was a dying art, and would have been killed by printed book and Reformation had not Holbein revived it by painting miniature portraits, or 'limnings' as the Elizabethans called them, a corruption of 'illuminating'. These tiny pictures, painted with fine brushes in opaque water-colour on round or oval pieces of parchment, resemble the medallions of thirteenth-century stained glass and book illumination, not only in their dependence on line – shadows were not brushed in, but hatched with the point – but also in the brilliant blue of their backgrounds. The exquisite portrait of Mrs Pemberton, an almost abstract design in black and white on blue, with a splash of red near the centre, is perhaps Holbein's finest work in this medium. He died of the Plague in 1543, soon after painting it, bequeathing his art to the greatest of all miniature painters, Nicholas Hilliard, born in Exeter four years later.

Hilliard was to write: 'Holbein's manner of limning I have ever imitated and hold it for the best, by reason that of truth all the rare sciences, especially the arts of carving, painting, goldsmiths, embroiderers, together with the most of all the liberal sciences, came first unto us from the strangers, and generally they are the best and most in number.' It was an odd reason to give for imitating Holbein, and was by no means altogether true, though it was true that Holbein's most famous successors were foreigners, as were to be the best painters in England for the next hundred and fifty years. The Renaissance, which had reached France and north-west Europe during the feudal struggle of York and Lancaster, had sapped English confidence in its native art, yet John Bettes, 'anglois', judging from his only signed picture, of a man in a black cap,

An English and a Flemish painter: (*Left*) *A Man in a Black Cap*, by John Bettes, 1545. (*Right*) *Lord Darnley and his Brother*, by Hans Eworth, 1563.

painted in 1545, was a not unworthy follower of Holbein. The influx from the Netherlands was beginning, and within a few years of Holbein's death Guillim Scrots was in the service of Henry VIII. A painter of more than common merit, he favoured the full-length standing portrait introduced by Holbein, the fine *Earl of Surrey*, for example, and if the *Young Man in Red* at Hampton Court be his, he was the first to paint such a portrait with an open-air background. Scrots seems to have left England at the beginning of Mary's reign, and it was probably his countryman, Hans Eworth, a shadowy figure, who painted the Catholic Queen, a portrait in which the thin, fanatical face is emphasized by the angular detail of her dress, her loneliness by the shadowy background of an empty room, an effect that was repeated in the poignant picture of the young Lord Darnley and his little brother, two boys in black standing in an empty Tudor gallery. Such pictures might almost be illustrations of Elizabethan tragedy, and equally well the painting of Sir John Luttrell being rescued from shipwreck by Peace, if the lady were not so like a Roman goddess, might illustrate a medieval morality.

Title-page of John Skelton's *Garlande of Laurell*, 1523.

The age of allegory was not yet over, and in literature was carried into the Tudor century by John Skelton in his play *Magnificence*. The great man, Magnificence, discards his virtuous counsellors in favour of Cloaked Collusion, Crafty Conveyance, and other vices, as a result of which he is, literally, beaten down by Adversity. The play is too long, without dramatic tension, much of it conventional moralizing, meaningless as the Last Judgment paintings above the chancel arches of churches, yet it would be visually effective, as when Poverty appears, 'lousy and unliking and full of scurf', and when we realize that it was a satire directed against Wolsey it gains point and becomes prophetic, though, unlike Magnificence, Wolsey did not find help in Redress and Circumspection and recover his estate. Much of Skelton's non-dramatic poetry was satire aimed at Wolsey, the proud prelate of the unreformed Church, as in *Colin Clout*, or more generally against the abuses of the age, as in *The Tunning of Elinor Rumming*, a description of the 'boosy, scurfy and lousy' creatures who swilled Elinor's noppy ale. Partly because of changes in pronunciation, notably the dropping of the final *e*, English prosody, like some of the other arts, had degenerated in the course of the fifteenth century, until the form given to verse by Chaucer was sometimes little more than rhyming prose. The verse of *Magnificence* is held together by rhyme, alliteration, and a doggerel rhythm, but for his poems Skelton invented a short, rapidly turning line that restored to verse form of a sort,

ragged,
Tattered and jagged,
Rudely rain-beaten,
Rusty and moth-eaten.

As employed by him it was equally effective in satire, in the mock-pathos of *Philip Sparrow*, and the lyric *To Mistress Margery Wentworth*:

With marjoram gentle,
The flower of goodlihood,
Embroidered the mantle
Is of your maidenhood.

Skelton was the most considerable poet in the barren century between Chaucer and the Reformation, ranging from the coarsest virulence to the utmost delicacy, but because he was an eccentric he was forgotten, and it is only recently that his merit has been rediscovered.

One of Skelton's poems, *Woefully arrayed*, was set to music by his great contemporary William Cornish, who thus began the happy partnership that was to be celebrated in Elizabethan times by Richard Barnfield in his sonnet: 'If Music and sweet Poetry agree, As they must needs, the sister and the brother.' Cornish was himself a poet, author of the haunting 'The knight knocked at the castle gate', and a man of many accomplishments: playwright, actor, Gentleman of the Chapel Royal, and main organizer of the revels at the Court of the youthful Henry VIII, whose favourite he was. The Chapel Royal, established in the twelfth century, was the sovereign's private choir, in Tudor times consisting of some thirty Gentlemen and twelve boys, who accompanied the Court on its travels, as when they went to France in 1520 and at the Field of the Cloth of Gold sang with the corresponding royal choir before the two kings. Cornish had become Master of the Children of the Chapel Royal on Henry's accession in 1509, and it was he who first formed them into a dramatic company for the performance of plays at Court, a venture with momentous consequences.

Cornish's most distinguished colleague in the Chapel was Robert Fayrfax, organist of St Albans Abbey, and another great composer. Most of their music, like that of all professionals before the Reformation, was written for the Catholic Church: Masses, sequences such as the 'Stabat Mater', and motets. The motet was a polyphonic refinement of the conductus, in which the length of the notes in the various parts might differ from one another. Often, however, there was little relation between the parts, which might be three or four well-known tunes, sometimes secular, more or less harmoniously arranged. Cornish and Fayrfax improved on this, though their polyphony was not yet fully articulated, the parts still being independent rather than related, repeating, echoing one another, an interweaving of similar, yet different, melodies. One difficulty was that the old modal scales did not lend themselves to modulation, in spite of the device known as 'musica ficta', the sharpening and flattening of notes to make them harmonically acceptable, and as change of key is of the essence of polyphony, it was not until our modern scales began to be adopted later in the century that the art could be perfected. This did not affect folk-music, which, like ballads, must often have been communal compositions, generally modal melodies without harmonic elaboration, and Early Tudor times seem to have been a great period for the making of such music: 'Green-sleeves', for example.

The 1520s brought a change, for in this decade Fayrfax, Cornish and Skelton died, and were succeeded by young men born at about the turn of the century: by the composers John Taverner, Christopher Tye, Thomas Tallis, John Shepherd, and John Merbecke, and the poets Thomas Wyatt and the Earl of Surrey. It was also the decade in which Holbein came to England, William Tyndale went to Germany to complete his translation of the New Testament, Lord Berners translated Froissart's *Chronicles*, and More's recently written *Utopia* was translated into German. All these men were to be affected by the Reformation – for some of them, indeed, it meant death – but on the whole musicians fared better than writers during the twenty-five confused years between England's severance from Rome and Elizabeth's religious settlement.

Members of the Chapel Royal Choir. In Shakespeare's time the Children presented plays at Court and in their own Blackfriars Theatre.

Thomas Tallis (*c.* 1505–85), greatest of early Tudor composers.

Two poets of the reign of Henry VIII:
(*Right*) Sir Thomas Wyatt, 1503–42:
a drawing by Holbein.
(*Far right*) The Earl of Surrey, 1517?–47:
a painting by Guillim Scrots.

Tallis, composer of the celestial motet *Spem in alium*, for eight five-part choirs, remained an obstinate though moderate Catholic all his long life, and in Elizabeth's reign accommodatingly changed Catholic motet into Protestant anthem by substituting English words for Latin. Taverner, Master of the Children at Cardinal College (Christ Church), Oxford, was imprisoned for heresy by its founder, Wolsey, but pardoned, 'being but a Musitian'. But a musician to be reckoned with, and his Mass, *The Western Wind*, despite the interdict of the Catholic Church, was unashamedly based on a popular folk-song. Merbecke, a Calvinist, was condemned to death for heresy, but escaped, and in 1549 furnished the music for Edward VI's first 'Booke of Common Praier, Noted', adaptations of Catholic plainsong to the rhythms of English prose. In the same year came Thomas Sternhold's metrical version of *Certayne Psalms* and the four-voice settings of Robert Crowley. The 'peevish and humoursome' Tye contributed a metrical version of the Acts of the Apostles, 'wyth notes to eche Chapter to synge and also to play upon the Lute'. It was fortunate that the art of printing music had been perfected, the first book of music to be printed in England, a collection of songs, having come from the

The first book of music printed in Britain. A lyric from Wynkyn de Worde's collection of songs, 1530.

press of Wynkyn de Worde in 1530. The age of instrumental music and accompanied song had arrived, and with it a new generation of composers. When Elizabeth succeeded Mary in 1558 William Byrd was fifteen.

In the previous year the stationer Richard Tottel had printed an anthology with the remarkable title, *Songes and Sonettes*, remarkable because the sonnet was then an unknown form in English. These were the contribution of two young men, Sir Thomas Wyatt, a much-travelled diplomat who had died in 1542, and the Earl of Surrey, executed on a frivolous charge of treason five years later. They took the sonnet from Petrarch, though Wyatt varied it slightly by clinching it with a rhyming couplet, as did Surrey, who was even freer in his adaptation, preferring the alternate rhyme of three quatrains before the final couplet, the form that was to be adopted by the Elizabethans. In this way they restored the discipline and form that English verse had so sorely lacked since the death of Chaucer. Wyatt also experimented with a number of other metrical forms, notably the *terza rima* of Dante, and, though sometimes stiff owing to his insistence on strict scansion, he had a passion, simplicity, and purity of diction that made him the first great lyric poet in our language:

> My lute, awake! perform the last
> Labour that thou and I shall waste,
> And end that I have now begun;
> And when this song is sung and past,
> My lute be still, for I have done.

Surrey was even more important as an innovator, for as the medium for his translation of part of Virgil's *Aeneid* he employed the unrhymed iambic pentameter, the first poet deliberately to write blank verse, verse that no longer relied on the ornamental conventions of alliteration and rhyme, but was dependent on the harmonious relation of words and syllables, and, like the music of the period, on counterpoint, the contrapuntal interweaving of an imposed and varied secondary rhythm with the regular iambic metre. Here is his description of Pyrrhus attacking Priam's palace:

> And he an axe before the foremost raught,
> Wherewith he gan the strong gates hew and break,
> From whence he beat the staples out of brass;
> He brake the bars, and through the timber pierc'd
> So large a hole, whereby they might discern
> The house, the court, and secret chambers eke
> Of Priamus and ancient kings of Troy,
> And armed foes in th'entry of the gate.

There is little counterpoint here, as all the lines, except perhaps the last, are absolutely regular, and the caesura, the short mid-line pause, comes almost always after the fourth syllable; yet there is a remarkable freedom in the treatment of the three middle lines, which run over without pause into their successors. This device is not so important in rhyming as in blank verse, which must have variety if monotony is to be avoided, but three consecutive run-on lines are exceptional in Surrey's *Aeneid*, as they are in the first attempts to employ the new medium in the drama.

The translation of the Bible into English had in a sense made the morality play redundant. Before the Reformation the only authorized version of the Bible was the Latin Vulgate, the province of priests, and for the stories of the Old and New Testaments the common people were dependent largely on their dramatic and visual representation in play, wall-painting, and stained glass, but in 1539 Henry VIII ordered an English version to be set up and read in churches, and at last all men could hear the written word and interpret it in their own imaginations. This version was the Great Bible, the work mainly of Miles Coverdale, though much of it was taken from the translation of Tyndale, recently burned abroad as a heretic. In this way the ordinary people of England grew accustomed to hearing the language and rhythms of great prose, soon to be rivalled by that of Cranmer's Book of Common Prayer, no mean preparation for those who were to become the audiences of the Elizabethan theatre.

The Reformation had also made the morality play redundant, for the morality was essentially a dramatized sermon, and the Sunday preachings of the Protestant Church were enough to last most men for a week. They wanted something more entertaining than homilies for their recreation, something like the interpolated comedy in the miracle plays and farcical episodes in folk-plays. In this way the Interlude developed, as its name suggests, a short play presented in the interval between other forms of entertainment. Skelton called his *Magnificence* 'a goodly interlude and a mery', but it was neither an Interlude nor merry, though it was a definition, and one of the earliest examples is Henry

'Matthew's Bible', 1537, the first complete English version. 'Thomas Matthew' was an *alias* ▶ for John Rogers, the editor. Most of the translation was by William Tyndale.

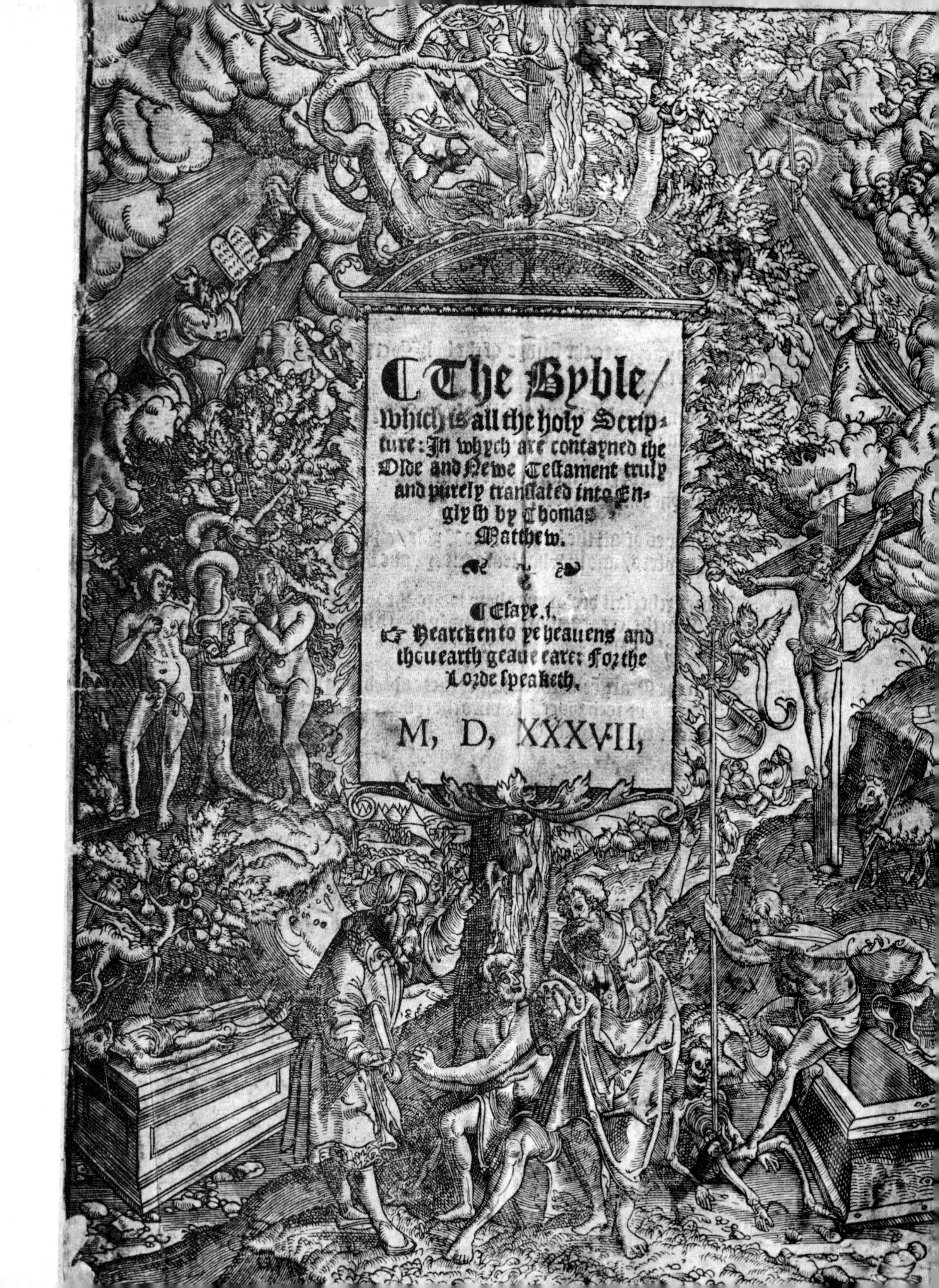

¶ The Byble/
which is all the holy Scrip-
ture: In whych are contayned the
Olde and Newe Testament truly
and purely translated into En-
glysh by Thomas
Matthew.

¶ Esaye .i.
☞ Hearcken to ye heauens and
thou earth geaue eare: For the
Lorde speaketh.

M, D, XXXVII,

Medwall's *Fulgens and Lucres*, the story of how the patrician Lucrece accepts a plebeian suitor, a play acted in the intervals of feasting in the hall of Cardinal Morton about 1490.

The new form produced its own master, John Heywood, who, before the Reformation, wrote a number of diverting Interludes. One was *The Play of the Weather*: the trials of Jupiter in trying to reconcile the demands of his petitioners for different kinds of weather; another *The Four PP*, a Palmer, Pardoner, Pothecary, and Pedlar who wager as to who shall tell the biggest lie, the Pardoner winning with his assertion that he has never seen a woman out of patience. Although a staunch Catholic, Heywood had no use for the four P's, and his most amusing play is *The Pardoner and the Friar*, in which the two men compete in extracting money from their audience and finally fall to blows, a theme that was to be adapted by Marlowe in his *Jew of Malta*. Some of the Pardoner's lines are lifted straight from Chaucer, on whom he improves by producing among his relics 'the blessed arm of sweet St Sunday' and 'of All-hallows the blessed jawbone', though he does not improve on Chaucer's verse, his dialogue being for the most part doggerel and rhyming prose. Another writer of Interludes was 'bilious' Bishop Bale who, however, in *God's Promises* retained the Biblical characters of the miracle plays, while in *King John*, written about 1547, the characters are abstractions of the moralities, the King being poisoned by Dissimulation in the guise of a monk, though John himself is a real character, and Bale's *King John* has some claim to be considered our first history play.

While the native drama was thus evolving from religious to secular themes and characters, there was another form of development in schools and universities, where the Renaissance had led to the study of Latin plays: the comedies of Plautus and Terence, and Seneca's Latin versions of the great Greek tragedies. The acting of these classical plays soon followed, the first recorded performance being of 'a goodly commedy of Plautus' at Greenwich Palace in 1519, and Wolsey, not to be outdone by the King in grandeur – his Cardinal College at Oxford even anticipated Henry's foundation of Trinity, Cambridge – followed with a performance of the *Menaechmi* in his palace of York Place, soon to become the King's Palace of Whitehall. The next stage was the writing of Latin plays in imitation of the ancient masters, and finally of plays in English after the same classical models. In this way the popular and academic streams were brought together, and the lively but amorphous Interlude was given a classical structure and coherence, much as Wyatt and Surrey gave form to lyric and narrative – though not dramatic – verse. Thus, the first 'regular' English plays, obeying, that is, the 'rules' of classical construction, were written in doggerel. Although the plot of *Gammer Gurton's Needle* is merely the old woman's loss of her needle and its discovery in Hodge's breeches, it *is* a plot of sorts, something more than a mere succession of incidents, and the characters are real people, English villagers of about 1550: the kind of farce that

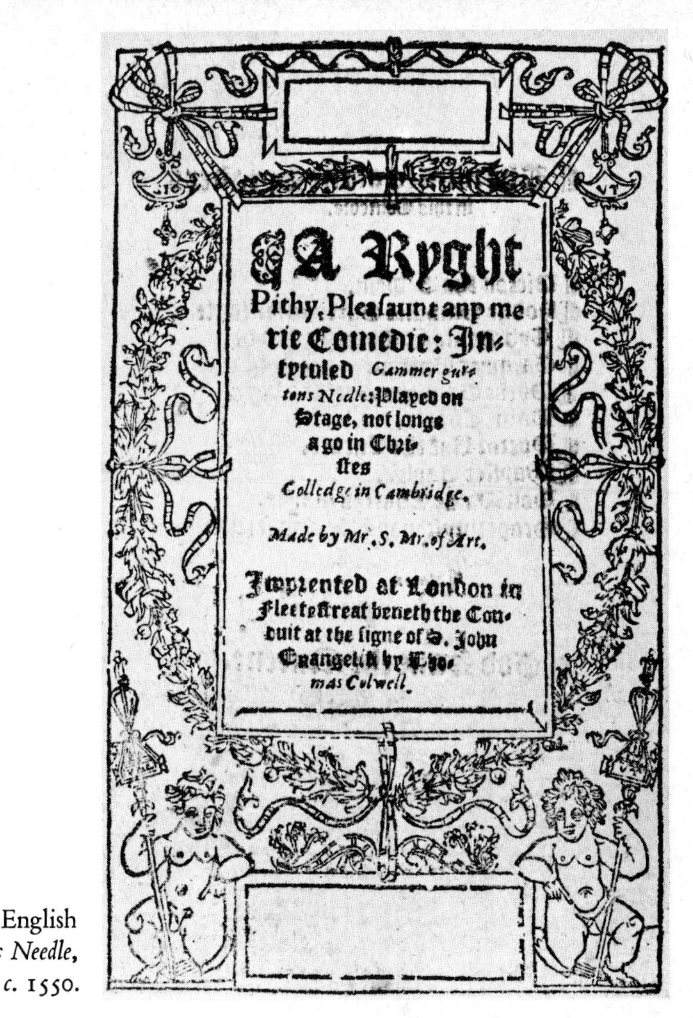

A Ryght
Pithy, Pleasaunt anp me-
rie Comedie: In-
tytuled Gammer gur-
tons Nedle: Played on
Stage, not longe
a go in Chri-
stes
Colledge in Cambridge.

Made by Mr. S. Mr. of Art.

Imprented at London in
Fleetestreat beneth the Con-
duit at the signe of S. John
Evangelist by Tho-
mas Colwell.

Title-page of the first extant English comedy, *Gammer Gurton's Needle*, *c.* 1550.

the Cambridge undergraduates who played it would enjoy. *Ralph Roister Doister*, of about the same date, was probably written for Eton schoolboys by their former headmaster, Nicholas Udall, and is a five-act comedy in imitation of Plautus, Ralph being the stock braggart of Latin comedy, and Mathew Merrygreek the sycophant, though the other characters come from the native Interlude. Here is the opening of Ralph's love-letter to Widow Custance:

> Sweet mistress, whereas I love you nothing at all,
> Regarding your substance and riches chief of all;
> For your personage, beauty, demeanour and wit
> I commend me unto you never a whit.

Evidently Shakespeare knew the play, for when he came to write *A Midsummer Night's Dream* some forty years later he borrowed this device of false punctuation, and in his Plautian *Comedy of Errors* adopted its rhyming doggerel.

Many of these Early Tudor Interludes and farces were performed by amateurs in the halls of schools, colleges, and inns of court, others by professional troupes of entertainers who wandered about the country playing where they could, some of them being in the service of the nobility, and Henry VIII had a company of eight men. There were no public theatres, but in London the yards of great inns served, the first recorded performance in one of them being at the Boar's Head in 1557. This was the year before the accession of Elizabeth, when young Sackville and Norton were considering the writing of a tragedy in the manner of Seneca.

Title-page of Henry Medwall's interlude, *Fulgens and Lucres*, apparently the first English printed play, *c.* 1515.

8 The Elizabethans 1558–1603

When Elizabeth, aged twenty-five, succeeded her half-sister Mary she faced a hostile Catholic Europe with an empty Treasury, and, although a scholar, a lover of the arts, and an accomplished musician, she could afford no extravagance of patronage. What she did cost her little: Roger Ascham, who had taught her Latin and Greek and written two admirable books on education, *Toxophilus* and *The Scholemaster*, she retained as her private tutor; she appointed Richard Edwards, musician and poet, Master of the Children of her Chapel, and brought young William Byrd from Lincoln to join Tallis as her organist. But she dismissed her eight Interlude players, who disgraced themselves at one of their first performances, playing 'shuche matter that they wher commondyd to leyff off', and for her dramatic entertainment turned to the choirboys of her Chapel and St Paul's, and to the men's company of players formed by her favourite, Robert Dudley, Earl of Leicester. Patronage was to come from courtiers, not from the Court; as for royal building, that was out of the question, and architecture was to become the province of devotees of the new cult of Gloriana.

With the establishment of the Reformed religion, it was inevitable that the Catholic cult of the Virgin Mary should be transformed into a cult of the Virgin Queen, and fostered, whether consciously or not, by those who had most to gain from the religious settlement. These were the new Protestant gentry, particularly the new courtiers who, instead of building Lady Chapels in cathedrals, were to build country-houses in which to entertain their Queen on her summer progresses. They were also the men who revitalized the aristocracy, added a new zest to life, and inspired a vigorous spring-like age of hope and expectancy, of elaborate display, euphuism, and fancy, who rejuvenated the obsolescent art of the Middle Ages by grafting it with that of Renaissance Italy and ancient Rome which they discovered on their European travels. Greece, now a province of the infidel Turk, was to remain almost unknown and unvisited for another two centuries. Few of them understood the fashions they brought back, and many of them came from the Netherlands, where classical forms had undergone strange distortions, and whence the great influx of refugees from Catholic persecution had begun, and Elizabethan architecture is essentially the application of classical or pseudo-classical detail to a native and still medieval fabric.

The Doric Order, by John Shute. From the first English book on architecture. 1563.

In 1563 John Shute published his *First and Chief Grounds of Architecture*, in which he reproduced drawings of the five classical orders, though most of his material was derived from the recently published work of the Italian architect Sebastiano Serlio, and more influential were the numerous Flemish books illustrating their curly and spiky strapwork, a sort of cut-out ornamentation somehow derived from classical originals, with which the Elizabethans gaily decorated the title-pages of their books and the façades of their buildings. When, therefore, Sir Thomas Gresham began his Royal Exchange in 1566, it was not only designed in Flanders but also built under Flemish direction, largely with material imported from Flanders.

It was only fitting that the first of the great houses built by Elizabeth's courtiers should have been the work of her chief minister, William Cecil, Lord Burghley. Theobalds, a red-brick palace in Hertfordshire, was begun in the year of Shakespeare's birth, 1564, but has long since perished, so that we do not know how much it was influenced by foreign models. Longleat, however, remains. Built in Wiltshire between 1568 and 1580, by Sir John Thynne and his master mason, Robert Smythson, it is both medieval and classical in plan, a courtyard house, but symmetrical and extrovert; in elevation like Thynne's Somerset House, French in its coupling of windows in the bays, Flemish in the ornament of its parapet, and yet unmistakably English, for there is nothing like it in any other country, and it remains one of the great achievements of the Elizabethan Age. Other houses dedicated to Elizabeth soon followed, three of them in Northamptonshire: Kirby Hall, with an astonishing pastiche of a porch and giant Ionic pilasters between mullioned windows, Christopher Hatton's Holdenby, apparently modelled on Theobalds, and Burghley House, in plan resembling Longleat, though its angle-towers are French-inspired, as is the somewhat clumsy clock-tower in the courtyard. Then came Wollaton, Nottinghamshire, built by Smythson for a Derbyshire businessman. Most

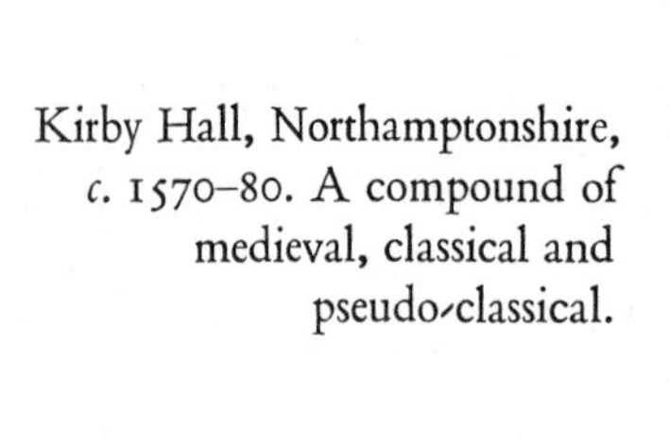
Kirby Hall, Northamptonshire, *c.* 1570–80. A compound of medieval, classical and pseudo-classical.

Longleat: one of the first great Elizabethan country-houses, built by Sir John Thynne, 1568–80. Note the Flemish strapwork on the parapet.

Wollaton Hall, Nottinghamshire, *c.* 1580–8, remarkable for its central hall lit by clerestory windows.

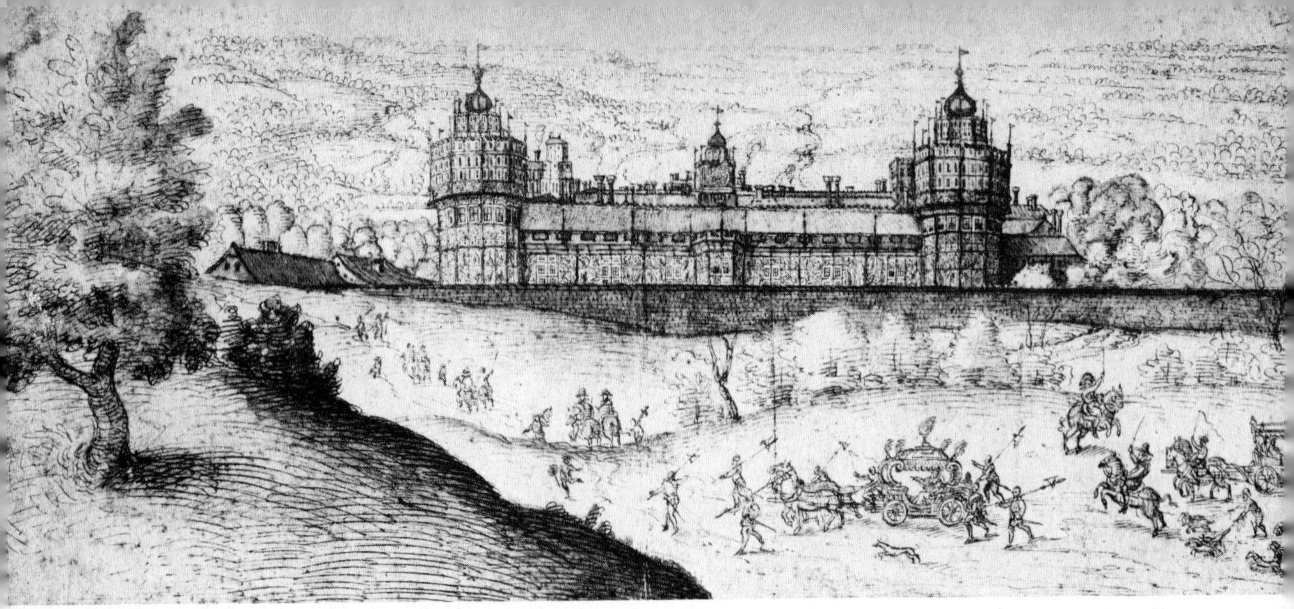

Nonsuch Palace, Surrey, *c.* 1538–58. It was a favourite residence of Queen Elizabeth—'Nonsuch of all other places she likes best'—but demolished in the 1680s.

ostentatious of Elizabethan houses, it is square in plan, not unlike Longleat in elevation, but with angle-towers, extravagant strapwork gables, and a hall with great chamber above rising monstrously out of its middle. It was finished in 1588, Armada year.

Smythson was buried at Wollaton, where his epitaph calls him 'Architector and Survayor', though there was no profession of architect in our sense of the word. Although surveyors like John Thorpe made 'platts' and sometimes 'uprights', plans and elevations, a building was designed and modified as it grew, generally by its owner, who told his master mason what he wanted and gave him a book of decorative design to work from, perhaps Shute's classical orders or de Vries's strapwork and cartouches. Rarely was a sculptor consulted, and in nothing were the Elizabethans more English than in their lack of interest in sculpture. It is true that Gresham's Royal Exchange was adorned with statues of the English kings, yet even these, like the rest of the ornament, were presumably Flemish. But if the new men of the reign were little concerned with sculpture as an art, they were much concerned with self-preservation and the founding of families, and indirectly therefore with sculpture, for the best way to impress posterity was the erection of funeral monuments: ornate, painted, and gilded tombs on which they, their wives and children lay or kneeled in effigy. Flemish sculptors were there to supply them, particularly on Bankside, in Southwark, where the Globe Theatre was soon to be built.

One of the first of these Flemish workshops was established by William Cuer (or Cure), who was employed by Henry VIII when building Nonsuch, and it was probably Cuer who introduced the French fashion of kneeling figures, which was to become increasingly common, for a living posture is more suggestive of permanence than a lifeless one. In Early Elizabethan times they were generally confined to wall-monuments, and to small praying figures of children whose parents lay under a canopy decorated with strapwork and supported by classical columns. Another Bankside workshop was that of Gheerart Janssen, anglicized as Gerard Johnson, who fled from Amsterdam about 1567 and married an Englishwoman who bore him five sons, two of whom, Nicholas and Gerard, followed their father's calling. Gerard Johnson the Elder's most important work was the Southampton tomb in Titchfield church, for which the second Earl, who died in 1581, left an extravagant sum of money. It is an unusual monument, the Earl and his father lying on either side of his mother, who is raised a degree above them; at the four corners are obelisks, symbols of eternity, and on one side of the tomb kneels the boy who was to become the third Earl and Shakespeare's patron. It may have been more than coincidence that, some thirty years later, Gerard Johnson the Younger was commissioned to make Shakespeare's monument in Stratford church.

The Elizabethans were more interested in painting than in sculpture, though again, not so much in painting as an art as in portraits that would perpetuate their memory. Yet there was no great demand for pictures to hang on their walls, for they preferred to cover them with tapestries that helped to keep their houses warm. Wolsey and Henry VIII had insulated Hampton Court with Flemish tapestries, whence came the name 'arras' for these hangings, and early in Elizabeth's reign Richard Hickes with the aid of Flemings established a

The Southampton tomb at Titchfield, by Gerard Johnson the Elder, 1592. The boy kneeling below his father's effigy is the third Earl, Shakespeare's patron.

Further Flemish influence. Warwickshire tapestry, or 'arras', one of a set representing the seasons—this one is *Summer*. Hatfield House.

(*Right*) Two Elizabethan portraits of the 1570s:
Lady Kytson, by George Gower.
Nicholas Hilliard miniature: self-portrait.

workshop in Warwickshire, so becoming, it was said, 'the only auter and beginner of tapestry and Arras within this realm'. Like the sculptors, the principal portrait painters were also Netherlanders. Hans Eworth was active until *c.* 1580, and it may have been he who in 1569 painted the first known portrait of Elizabeth as Queen, a group in which she plays Paris and confounds the three goddesses by awarding the apple – in the form of an orb – to herself. The cult of the Virgin Queen had begun. Other Flemish painters who settled or were born in England were Marcus Gheeraerts and John de Critz, and many more visited the country, notably Cornelis Ketel, who painted a

Queen Elizabeth confounding the Goddesses, an allegory by Hans Eworth, 1569. Apparently the young Queen would not sit for her portrait, and this is the first known painting of her as Queen, aged 36.

full-length portrait of Martin Frobisher, so bringing this style of portrait back into favour. Another distinguished visitor was the Italian Federico Zuccaro, on whom a number of so-called portraits of Shakespeare have been fathered, though he was here only for a year, when Shakespeare was ten.

There was, however, at least one eminent English portrait painter at this time: George Gower, who in 1581 became Serjeant Painter to the Queen. His known paintings are few, but the portrait of Lady Kytson is in the true English tradition, with an emphasis on line, pattern, and decorative detail that give it a delicacy and gaiety so often lacking in Flemish work. More sombre is the portrait of himself holding his palette and brush, painted appropriately enough in 1579, the year in which the Elizabethan Renaissance may be said to begin.

If the Elizabethans had little room for pictures on their walls, they had room for the miniatures, or 'limnings', in which Holbein had preserved the medieval art of illumination, for these, encased in lockets, they could carry with them, and these 'pictures in little' were the most prized of all forms of portrait, partly because the finest of all English artists painted them. This was Nicholas Hilliard, born at Exeter in 1547, son of a goldsmith and himself a goldsmith, a training that accounts for the exquisite delicacy and brilliance of his work. This he achieved by insisting on line: shadows, he wrote in his *Art of Limning*, must be drawn with the point, not 'smutted' with the flat of the brush, and these jewel-like paintings are the visual counterpart of Elizabethan lyric and plucked music of virginal and lute.

The vogue of virginal, lute, and music-making in the home had begun, made possible by the printing of music and encouraged by the publication in 1561 of Castiglione's *Cortegiano*, translated as *The Courtier* by Sir Thomas Hoby, soon to lie on his side in armoured effigy with his brother Philip, the first Englishmen to do so. The book is a discourse about the qualities that go to make a real gentleman, one of them being a proficiency in music. The virginal, first version of the harpsichord, was the instrument of Queens – Mary and Elizabeth played it well – its early music entirely English, and for it composers,

A sixteenth-century Italian virginal belonging to Queen Elizabeth. The strings of the virginal, like those of the later spinet and harpsichord, are plucked, not struck as on the piano.

notably Byrd, developed the form of variations on an air. The lute became popular in Early Tudor times – Wyatt's famous poem is addressed to his lute – but really came into its own as the perfect instrument for the accompaniment of Elizabethan lyrics, music indeed to hale souls out of men's bodies. Virginal and lute were essentially solo instruments, but for a group of performers there was the chest of viols, a set of instruments of various sizes, usually two treble, two tenor, and two bass, played with the hand under the bow, and normally held downwards like a cello. This was whole consort, but there was also broken consort, in which different kinds of instrument took part, the strings supplying chords to the contrapuntal melodies of hautboy and recorder. The favourite music for broken consort was the fancy, or fantasia, which, as the name suggests, left the composer free to pursue his fancy unfettered by regular form, each section, complete in itself, being inspired by its predecessor.

The drama, rudimentary though it remained for the first half of Elizabeth's reign, had a musical contribution to make. Thus, in the tragedy *Gorboduc*, produced in the winter of 1561 both in the Inner Temple and at Court, each act was introduced by a dumb show accompanied by music played on instruments appropriate to the theme: viols, cornets, flutes, hautboys, and finally drums and flutes. Twenty years later, when *Love and Fortune* was performed at Court, the triumphs of Venus were symbolized by 'a noise of viols', those of Fortune by trumpets, drums, and cornets, and symbolic instrumental music was employed throughout the Elizabethan-Jacobean drama. However, until the formation of really competent men's companies of actors, about 1580, the Queen preferred the performances given by the choirboys of her Chapel and St Paul's, boys who could sing like angels, and trained by skilled musicians like Richard Edwards, two of whose plays she saw before his death in 1566. Then, at the Christmas Revels there were masques, elaborate charades followed by dancing to music with anglicized Italian names: galliard and pavan, almain and coranto.

Scenes from the life of Sir Henry Unton, *c.* 1557–96. On the left a consort of viols, on the right a drum. Below are masquers and musicians: violin, flute, lute, cittern, bass viol. ▶

Although it was an age primarily of secular and domestic music, it was also an age in which some of our great Church music was composed. When Archbishop Parker issued his metrical *Whole Psalter* in 1567 it was with nine tunes by Tallis, one of which is still known as 'Tallis's Canon', and another has been popularized by Vaughan Williams' *Fantasia on a Theme by Tallis*. For his nine tunes Tallis employed the eight modes, but the mode was dying out and being superseded by the major and minor scales in which modulation, essential to polyphonic composition, was so much easier. In 1575 Elizabeth granted Tallis and Byrd, even though they were Catholics, the monopoly of music printing, and in that year they published their *Cantiones Sacrae*, Latin motets for five and six voices. This was the last of Tallis's music to be published in his lifetime, and he died, 'very aged', ten years later. But an even greater than Tallis remained, his pupil William Byrd, aged only forty when his master died, the peer of Palestrina, Victoria, and de Lassus, and composer of every form of music, from fancy to Anglican anthem and Roman motet and the splendid Masses for four and five voices. It is possible that some of his *Sonnets and Songs*, published in Armada year, were written for the Court plays given by the Chapel Royal Children, including the first comedies of John Lyly.

William Byrd, 1543–1623, greatest composer of the golden age.

The Elizabethan drama began, after a fashion, with the production of *Gorboduc* in 1561, the joint work of two young men, Thomas Sackville, who was to become first Earl of Dorset and build Knole House in Kent, and Thomas Norton, whose fanatical Puritanism later led to his imprisonment and early death. The play is important as the first to be written in blank verse, and the first 'regular', that is 'classical' English tragedy, but as a work of art it is of no importance at all. The blank verse is monotonous as a metronome, and hammers out the lines into speeches of epic proportions, culminating in the moral:

> For right will always live, and rise at length,
> But wrong can never take deep root to last.

However, it set an example of formal construction in five acts, though an arid Senecan form, a tragedy of blood and revenge without any action on the stage, a rhetorical *tour de force*. The plays of Seneca were translated, and English drama might have been fettered, like the Italian, by the 'rules' invented by neo-classical pedants, had not the native tradition been kept alive in such plays as *Cambyses*, 'a lamentable tragedy mixed full of pleasant mirth'.

The popular demand for such tragical mirth was growing, and in 1576 James Burbage built the Theatre, the first playhouse in England, just outside the north wall of London. As in the medieval 'rounds' the audience stood or sat about an open 'yard' into which projected a large apron stage, a circus-like arrangement eminently suitable for the buffoonery that composed much of the plays. In the same year the Children of the Chapel Royal secured a long narrow room in Blackfriars for the performance of their plays, in which music was more important than 'feats of activity'. London now had its theatres, but in 1576, nearly twenty years after Elizabeth's accession, there was still no sign of a dramatic renaissance.

Nor was there any sign of a literary renaissance, and even Sackville's 'Induction' to *A Mirror for Magistrates* is a poem that might have been written a hundred and fifty years before, except perhaps the description of Sleep:

> The body's rest, the quiet of the heart,
> The travail's ease, the still night's fere was he,

lines that were to inspire Sir Philip Sidney's most famous sonnet:

> Come, sleep, O sleep, the certain knot of peace,
> The baiting place of wit, the balm of woe,
> The poor man's wealth, the prisoner's release,
> The indifferent judge between the high and low.

It must have been about 1579 that Sidney wrote this sonnet, the memorable year in which three books introduced the golden age of Elizabethan literature. One was Sir Thomas North's translation of Plutarch, *The Lives of the Noble Grecians and Romanes*, written in a prose that Shakespeare in his Roman histories was to render into verse with minimum alteration. Another was John Lyly's *Euphues*, a moralizing romance in a very different style, an affected prose compounded of classical allusion and unnatural history, the equivalent of the hybrid ornament then being applied to the fronts of country-houses and, quite inappropriately, to the chapter-headings of North's *Plutarch*. Finally, more

Beginning of the golden age of literature: North's *Plutarch*: chapter-heading with strapwork ornament. Sir Philip Sidney (?). A miniature by Isaac Oliver.

1

THE LIVES OF THE NOBLE GRECIANS AND ROMANES, COMPARED TOGETHER BY THAT graue learned Philoſopher and Hiſtoriographer, Plutarche of Chæronea.

Theſeus.

A LIKE as hiſtoriographers deſcribing the world (frende *Soſsius Senecio*) doe of purpoſe referre to the vttermoſt partes of their mappes the farre diſtant regions whereof they be ignoraunt, with this note: theſe contries are by meanes of ſandes and drowthes vnnauigable, rude, full of venimous beaſtes, SCYTHIAN iſe, and froſen ſeas. Euen ſo may I (which in comparinge noble mens liues haue already gone ſo farre into antiquitie, as the true and certaine hiſtorie could lead me) of the reſt, being thinges paſt all proofe or chalenge, very well ſay: that beyonde this time all is full of ſuſpicion and dout, being deliuered vs by Poets and Tragedy makers, ſometimes without trueth and likelihoode, and alwayes B without certainty. Howbeit, hauing heretofore ſet foorth the liues of *Lycurgus* (which eſtabliſhed the lawes of the LACEDÆMONIANS) and of king *Numa Pompilius*: me thought I might go a litle further to the life of *Romulus*, ſence I was come ſo nere him. But conſidering my ſelfe as the Poet *AEſchilus* did:

VVhat champion may vvith ſuch a man compare?
or vvho (thinke I) ſhalbe againſt him ſet?
VVho is ſo bold? or vvho is he that dare
defend his force, in ſuch encounter met?

A

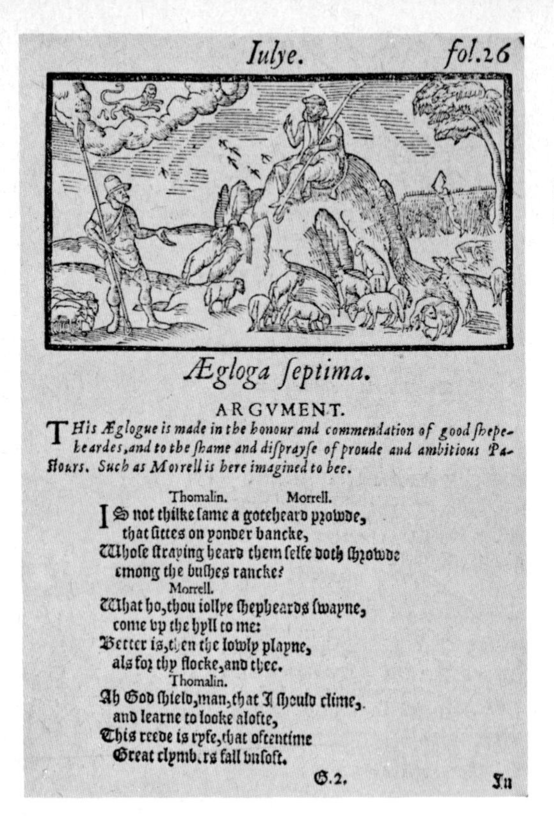

Iulye. *fol.26*

Ægloga ſeptima.

ARGVMENT.

THis Æglogue is made in the honour and commendation of good ſhepeheardes, and to the ſhame and diſprayſe of proude and ambitious Paſtours. Such as Morrell is here imagined to bee.

Thomalin. Morrell.

IS not thilke ſame a goteheard prowde,
that ſittes on yonder bancke,
Whoſe ſtraying heard them ſelfe doth ſhrowde
emong the buſhes rancke?

Morrell.

What ho, thou iollye ſhepheards ſwayne,
come vp the hyll to me:
Better is, then the lowly playne,
als for thy flocke, and thee.

Thomalin.

Ah God ſhield, man, that I ſhould clime,
and learne to looke alofte,
This reede is ryfe, that oftentime
Great clymbers fall vnſoft.

G.2. In

The Shepherd's Calendar, Spenser's first publication, 1579. Woodcut illustrating the seventh Eclogue, July.

(*Right*) Title-pages of the two most influential pre-Shakespeare plays: *Gorboduc*, by Sackville and Norton, the first blank-verse play. *Tamburlaine*, Marlowe's first play.

important though less immediately influential than *Euphues*, was young Edmund Spenser's first publication, *The Shepherd's Calendar*. It is by no means a great poem: another compound of medieval and classical, the diction is deliberately Chaucerian, but it is Elizabethan in its song to the Queen, 'the flower of virgins', its catalogues of flowers, and graceful metrical forms.

Spenser dedicated his poem to Sir Philip Sidney. Although none of Sidney's work was published until after his death in 1586, he was at this time writing his sonnets to Stella, and his *Arcadia* for his sister, the Countess of Pembroke. Every inch a humanist, a defender of the classical delight in this life against the medieval insistence on the next, he directed his *Defence of Poesy* against the Puritans who thought poetry mere feigning and plays positively immoral. On the contrary, Sidney argued, poetry and plays teach virtue, and he singled out *Gorboduc* for special commendation as a moral tragedy 'climbing to the height of Seneca his style', though even that play failed to obey the unities of place and time. He was a stickler for neoclassical regulation, though nothing could be less classical than his romantic, rambling, make-believe *Arcadia*, and he is at his best when he forgets rules and moralizing, and looks in his heart and writes.

No doubt the popular plays, long since perished, performed at the Theatre were anything but models of morality, but the Puritans had less reason to

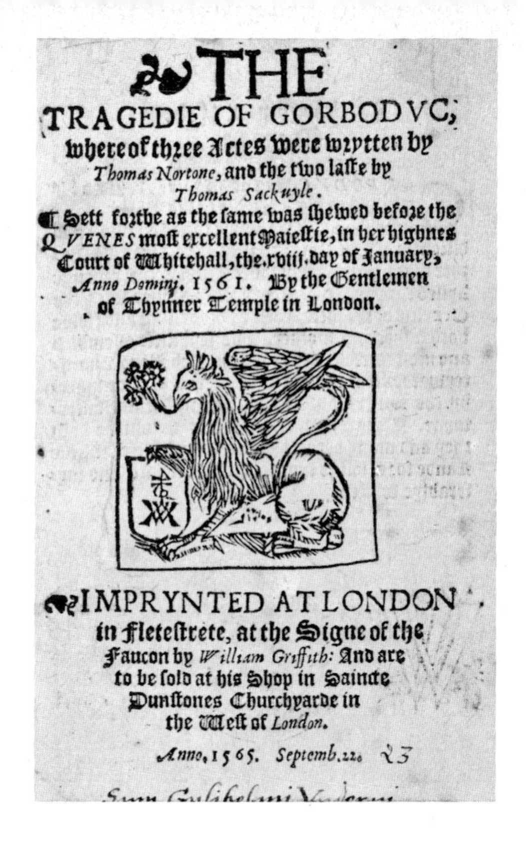
THE
TRAGEDIE OF GORBODUC,
whereof three Actes were wrytten by
Thomas Nortone, and the two laste by
Thomas Sackuyle.
Sett forthe as the same was shewed before the
QVENES most excellent Maiestie, in her highnes
Court of Whitehall, the .xviij. day of January,
Anno Domini. 1561. By the Gentlemen
of Thynner Temple in London.

IMPRYNTED AT LONDON
in Fletestrete, at the Signe of the
Faucon by William Griffith: And are
to be sold at his Shop in Saincte
Dunstones Churchyarde in
the West of London.
Anno, 1565. Septemb. 22.

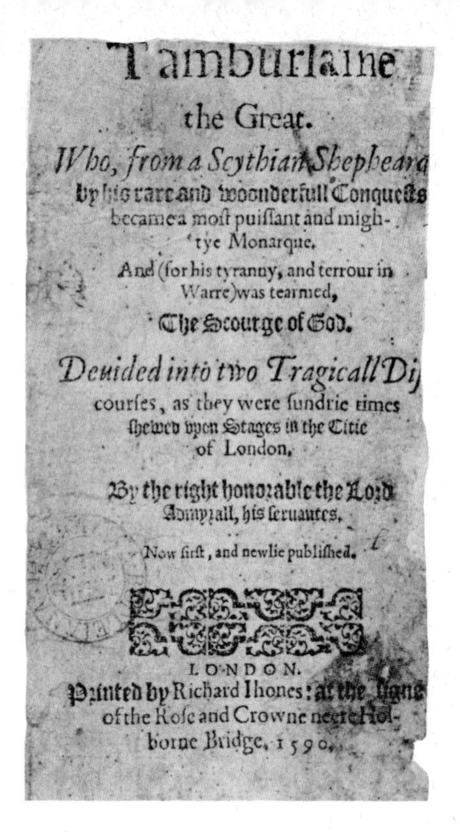
Tamburlaine
the Great.
Who, from a Scythian Shepheard
by his rare and woonderfull Conquests
became a most puissant and migh-
tye Monarque.
And (for his tyranny, and terrour in
Warre) was tearmed,
The Scourge of God.
Deuided into two Tragicall Dis-
courses, as they were sundrie times
shewed vpon Stages in the Citie
of London.
By the right honorable the Lord
Admyrall, his seruauntes.
Now first, and newlie published.

LONDON.
Printed by Richard Ihones: at the signe
of the Rose and Crowne neere Hol-
borne Bridge. 1590.

attack those of Lyly, written for the boys of the Chapel Royal and St Paul's. His first comedies, *Campaspe* and *Sapho and Phao*, were presented at Court in 1584: gossamer fairy-tales, with delicate prose dialogue and songs set to music by Byrd, they raised the native drama to another plane. Then, at these same memorable Revels the Children presented George Peele's first play, *The Arraignment of Paris*, a comedy in blank and rhyming verse, in which, as in Eworth's allegorical painting, 'the nymph Eliza' received the apple. The allegory might have been interpreted in another way, with the apple as the symbol of the drama, for the true Elizabethan drama had begun.

The young university men who were to revolutionize the theatre were gathering in London. Besides Lyly and Peele, there were Thomas Lodge, Robert Greene, and Thomas Kyd, and then in 1587 Christopher Marlowe arrived from Cambridge, at about the same time as the twenty-four-year-old Shakespeare from Stratford. A new theatre, the Rose, had just been built on Bankside near the Flemish sculptors' workshops, and it was probably there, in the autumn of 1587, that Marlowe's *Tamburlaine* was first performed. It was the most momentous performance in the history of the English theatre, for here was a play that combined a loose classical form with a native vigour and variety, written in blank verse such as had never before been heard, a violent poetry of 'high astounding terms' that proclaimed the end of the drama of clowns and 'rhyming mother wits', and the beginning of a drama of poets, at the same time trumpeting the arrogant aspirations of Renaissance man:

> Our souls, whose faculties can comprehend
> The wondrous architecture of the world,
> And measure every wandering planet's course,
> Still climbing after knowledge infinite,
> And always moving as the restless spheres,
> Will us to wear ourselves, and never rest
> Until we reach the ripest fruit of all.

It was to be the basic theme of all Marlowe's plays.

Inspired by *Tamburlaine*, the other young poets in the capital poured their genius into the writing of plays in emulation of Marlowe, and between 1588, Armada year, and 1593 revolutionized the English drama with a series of blank-verse comedies and tragedies that owed little to classical models save structure, and nothing at all to pedantic neoclassical rules. Greene's first play, *Alphonsus*, in which he tried to out-Tamburlaine *Tamburlaine*, was a failure, and he followed it with the comedy *Friar Bacon and Friar Bungay* and the imaginary Scottish history *James IV*, both written with a rare lightness of touch. Lodge was much heavier handed in his *Wounds of Civil War*, and turned to prose in the euphuistic romance *Rosalynde*, important as the source of *As You Like It*. Peele was the most successful exploiter of Marlovian rhetoric; the rant of his *Battle of Alcazar* was later to be burlesqued by Shakespeare, but *David and Bethsabe*, the only Elizabethan dramatization of a Bible story, is tempered with lush and sensuous poetry and his *Old Wives' Tale* is one of the most delightful comedies of the period. Far more influential than all these was Kyd's *Spanish Tragedy*, first of the popular tragedies of blood, and of ghosts calling for revenge, the immense success of which was to be repeated in *Hamlet*. At this time, however, Shakespeare seems to have been fascinated by English history and the recently published *Chronicles* of Holinshed, and wrote the three parts of *Henry VI* and *Richard III* before trying his hand at horrors in *Titus Andronicus*.

Dr Faustus, Marlowe's second play, performed *c.* 1589. Woodcut from the seventh edition.

A scene from *Titus Andronicus*: 'Tamora pleadinge for her sonnes going to execution.' The first illustration to Shakespeare, probably by Henry Peacham, 1595.

Meanwhile, Marlowe followed *Tamburlaine* with *Dr Faustus*, the tragedy of another aspiring hero, who sold his soul to the Devil in return for 'knowledge infinite', and spoke immortal poetry to Helen of Troy. Then, after the melodramatic *Jew of Malta*, it was Marlowe's turn to be influenced by his pupil, and in *Edward II* he took Shakespeare's history plays as his model. There is a difference in treatment, however; although *Henry VI* and *Richard III* are full of murder and violence, Shakespeare did not, like Marlowe, exploit cruelty for its own sake; there was a glittering streak of cruelty in Marlowe's make-up, and the difference between the two great poets may be seen in their handling of the murder of kings, of Henry VI and Richard II in Shakespeare, of Edward II in Marlowe. The difference can also be seen in their two erotic poems. In Marlowe's splendid *Hero and Leander* there is neither pity nor humanity, love is an animal passion, and Hero's gown is stained 'with the blood of wretched lovers slain'. *Venus and Adonis*, however, is a mere exercise in eroticism, passion as artificial as the poetry; there is no cruelty, and Shakespeare, one feels, was more interested in natural history, the dive-dapper, snail, and hunted hare of his imagery, than in the amorous advances of the sweating Venus.

The inspiration of the two poems was Spenser's *Faerie Queene*, the first three books of which appeared in 1590. Although its purpose was didactic, a moral epic in which the hero of each of the twelve proposed books was to symbolize one of the Virtues, it is the most sensuous of poems, and the most musical, for

Edmund Spenser (*c.* 1552–99) sings of 'Knights and Palladines' in *The Faerie Queene*, the first three books of which were published in 1590.

THE FAERIE
QVEENE.

Diſpoſed into twelue books,
Faſhioning
XII. Morall vertues.

LONDON
Printed for William Ponſonbie.
1590.

Spenser loaded every rift with ore, every line of his long languorous stanzas with Renaissance ornament, and among the more memorable passages are the voluptuous ones, such as the description of the Bower of Bliss:

> The joyous birds, shrouded in cheerful shade,
> Their notes unto the voice attempered sweet;
> Th' angelical soft trembling voices made
> To th' instruments divine respondence meet;
> The silver sounding instruments did meet
> With the bass murmur of the waters' fall;
> The waters' fall with difference discreet,
> Now soft, now loud, unto the wind did call;
> The gentle warbling wind low answered to all.

The Faery Queen was, of course, Elizabeth, and it was now, after the defeat of the Armada, that the artists, most of them unknown, who painted her portraits transformed her into a legendary figure with a mask-like face, Gloriana, allegorical and decorative as the poetry of Spenser, formal and conventional as a sonnet.

Sidney's sonnets, *Astrophel and Stella*, were published in 1591, and inspired the writing of a score of similar sequences before the end of the century. Among the best were Spenser's *Amoretti* and Michael Drayton's *Idea*, but neither of these rises to the heights of the finest things in Samuel Daniel's *Delia*, to the splendour of such lines as these, with their emphasis on initial vowels:

> Let others sing of knights and paladins
> In aged accents and untimely words;
> Paint shadows in imaginary lines,
> Which well the reach of their high wits records:
> But I must sing of thee, and those fair eyes
> Authentic shall my verse in time to come . . .
> These are the arks, the trophies I erect
> That fortify thy name against old age;
> And these thy sacred virtues must protect
> Against the dark, and Time's consuming rage. . . .

Spenser must have been proud to have the knights and archaic diction of the *Faerie Queene* described in poetry like this. *Delia* was published in 1592, and it may well have been this sonnet that prompted Shakespeare to begin his sequence, for nothing could be more Shakespearean both in matter and manner, but unlike the other sequences, Shakespeare's is addressed not to a woman but mainly to the young man described in the opening sonnet:

> Thou that art now the world's fresh ornament
> And only herald to the gaudy spring,

and this is the princely poetry in which he was to write his next series of plays.

Queen Elizabeth: said to have been painted after her visit to Ditchley in Oxfordshire, on the map of which she is standing, 1592.

Perhaps it was no accident that while Spenser was meditating the verbal harmonies of *The Faerie Queene* Byrd was composing his *Songs of Sundry Natures*, among which were some to be accompanied by viols, the earliest English madrigals of any importance, though voices were soon to replace viols. At about the same time, 1588, Nicholas Yonge published *Musica Transalpina*, a collection of Italian madrigals, and the form was taken up and developed by Thomas Morley, who in 1594 published his *Madrigals to Four Voices*, the first book of madrigals by an English composer. The most characteristic form of Elizabethan music, therefore, coincided with the new blank-verse drama and the sonnet sequences, with the great outburst of poetry after the defeat of the Armada.

The madrigal was a secular form of the motet, a contrapuntal interweaving of a number of melodies for unaccompanied voices, though in the madrigal there was normally only one voice to a part, and the words were the love-songs and lyrics of the age. As in the motet, therefore, the music of the madrigal must be followed horizontally, a music more difficult to appreciate than the vertical and simultaneous concord of harmony. For much the same reason blank verse is more difficult to appreciate than rhyme, and Shakespeare's development of blank verse curiously resembles the polyphony of the contemporary madrigal.

Because in English the accent of words of two and three syllables generally falls on the first, and of four syllables on the first and third, the rhythm of English prose is a falling one. But the characteristic rhythm of English verse is the rising one of the iambic metre, and this, for two reasons, is emphasized by rhyme: because rhyme is nearly always on a final accented syllable, and because it is more effective if followed by a pause, as in *Hero and Leander*:

> So that the truce was broke, and she, alas!
> Poor silly maiden, at his mercy was.
> Love is not full of pity, as men say,
> But deaf and cruel where he means to prey.

The trochaic disyllables, *silly*, *maiden*, *mercy*, *pity*, *cruel*, are not strong enough to set up a counter-rhythm, because their effect is neutralized by the clinching

A
PLAINE AND
EASIE INTRODVCTI-
ON TO PRACTICALL
MVSICKE,
Set downe in forme of a dialogue:
Deuided into three partes,
The first teacheth to sing with all
things necessary for the knowledge of
pricksong.
The second treateth of descante
and to sing two parts in one vpon a plainsong or
ground, with other things necessary
for a descanter.
The third and last part entreateth of com
position of three, foure, fiue & more parts with
many profitable rules to that effect.
With new songs of .2.3.4. and .5 parts.

by Thomas Morley, Batcheler of musick, & one of the gent. of hir Maiesties Royall Chappell.
Imprinted at London by Peter Short dwelling on
Breedstreet hill at the signe of the Starre. 1597.

Thomas Morley's famous *Introduction*, 1597, a book that was much used during the next two centuries.

rhyme. But blank verse allows a greater freedom of rhythmical variation, for there is no reason why a line should not end in a trochaic word and flow over without pause into the next, as in the first speech of Richard III:

> He capers nimbly in a lady's chamber
> To the lascivious pleasing of a lute.

Here the counter-rhythm of the disyllables in the first line is very pronounced, all the more so because three of them are emphasized by assonance, the repetition of the long *a* of the accented syllables: *capers*, *lady's*, *chamber*. Shakespeare employs the same device a few lines later in, 'Cheated of feature by dissembling nature', and here the counter-rhythm is even more pronounced, because it is introduced by the reversed beat of the first foot.

Early blank verse, that of *Gorboduc*, for example, is so dull because it is so regular:

> There resteth all. But if they fail thereof,
> And if the end bring forth an ill success,
> On them and theirs the mischief shall befall,
> And so I pray the gods requite it them.

There must be something to compensate for the loss of the ornament of rhyme, which like harmony in music is a vertical concord; there must be variety, the

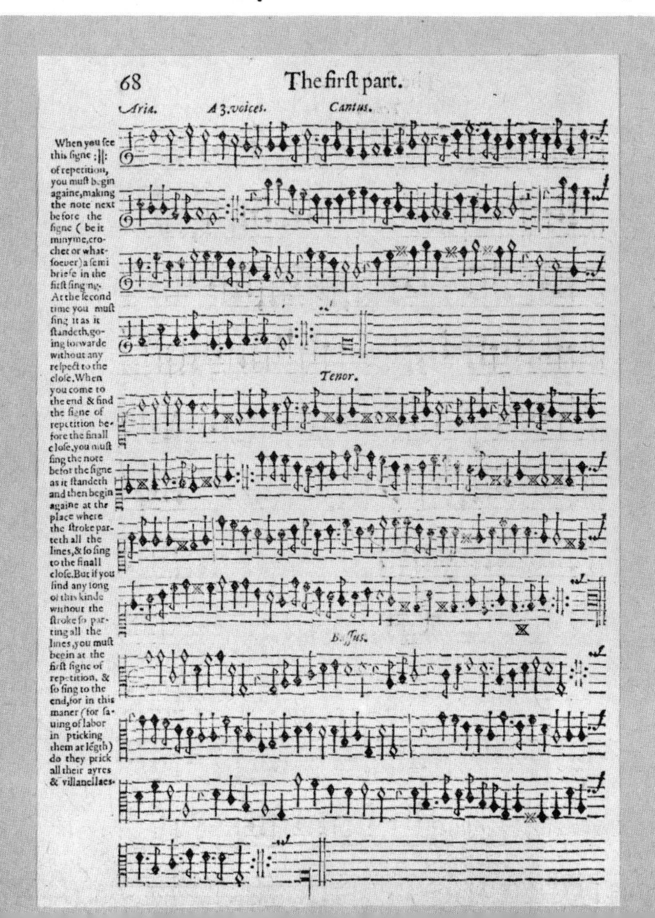

68 The firſt part.

Aria. *A 3.voices.* *Cantus.*

When you ſee this ſigne :||: of repetition, you muſt begin againe, making the note next before the ſigne (be it minyme, crochet or whatſoever) a ſemibriefe in the firſt ſinging. At the ſecond time you muſt ſing it as it ſtandeth, going forwarde without any reſpect to the cloſe. When you come to the end & find the ſigne of repetition before the finall cloſe, you muſt ſing the note befor the ſigne as it ſtandeth and then begin againe at the place where the ſtroke parteth all the lines, & ſo ſing to the finall cloſe. But if you find any ſong of this kinde without the ſtroke ſo parting all the lines, you muſt begin at the firſt ſigne of repetition, & ſo ſing to the end, for in this maner (for ſauing of labor in pricking them at lẽgth) do they prick all their ayres & villanellaes.

Tenor.

'The first part teacheth to sing.' At this time bar lines were normally inserted only in full scores of choral and instrumental music.

interweaving of a secondary falling rhythm with the primary rising one of the metre, a counterpoint of prose and verse rhythms, and this, like the interwoven melodies of the madrigal, is heard horizontally. Even the mighty line of Marlowe's blank verse has little variety, is melodic rather than contrapuntal, and it was Shakespeare who, in the last decade of the sixteenth century, developed the verbal polyphony of blank verse until in *Twelfth Night* it became the complex and extended counterpoint of:

> 'Tis beauty truly blent, whose red and white
> Nature's own sweet and cunning hand laid on:
> Lady, you are the cruellest she alive
> If you will lead these graces to the grave
> And leave the world no copy.

Here, in this most musical of speeches, without the aid of feminine endings a counter-rhythm is induced by assonance, alliteration, and juxtaposition of verbal trochees: *beauty truly, laid on, lady, nature, graces, cruel, cunning, copy.*

Shakespeare did not achieve this dramatic poetry without a struggle, all the more severe because for some years he had little or no competition. By 1594, when he published his second long poem, *The Rape of Lucrece*, and the theatres reopened after two years of the Plague, Marlowe and the rest of the University Wits who had carried through the first phase of the dramatic revolution were

A
PLEASANT
Conceited Comedie
CALLED,
Loues labors loſt.

As it vvas preſented before her Highnes
this laſt Chriſtmas.

Newly corrected and augmented
By W. Shakeſpere.

Imprinted at London by *W.W.*
for *Cutbert Burby.*
1598.

Love's Labour's Lost: the first quarto, 1598, though written *c.* 1594. This is the first play to be published with Shakespeare's name.

either dead or no longer writing for the stage. Tom Nashe remained, but he was primarily a pamphleteer, though his *Unfortunate Traveller*, published in this year, has claims to be called the first historical and realistic novel in English. Shakespeare was not in realistic vein; he had begun his sonnet sequence, and his next plays, written partly in rhyme, reflect this lyric impulse. After the Plautian *Comedy of Errors* and farcical *Taming of the Shrew* came his first romantic comedy, *The Two Gentlemen of Verona*, which contains his first lyric, 'Who is Silvia?', the scintillating courtly comedy of *Love's Labour's Lost*, and silvery, moon-drenched *A Midsummer Night's Dream*. *Romeo and Juliet*, an essay in romantic tragedy, was followed by two more English histories, *Richard II* and *King John*, in which the grimness of the story was relieved by the poetry, not as in the earlier histories emphasized by a hammering rhetoric and arid imagery of destruction. The blank-verse plays of the Wars of the Roses had been too rhetorical, their dialogue too studied and inflated to be creative of character, and the largely rhyming plays of this next period were too lyrical to be fully dramatic. We remember the poetry of Theseus, but the man we remember is Bottom – and Bottom speaks prose. Up till now Shakespeare had confined prose to his comic characters, but in *The Merchant of Venice* he applied it to the protagonist, Shylock; the play thus became a transitional one, and lyrical dialogue is heard for the last time in the last act:

> Sit, Jessica. Look how the floor of heaven
> Is thick inlaid with patines of bright gold:
> There's not the smallest orb which thou behold'st
> But in his motion like an angel sings,
> Still quiring to the young-eyed cherubins.

Shakespeare never wrote poetry more beautiful than this of his lyrical period, but he was to write far greater dramatic poetry, poetry creative of character and action, and he learned how to do so by writing prose.

With the exception of *Julius Caesar*, all the plays of his middle period, from *Henry IV* to *Twelfth Night*, contain more prose than verse, for not only clowns but heroes and heroines speak it, and it was largely out of prose that Shakespeare created so many of his most familiar characters, from Falstaff and Prince Henry to Benedick and Beatrice, Malvolio and Viola. It was a salutary discipline, for prose invites neither rhetorical nor lyrical elaboration, and from this discipline emerged the magnificent medium, the dramatic poetry, of *Hamlet* and the later tragedies.

The plays of Shakespeare are so much the greatest monument of the last decade of Elizabeth's reign that it is easy to forget that even without them these years would be among the most wonderful in the history of the arts in England. By the end of the century a new generation of dramatists had appeared, one of them the kindly and improvident Thomas Dekker, whose comedy of magic, *Old Fortunatus*, was as romantic as *As You Like It*, his *Shoemaker's Holiday* as

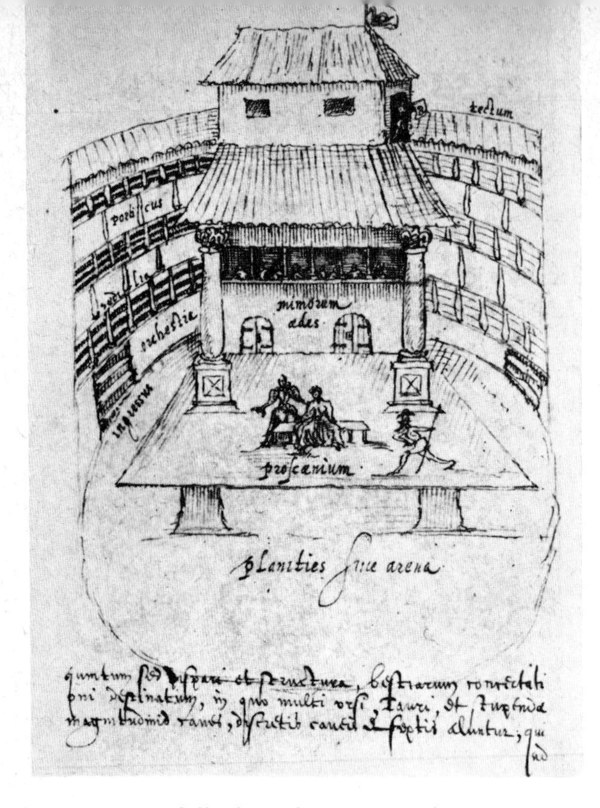

The Swan Theatre, London. A sketch made *c.* 1596, but discovered only in 1888. It is the only illustration we have of the interior of an Elizabethan theatre.

The second Globe Theatre, rebuilt in 1614, and the 'Beere bayting h[ouse]'. (The names are interchanged on this engraving.) This is the earliest representation of a theatre exterior. ▶

full of good spirits as *The Merry Wives of Windsor*. More important than Dekker was young Ben Jonson, in whose *Every Man in his Humour* Shakespeare acted when it was first produced in 1598. Brought up on the classics at Westminster School by the great antiquary William Camden, Jonson was convinced that Shakespeare was on the wrong lines, that comedy should not be romantic and remote, but realistic and contemporary, that its purpose was to purge society of its follies and vices by holding them up to ridicule in characters who, like those in the moralities, symbolized some excessive 'humour', or temperament. Jonson's comedy, therefore, was one of types rather than individuals, but it was something new, brilliantly done, and appealed to the audience of the newly built Globe Theatre.

The triumphs of the latter years of the reign were not confined to drama. Before he died in 1599 Spenser wrote three more books of *The Faerie Queene* and his two great marriage odes, *Epithalamion* and *Prothalamion*. Unlike so many of his contemporaries, he was not a lyric poet; the form was too delicate, too confined for the slow, symphonic music of his verse, which needed a series of long intricate stanzas for its full development, the stanzas of these odes leading up to the refrains, 'That all the woods may answer and your echo ring', and 'Sweet Thames, run softly, till I end my song'. Another important poem of the period was Daniel's *Musophilus*, a defence of poetry and eulogy of the English tongue, which prophetically he saw would one day be the language of the New World of the West. Daniel was the quietest, gentlest of the Elizabethan poets,

George Chapman the noisiest, and his translation of *Seven Books of the Iliads* gave full scope to his 'loud and bold' rhetoric. It was splendid, though not Homer, nor was his conclusion of the unfinished *Hero and Leander* Marlowe, though the best thing he ever wrote. Another, but very different, Homeric poem was the *Orchestra* of Sir John Davies, a long didactic poem in which Antinous tries to persuade Penelope to dance, for Love taught disordered Nature to observe the measure of a dance, and

> The turning vault of heaven formed was,
> Whose starry wheels he hath so made to pass,
> As that their movings do a music frame,
> And they themselves still dance unto the same.

Lorenzo says much the same thing to Jessica in *The Merchant of Venice*, and in *Troilus and Cressida* Ulysses summarizes Shakespeare's concept of a natural order, measure, harmony, the disturbing of which leads to anarchy and tragedy:

> The heavens themselves, the planets and this centre
> Observe degree, priority and place . . .
> Take but degree away, untune that string,
> And, hark, what discord follows!

This is also one of the principal themes in Richard Hooker's *Laws of Ecclesiastical Polity*, a defence of the Established Church of England, written in prose that is itself an example of harmony and measured order: 'If celestial spheres should forget their wonted motions, and by irregular volubility turn themselves any way as it might happen . . . what would become of man himself, whom these things now do all serve ? See we not plainly that obedience of creatures unto the law of nature is the stay of the world ?' The great majority of Elizabethans agreed, though Francis Bacon had his reservations, and in the ten *Essays* that he published in 1597, in terse and aphoristic prose offered his worldly advice to those ambitious as himself, matter very different from the meditations of Montaigne, whose *Essays* were translated into English by John Florio. But more popular than the spiritual explorations of the new literary form of the essay, and far more influential, were the stories of physical exploration in Richard Hakluyt's *Principal Navigations of the English Nation*, some told by Hakluyt himself, others by the survivors of these voyages and discoveries.

These too were among the triumphs of Elizabeth's reign, but if, as Daniel wrote, its 'best glory' was its literature, it was also the golden age of English music, the only time in England's history, before the present, when it could be said that her composers were the peers of those anywhere else in the world. Byrd was only fifty in 1593, and in the next ten years led the way in every form of musical composition, though he was not represented in the anthology of madrigals, including those of the two greatest masters of the form, Thomas Weelkes and John Wilbye, which Morley assembled to celebrate the Queen in 1601, with the title of *The Triumphs of Oriana*. In his *Plain and Easy Introduction to Practical Music* Morley had described the madrigal: 'Next unto the motet this is the most artificial, and to men of understanding the most delightful. If, therefore, you will compose in this kind, you must possess yourself with an amorous humour . . . so that you must in your music be wavering like the wind,

The most popular of all English madrigals. One of Thomas Weelkes's contributions to Morley's collection, *The Triumphs of Oriana*, celebrating the Queen.

A North American Indian in body paint. A sketch made by John White, the first English water-colourist, who led an expedition to Virginia in 1587.

sometime wanton, sometime drooping, sometime grave and staid, otherwhile effeminate, and the more variety you shall show the better you shall please.' But when Morley died, aged only forty-six, in the same year as the Queen, there were already signs that the brief age of the madrigal was almost over. Every educated man and woman was expected to be able to sing a part in a madrigal, but if a voice were lacking it might be replaced by lute or viol. Then in 1597 John Dowland published his first *Book of Songs*, 'so made that all the parts together, or either of them severally, may be sung to the lute', and in the year of *Oriana* appeared the first books of solo songs with lute accompaniment, one by Robert Jones, the other by Thomas Campion. One of the most accomplished men of the age, a lawyer turned physician, Campion wrote the words as well as music of his songs, graceful and delicate lyrics, many of them unrhymed, in which indeed, as Barnfield wrote, 'Music and sweet Poetry agree'. It was a pity that the communal music-making of the madrigal was going out, but the piercing purity of the Elizabethan lute song more than made amends.

The lyricism of Hilliard's miniatures is the counterpart of this music, but Hilliard's ideal of preserving the brilliance and linear quality of medieval glass was being challenged by his rival, Isaac Oliver, the son of Huguenot refugees, who favoured the chiaroscuro of oil-painting. Painting had killed the art of stained glass, and 'smutting and darkening for the rounding' was to kill the art of the miniature, yet Hilliard wrote his *Art of Limning* in 1600, outlived Oliver, and was among those who carried something of the Elizabethan spirit into the gloomier century of the early Stuarts. Another was John White, whose

Montacute House, Somerset. Statues of the Nine Worthies are between the upper windows.

water-colours of Red Indians and North American wild life are among the most remarkable works of art of the age of Shakespeare.

The great country-houses were still going up to receive and honour Gloriana: Montacute in Somerset, and many-windowed Hardwick Hall in Derbyshire, built by another Elizabeth, Bess of Hardwick, Countess of Shrewsbury. But the Queen never visited them, never saw the glowing stone and rustic sculptures, the Nine Worthies, of the one, never climbed the great staircase or walked down the Long Gallery to the Presence Chamber of the other. She died on 24 March 1603.

Hardwick Hall, Derbyshire. 'Not the longest of long galleries, but the noblest in the use of space.'

9 *The Early Seventeenth Century 1603–1660*

For the last twenty years of her reign Elizabeth's patronage of the arts had been limited by the cost of the war with Spain, but one of the first acts of James I was to make peace, and he and his young Queen, Anne of Denmark, could afford to be more liberal with the treasure of their new kingdom, so much wealthier than Scotland. But the heroic age was over, and James, more interested in horses than the arts, did little to deserve the triumphs of his reign.

Not least among these was the major work of Bacon, *The Advancement of Learning* and *Novum Organum*. Up till this time knowledge of the material world had been little more than the reckless and unrelated generalizations of medieval philosophy, but in these immensely important books Bacon distinguished between the fields of philosophy and science, and insisted on experimental research and inductive reasoning, from the particular to the framing of general laws, so preparing the way for the experimental science and great discoveries of the century. The new method soon bore fruit, and in the year of Shakespeare's death William Harvey established biology as a science by his experimental proof of the circulation of the blood.

Francis Bacon, Lord Verulam, promoter of experimental science.

Perhaps the decline of standards at Court was partly responsible for Shakespeare's turning to tragic themes, yet he had written *Hamlet* and perhaps *Othello* before James's accession, and the change was inevitable. With the perfected dramatic poetry now at his command, he could no longer be satisfied with writing romantic comedies, but applied it to the creation of tragic heroes, the exploration of their motives and consequences of their actions. So possessed was he by his subject that each of these great tragedies is unified, probably unconsciously, by a dominating image that is a symbol of the theme: of disease in *Hamlet*, for example, of physical torment in *Lear*.

Then, the plays are unified by the poetry itself. In *Macbeth* the atmosphere is one of physical confinement within the castle walls, of spiritual constriction within the curtain of fear, and to suggest such an atmosphere Shakespeare, again perhaps unconsciously, exploited the gutturals *k* and hard *c*, those of *lock* and *key* and *Clink*, the name of the prison near the Globe Theatre. Macbeth himself tells us that he is 'cabined, cribbed, confined' to doubts and fears; Lady Macbeth invokes the spirits of *cruelty* to *unsex* her, to *make thick* her blood, to *take* her *milk for gall*, and cries,

> Come, thick night,
> And pall thee in the dunnest smoke of hell,
> That my keen knife sees not the wound it makes,
> Nor heaven peep through the blanket of the dark
> To cry 'Hold, hold!'

With the same harsh gutturals she goads Macbeth into murdering Duncan, 'screw your courage to the sticking-place', and the horror is heightened when we hear Macbeth, planning the murder of Banquo, speak the same language: 'Come seeling night! . . . Light thickens, and the crow Makes wing to the rooky wood.'

It is one of the wonders of Shakespeare's genius that he could follow *Macbeth* with *Antony and Cleopatra*, for never were two tragedies more unlike. Instead of confinement, darkness, and ambiguity, all is now spaciousness, clarity, and light, an atmosphere of both physical and temporal extension that is created not only by the imagery but also by the emphasis on long vowels, and instead of the dramatic alliteration of *Macbeth* we have dramatic assonance. In the first speech we are told that Antony's eyes 'have glowed like plated Mars', and it is the broad, melancholy *a* of *Mars* that becomes the dominant vowel as the tragedy closes in, the vowel that we associate with all the most memorable passages: *barge, heart, charm, unarm, darkling, garland, remarkable, star, dark.* Then, having written this, the most splendid of his plays, having created his great tragic heroes, Hamlet, Othello, Timon, Lear, Macbeth, Antony, and Coriolanus, Shakespeare turned again to romance and the wildly improbable adventures of young heroines.

All four romances of Shakespeare's final period have a masque, or dance, or vision, and music plays a far larger part than in the earlier comedies. As in *King Lear*, the theme is reconciliation and restoration of daughter to father, in *The Tempest* of all men to themselves, and in all but *Cymbeline* the background is the sea, first heard in the storm scene of *Pericles*. In *The Winter's Tale* Shakespeare seems to be striving for an ever greater compression, to break down the constraint of metre until verse is scarcely distinguishable from prose, almost to create an abstract poetry, but in *The Tempest* he returned to the earlier lyricism, modified however by the polyphonic music of his maturity, the complex counterpoint of opposing rhythms. It is the most perfect of his plays, and this may be why his friends Heminge and Condell, although they knew it to be his last, placed it first in the collected edition of the Folio, published in 1623, seven years after his death.

Two collected editions of plays: Ben Jonson: First Folio, 1616, which may have inspired the editing of the Shakespeare: First Folio, 1623, containing his thirty-six plays.

Robert Johnson set Ariel's songs, 'Full fathom five' and 'Where the bee sucks', to lute accompaniment, and these are among the most perfect settings of this great age of lute song. No other country had such a wealth of lyric, and this is why the English lute song is without a parallel elsewhere. In his *First Booke of Ayres*, 1600, Morley had set 'It was a lover and his lass' from *As You Like It*, and further books of airs and songs soon followed, one by Robert Jones and another by Campion and his friend Philip Rosseter. Campion published three more books, for which he wrote both words and music, but the greatest lutenist of all was John Dowland, lutenist to kings, to Christian IV of Denmark as well as to James I, and his music was played and published throughout Europe. The lute owed its popularity partly to its harmonic range, greater than that of the viol, while at the same time it was easily portable, unlike keyboard instruments. Yet exquisite music for the virginal was composed in the early years of James I's reign, one of the great masters being John Bull, first Professor

(*Left*) From the early seventeenth-century Fitzwilliam Virginal Book, an invaluable collection of early English keyboard music. 'O mistris myne' is an air by Byrd, to words by Shakespeare.

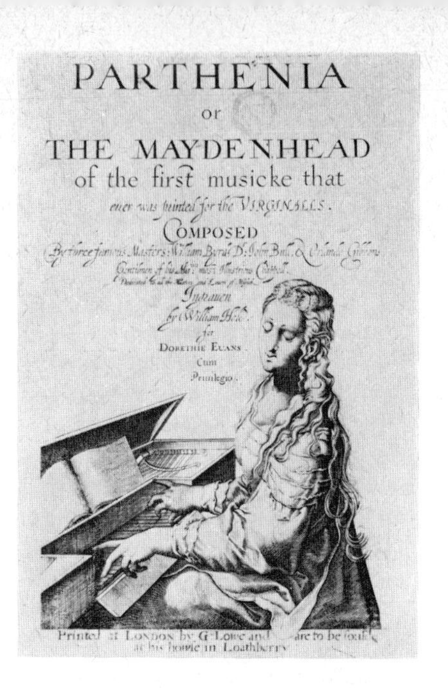

(*Right*) *Parthenia*, 1611: the first music to be printed in Britain from engraved plates instead of types.

of Music at Gresham College. Doctor of Music to the King and musical tutor of Henry, Prince of Wales, in 1611 he was associated with the oldest and youngest composer of this golden age, Byrd and Orlando Gibbons, in the publication of *Parthenia*, 'the first musicke that euer was printed for the Virginalls'. It was at about this time that Francis Tregian, a Cornish Catholic recusant, occupied his time in prison by compiling the most valuable of all anthologies of early English keyboard music, the Fitzwilliam Virginal Book.

Even if Shakespeare had not written his great tragedies in the first decade of James's reign, the period would still have been one of the most memorable in the history of English drama. Jonson, too, tried his hand at tragedy, but *Sejanus*, a classical counterblast to the romantic *Hamlet*, was a failure, and he turned again to comedy in *Volpone*, a terrifying exposure of greed, *The Silent Woman*, written in prose and a lighter vein, and *The Alchemist*, in which Sir Epicure Mammon anticipates the Restoration drama, yet speaks poetry of Marlovian arrogance. His last great play, for after this his genius declined, was *Bartholomew Fair* in 1614, a boisterous anti-Puritan comedy, as crammed with characters as the scene it represents.

Partly because of Jonson, partly because of the growing wealth of the middle classes, the dramatists of the early seventeenth century took a greater interest in realism and bourgeois life, and while Shakespeare was writing his domestic tragedy of *Othello*, the gentle and prolific Heywood was engaged on his very different masterpiece, *A Woman Killed with Kindness*, in which an unfaithful wife is forgiven by her husband and dies of remorse. It is a melancholy rather than a tragic play, but then it was a melancholy age, the age ushered in by *Hamlet*, satirized by Jonson, and soon to be analysed with whimsical pedantry in Robert Burton's *Anatomy of Melancholy*. Even Dekker's cheerfulness in

John Bull (*c.* 1562–1628), one of the great composers of virginal music, and a contributor to *Parthenia*. He died at Antwerp, where he had been cathedral organist for eleven years. ▶

AN ÆTATIS SVÆ 2
1589

The Honest Whore is tinged with melancholy, and the greatest of all tragic poets apart from Shakespeare, John Webster, was 'possessed by death':

> They'll remarry
> Ere the worm pierce your winding-sheet, ere the spider
> Make a thin curtain for your epitaphs.

The lines come from *The White Devil* of *c.* 1610, but it was soon to be followed by an even finer play, *The Duchess of Malfi*, a tragedy of darkness and horror and dazzling poetry.

The Elizabethan tradition of rhetoric on the grand scale was perpetuated by Chapman in his tragedies of contemporary French history, *Bussy D'Ambois*, *Biron*, and *The Revenge of Bussy D'Ambois*, but Chapman was essentially an epic poet, the translator of Homer, with the old-fashioned view that his business was to instruct and inculcate virtue, and by the time Shakespeare died in 1616 the great age of English drama was almost over. Most of it had been written for the large public theatres like the Globe, for an audience that was a cross-section of society, from the young aristocrats of the inns of court to humble apprentices, the kind of audience that encouraged freshness and vigour of writing, but by 1609 manners had deteriorated. In that year Dekker published his *Gull's Hornbook*, giving ironical advice to a gallant on how to behave in a playhouse: let him arrive late and clatter his stool on the stage, laugh during a tragedy, show his displeasure by whistling or walking out in the middle of a scene. Shakespeare's company had just taken over the boys' private theatre at Blackfriars as a winter playhouse. It was small, roofed, warm, and comfortable, the seats correspondingly expensive, the audience confined to the wealthier classes, and it was mainly to please their sophisticated tastes that the new dramatists, John Fletcher and Francis Beaumont, wrote tragi-comedies such as *Philaster*, and tragedies like *A King and No King*, plays full of prettiness and pathos, but shallow and unnatural, enervated as the limp rhythms of their blank verse.

Another cause of the decline of drama was the Court masque. In Elizabeth's time this had been little more than an occasion for dressing up and dancing, but the new Queen wanted something more exciting, and for the Revels of 1604 commissioned Jonson to write *The Masque of Blackness*, in which she and her ladies were to take part. It was mainly mime, dancing, and song, but a spectacular and exceedingly expensive entertainment, largely because of the way in which it was presented by Jonson's collaborator, Inigo Jones. At one end of the hall was a stage framed by a proscenium arch with a painted curtain that rolled down in the Roman manner to reveal 'an artificial sea', the waves of which, and great floating shell of the blackamoors, were moved by the machinery beneath. It was revolutionary, for here was the beginning of the picture-frame stage with front curtain and elaborate scenery behind, and in the next ten years Jonson and Jones collaborated in masques of mounting

Henry, Prince of Wales
Had he lived, there might have been no Civil War.
Miniature by Isaac Oliver.

complexity and ingenuity. The Court masque inevitably influenced both drama and theatre, but the Elizabethans had not written for this kind of stage, with actors cut off from the audience, nor did their plays owe anything to scenery and adventitious spectacle, and their introduction hastened the decline of the drama.

Inigo Jones was a new phenomenon in England, a professional architect. The same age as Jonson, thirty at the beginning of James's reign, he had already been to Italy and studied Roman and Renaissance art and architecture at first hand, and learned to draw something more than mechanical plans and elevations, as his sketches for the costumes of *The Masque of Blackness* show. He designed a theatre for Whitehall Palace, and his association with the Court led to his being appointed Surveyor to Henry, Prince of Wales, who, although only seventeen, was already beginning to buy pictures that were to become part of the great collection of his younger brother Charles I.

The Ben Jonson–Inigo Jones collaboration in Court masques: (*Left*) Jonson's *Masque of Queens*, 1609: A Tribune, part of Jones's 'invention and architecture of the whole scene'. (*Right*) One of Jones's costumes for Jonson's *Masque of Blackness*, 1604, in which James I's Queen was leading lady.

This was in 1611, a memorable year in the history of the arts, the year of the writing of *The Tempest*, of the publication of *Parthenia*, and of the Authorized Version of the Bible, the splendid cadences and solemn, newly incorporated latinisms of which make it one of the major treasures of our literature. In this year also appeared the first published poem of John Donne, *An Anatomy of the World*, a disturbing poem mainly inspired by the revelations of Galileo, that the earth is not the centre of the universe, that the world 'is all in pieces, all coherence gone'. Donne, born in 1572, wrote much of his poetry in Elizabeth's reign, though little of it was published until after his death in 1631, when it profoundly influenced the work of Caroline poets, both Cavaliers and Anglican divines, for in 1615 the writer of erotic lyrics took orders and for the last ten years of his life was Dean of St Paul's. Unlike the smooth and conventional poetry of most of the Elizabethans, Donne's is rough and knotty, his passionate thought and sensual asceticism impregnated with wit, and often expressed in grim jests and grotesque imagery, an aspiring sinewy poetry that has something in common with the tall canvases of El Greco.

In 1611 Inigo Jones may have been helping with the design of Hatfield House, which the Earl of Salisbury was then building in Hertfordshire, and the semi-classical loggia bridging the two wings, with long gallery above, is either his or his inspiration. Hatfield is the last of the great country-houses, of which Theobalds, the work of Salisbury's father, Lord Burghley, was the first, built to receive the sovereign when on progress, the two exactly spanning the fifty years of Shakespeare's life. Still essentially Tudor, ultimately medieval therefore, with mullioned windows and great hall, it is nevertheless unmistakably Jacobean, less fantastic than Elizabethan houses, more severe, built mainly of brick, its windows smaller, an architecture of mass and horizontal roof-line rather than romantic silhouette.

Three contemporaries: (*from left to right*)
John Donne (1572–1631), first and greatest of the metaphysical poets.
Ben Jonson (1572–1637), a classical innovator in drama.
Inigo Jones (1573–1652), the first English classical architect.

Hatfield House, Hertfordshire. Jacobean Gothic with Renaissance loggia.

The Queen's House, Greenwich. A Palladian villa by Inigo Jones, and the first classical building in England, begun in the year of Shakespeare's death, 1616.

Prince Henry died in 1612, and in the following year Inigo Jones accompanied the second Earl of Arundel on a tour of Italy. Arundel, then only twenty-seven, was to become the first great patron, 'the father of *virtu*', in England, the man who brought English art into the European tradition, and to whom 'this angle of the world owed the first sight of Greek and Roman statues'. Jones spent his time studying the architecture of Italy, reading and annotating Palladio's recent *Quattro Libri dell'Architettura*, and on his return to England was appointed Surveyor of the King's Works, and in 1616 began the building of a Palladian villa at Greenwich, the Queen's House. So, in the year of Shakespeare's death, the Middle Ages came finally to an end, after the century when medieval art had been fertilized by an indirect contact with the Italian Renaissance, and flowered again in the hybrid art of the Tudor and Early Jacobean era. For the Queen's House was the first classical building in England, symmetrical, with a ground floor of rusticated masonry and above

A view of Whitehall *c.* 1758. The Banqueting House (*left*), built by Inigo Jones 1619–22. The Tudor 'Holbein Gate' (*centre*) was demolished 1759, the Horse Guards (*right*) completed 1758.

it a loggia with Ionic colonnade. It was not finished until 1635, but meanwhile, between 1619 and 1622, Jones built the Banqueting House in Whitehall, a huge double-cube room, with an exterior of two storeys, the pedimented windows separated by columns and pilasters, and crowned with a frieze and cornice that projects to emphasize the three central bays. Italian architecture, though modified by Jones's genius to suit the greyer skies, was established in England.

It was now, largely because of Arundel and Prince Charles, that painting in England became less insular, more an integral part of the art of Europe. The influence still came from the Netherlands, whence Paul van Somer arrived in 1616. He was not a very distinguished painter, but his large portrait of Queen Anne, with its horse, dogs, view of her favourite Palace of Oatlands, and Inigo Jones's scarcely finished gateway, is on a grander scale than Elizabethan portraiture, and the chiaroscuro, the lights emerging from a dark background, very different from the formal linear tradition. When van Somer died in 1622

(*Left*) Thomas, Earl of Arundel, by Daniel Mytens, *c.* 1618. The Earl points to his gallery of Roman statues, the first English collection of classical sculpture. (*Right*) Sir Nathaniel Bacon: self-portrait of a gentlemanly amateur, *c.* 1620.

he was succeeded as Court portrait painter by Daniel Mytens, a more important artist brought from Holland by Arundel, whose portrait he painted in the gallery of Arundel House, with the classical sculptures he had imported. This was early work, and not to be compared with the grace and colour mastery of his maturity, notably the splendid portrait of the Duke of Hamilton. The most remarkable Jacobean painter, however, and one who might have been the greatest, was an English amateur, Sir Nathaniel Bacon, younger brother of Sir Francis. In those days painting was scarcely a profession for a gentleman, though it was soon to become so, and only a few of his paintings remain, most of them self-portraits. But he also painted the remarkable *Cookmaid*, a combination of portrait and still-life in the new Dutch manner, and a miniature 'landskip' – the word was a recent importation from Holland – the first English essay in this new form of art.

James I died in 1625, and the decade of the 1620s claimed most of the Elizabethan poets, dramatists, musicians, and painters, the contemporaries of Shakespeare: from Daniel and Campion to Webster and Fletcher, Byrd and Dowland, Bull and Gibbons, Hilliard and Nathaniel and Francis Bacon. Donne followed in 1631, and his last sermon served as epitaph for all: 'The whole *world* is but an *universall churchyard*, but our *common grave*, and the life & motion that the greatest persons have in it, is but as the shaking of buried bodies in their grave, by an *earth-quake*.' Nothing better illustrates the grotesque ingenuity of Donne's thought, and the Jacobean obsession with death and dissolution, than his last words: '*Miserable riddle*, when the same *worme* must bee *my mother*, and *my sister*, and *my selfe. Miserable incest*, when I must be *maried* to my *mother* and my *sister*, and bee both *father* and *mother* to my own *mother* and *sister, beget* & *beare* that *worme*. . . .'

A new age began with the accession of Charles I, the princely patron who bought the great Mantua Collection, and whose visit to Spain in 1623, where he saw the royal portraits by Titian, Rubens, and Velazquez, led to his search for a comparable painter for the English Court. His attempt to win Rubens with a knighthood failed, though the great Flemish master undertook the painting of the panels for the ceiling of the new Banqueting House: an opulent

Inigo Jones's Banqueting House, Whitehall, with the ceiling painted by Rubens *c.* 1635.

Endymion Porter, patron of the arts, and friend of Charles I and Van Dyck, who painted this picture with himself on the right, *c.* 1635.

apotheosis of James I and an allegory of the birth of Charles. However, a knighthood, a pension, and a house induced a younger Flemish painter, Anthony Van Dyck, to settle in London in 1632, where he remained most of the time until his death ten years later. He was ideally suited to the task of Court Painter: a disciple of Titian, by the elegance of his style, idealization rather than flattery, he was able to portray his royal and aristocratic subjects as they would like to appear and be remembered, as indeed they are remembered, for his portraits have for ever fixed the image of Charles, his family, and the supporters of his claim to absolutism. They are the visual counterpart of the Cavalier poetry of the decade, of Thomas Carew and Suckling, charming and graceful, immensely accomplished, but rarely passionate and profound. He painted too much and too rapidly, and towards the end declined into mannerism, yet at his best, as in the portrait of himself and Endymion Porter, he rivals Velazquez in his use of colour, particularly his shimmering greys. One of the last commissions of Inigo Jones was the designing of the great double-cube room at Wilton House, for the display of Van Dyck's portraits of the Pembroke family.

The master mason who worked with Inigo Jones at the Banqueting House was Nicholas Stone, a Devonshire man who had been trained in Holland.

Wilton House, Wiltshire, partly rebuilt by Inigo Jones, *c.* 1650. The double-cube room with Van Dyck portraits, including the children of Charles I over the fireplace. ▶

VNG·IE·SER
VIRAY

Early Jacobean sculpture was in the main like that described by the Duchess of Malfi, 'the figure cut in alabaster kneels at my husband's tomb', but the Arundel Marbles and new knowledge of Italian art had their effect on Stone, and at about the time of Charles I's accession he carved the statues of Francis and Sir George Holles in Westminster Abbey, both in Roman armour, one seated, the other standing, something new in English funeral monuments, and apparently inspired by Michelangelo's Medici tombs. Charles's acquisition of the Duke of Mantua's collection of sculptures was another formative influence, and in Stone's figures of the Lyttleton brothers at Magdalen, Oxford, can be seen the beginning of an interest in the nude, for the classical drapery of the two boys leaves their arms and shoulders bare. Stone's most remarkable memorial, however, was the shrouded figure of Donne in St Paul's, the making of which Izaak Walton described a few years later: 'Several charcoal fires being first made in his large study, he brought with him into that place his winding-sheet in his hand, and having put off all his clothes, had this sheet put on him, and so tied with knots at his head and feet, and his hands so placed as dead bodies are usually fitted, to be shrouded or put into their coffin or grave. Upon this urn he thus stood, with his eyes shut, and with so much of the sheet turned aside as might show his lean, pale and death-like face. . . . In this posture he was drawn at his just height; and

Something new in English sculpture: a figure on a pedestal in Roman armour. The Francis Holles memorial, by Nicholas Stone, *c.* 1625.

when the picture was fully finished, he caused it to be set by his bed-side, where it continued and became his hourly object till his death, and was then given to his dearest friend, Dr Henry King, who caused him to be thus carved in one entire piece of white marble, as it now stands in that church.'

Stone, Master Mason to the Crown, worked, appropriately enough, in that material, and was thought of as a craftsman rather than as an artist, for sculpture in England had not yet gained recognition as an art. This lowly status was changed by the Frenchman, Hubert Le Sueur, brought across by Charles to do for him in the round what Van Dyck was to do for him on canvas. But, although Le Sueur had a high opinion of himself – he liked to sign his work Praxiteles Le Sueur – he was an indifferent sculptor, and is important mainly because he worked in bronze, a medium that had scarcely been used in England since the Middle Ages. His best-known work, the equestrian statue of Charles now in Trafalgar Square, must have disappointed the King, for the wooden-looking horse and his own boneless and vacuous face little resembled the mounted warrior depicted by Van Dyck, a picture painted in emulation of Titian's equestrian portrait of the Emperor Charles V. However, it had the distinction of being the first equestrian statue in England, as his bronze portrait busts of the King were the first of their kind, though little more successful, and

'John Donne undone.'
Effigy by Stone, 1631.
Stone was Inigo Jones's master mason
at the Banqueting House.

Van Dyck's portrait of Charles's head in three positions was sent to Bernini, who made a marble bust of very different quality. Thanks to Arundel and Charles I, the English were beginning to take an interest in sculpture, which was no longer confined to memorials in churches. Stone carved statues for the Royal Exchange and classical figures for the King, who also commissioned sculptures for his gardens, and English gentlemen followed the royal example.

Orlando Gibbons, died 1625, last of the great composers of the golden age.

There was no need for Charles to attract foreign composers to his Court, for in 1625 England was still the leading musical country of Europe, though with the death of Orlando Gibbons in that year the golden age was almost over. Ironically, Gibbons died on the journey to meet the new Queen, Henrietta Maria of France, who brought with her a number of musicians, not composers but performers, for the gap between the two was widening. This led to the decay of the lute song, for lute music was written in tablature, a special form of notation, and when composers were no longer skilled performers, composition languished. The death of so many of the older generation of composers and decline of the madrigal and lute song left England more open to foreign influence, mainly that of Italy and the new music of Monteverdi, a richer orchestration, recitative, and opera. Thus, in 1632 Walter Porter, probably a pupil of Monteverdi, published *Madrigals and Airs* for a number of voices, harpsichord, lutes, theorbos, bass viol, two violins or viols, with 'toccatos, sinfonias, rittornellos' and figured bass, a shorthand method of indicating bass notes. The age of polyphony and consort music was becoming one of harmony and orchestra, though not yet, in England, of opera.

The nearest approach to opera was the masque, in which music was still subordinated to verse and spectacle, being virtually confined to the incidental songs and dances, as in the most famous of all masques, *Comus*, with music by Henry Lawes, produced in 1634 at Ludlow Castle. Its author, John Milton, was only twenty-six, but his first published work, a sonnet to Shakespeare, had already appeared in the Second Folio of 1632, the year in which he wrote the companion poems, *L'Allegro* and *Il Penseroso*, in the graceful octosyllabic couplets that were the favourite verse form of the period. In the first of these Milton describes the delights of the cheerful man: the sights and sounds of the country, 'towered cities', the theatre of Jonson and Shakespeare, above all 'Lydian airs married to immortal verse'. In the second are the more sober pleasures of the contemplative man, who prefers silence, darkness, and organ music in the 'dim religious light' of churches. *Comus* combines the themes, though the opposition is intensified into one of worldly pleasure and temperance, a conflict that was to grow in the mind of the puritanical Milton, so that in his next poem, *Lycidas*, the elegiacs of this most musical of mourners were interrupted by an attack on the sycophantic Anglican clergy.

Whatever Milton may have meant by 'their lean and flashy songs', the phrase could scarcely be applied to those Anglican divines who were among

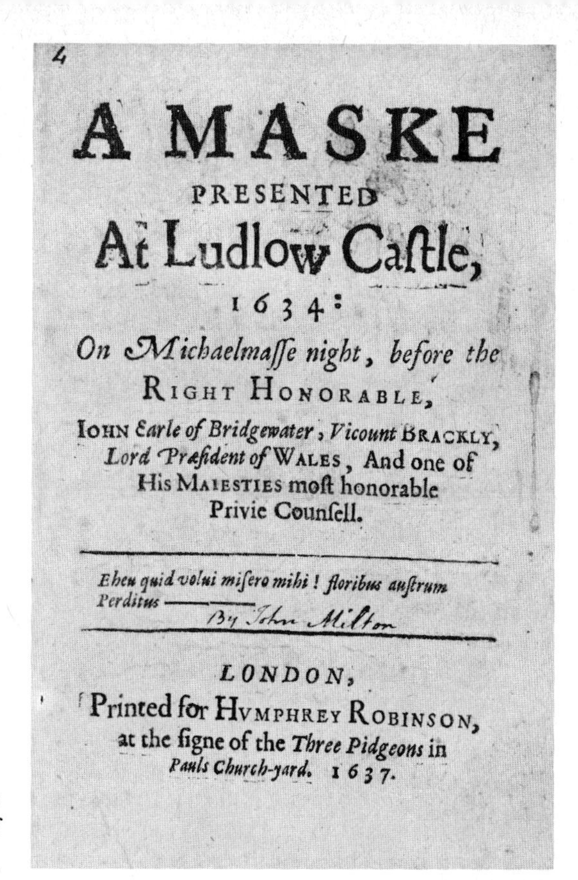
4

A MASKE
PRESENTED
At Ludlow Castle,
1634:
On Michaelmasse night, before the
RIGHT HONORABLE,
IOHN *Earle of Bridgewater; Vicount* BRACKLY,
Lord Præsident of WALES, And one of
His MAIESTIES most honorable
Privie Counsell.

Eheu quid volui misero mihi! floribus austrum
Perditus ——
By John Milton

LONDON,
Printed for HUMPHREY ROBINSON,
at the signe of the *Three Pidgeons* in
Pauls Church-yard. 1637.

The masque was *Comus*, the author a young scholar of twenty-six, John Milton.

the 'metaphysical' poets of the school of Donne: to the homely imagery of George Herbert's religious experiences, the more mystical meditations of Henry Vaughan, the passionate ecstasies of Richard Crashaw, or Henry King's most poignant of all love-poems, *The Exequy*, written to his dead wife:

> Stay for me there; I will not fail
> To meet thee in that hollow vale;
> And think not much of my delay:
> I am already on the way. . . .
> But hark! My pulse, like a soft drum,
> Beats my approach, tells thee I come;
> And slow howe'er my marches be,
> I shall at last sit down by thee.

As the decade of the 1620s took most of the great musicians born in Elizabeth's reign, that of the 1630s took the last of the dramatists: Dekker, Marston, Chapman, Jonson; Philip Massinger and John Ford survived until 1640, when only James Shirley remained, and with these three men the great half-century of the English drama, begun by Marlowe, came to an end. Inevitably it had declined into mannerism. In his tragedies, *The Roman Actor* for example,

Massinger modelled his style on Shakespeare, and Sir Giles Overreach in his great comedy, *A New Way to Pay Old Debts*, is another version of Jonson's Epicure Mammon. Ford was another, though inferior, Webster, whom he outstripped in horrors and the exploitation of unnatural passions, as in *'Tis Pity She's a Whore*, and with Shirley the epoch closes without any great distinction, his main claim to fame being the song, 'The glories of our blood and state'.

Plays and playhouses had always been opposed by the Puritans, whose assault had begun with the building of the Theatre in 1576: 'Satan hath not a more speedy way . . . to bring men and women into his snare of concupiscence and filthy lusts of wicked whoredom, than those plays and theatres are. . . .' Fortunately, the attack had died down, but it was resumed in the 1630s by William Prynne: 'Stage-plays, the very pomps of the Devil, are sinful, heathenish, lewd, ungodly spectacles. . . .' As the Queen played in masques, Prynne forfeited his ears for his temerity, but at last the Puritans carried the day, for when the Civil War began in 1642 the theatres were closed, not to be reopened until the Restoration in 1660.

It was a period of bitter controversy and pamphleteering, in which Milton, abandoning his beloved poetry, participated. Prose was not his natural medium, and without the discipline of verse his meaning is often obscured by Latin constructions, involution, and sheer length of sentence, but when deeply moved, as in his defence of a free Press in the *Areopagitica*, he could write with epigrammatic simplicity: 'A good book is the precious life-blood of a master spirit,' or in prose that is not far removed from his poetry, 'I cannot praise a fugitive and cloistered virtue, unexercised and unbreathed, that never sallies out and sees her adversary, but slinks out of the race where that immortal garland is to be run for, not without dust and heat.' But the greatest prose writer of the period, perhaps of any period, was Sir Thomas Browne: a metaphysical prose of

Sir Thomas Browne (1605–82), physician and prose writer of 'beautiful obliquities'.

The Compleat Angler or the Contemplative Man's Recreation.

Being a Discourse of

FISH and FISHING,

Not unworthy the perusal of most *Anglers*.

Simon Peter said, *I go a fishing: and they said, We also wil go with thee.* John 21.3.

London, Printed by *T. Maxey* for RICH. MARRIOT, in S. *Dunstans* Churchyard Fleetstreet, 1653.

Title-page of the first edition of *The Compleat Angler, or the Contemplative Man's Recreation*, by Izaak Walton, 1653.

fanciful conceits, resonant with latinisms, harmonized by assonance, and falling in long, melancholy cadences that echo like organ music in a vaulted chamber. His first work, *Religio Medici*, published at the outbreak of the Civil War, was followed by *Vulgar Errors*, *The Garden of Cyrus*, and *Urn Burial*, in the last chapter of which his style reaches its full splendour: 'Pyramids, Arches, Obelisks, were but the irregularities of vain-glory, and wild enormities of ancient magnanimity. But the most magnanimous resolution rests in the Christian Religion, which trampleth upon pride, and sits on the neck of ambition, humbly pursuing that infallible perpetuity, unto which all others must diminish their Diameters, and be poorly seen in Angles of contingency.' A very different kind of prose was written by Izaak Walton, who, unlike Milton, could be both cheerful and contemplative at once. He wrote a number of short *Lives*, including those of Donne and Herbert, but is best known and loved for his *Compleat Angler*, written in dialogue form and an artless conversational style descriptive of the delights of fishing and the mid-seventeenth-century countryside.

It was now that Thomas Hobbes published his *Leviathan* and inaugurated the great century of British philosophy. Experimental science, as Bacon had foreseen, had shown that natural phenomena can be naturally explained, but Hobbes went further, maintaining that matter and motion are the only ultimate realities, that even mind, or soul, is matter, and God, if there is one, beyond human knowledge. It followed that he rejected Hooker's belief in a divine order, the natural human condition being one of 'war of every man against every man', and an ordered society is his own defensive creation, for without it his life would be 'solitary, poor, nasty, brutish and short'. To materialism, therefore, he added the doctrine of absolutism, for there must be some absolute power to enforce the law and prevent the disintegration of society. As there could be no Divine Right of Kings, this absolute ruler was not necessarily a king, and for this reason the Royalists opposed him, notably the Earl of Clarendon, author of the great history of the Civil War, or as he called it, *History of the Rebellion*.

While Walton was communicating his happiness in prose, Robert Herrick, a Devonshire parson, was celebrating the flowers and festivals of the West Country in lyrics light and graceful as those of the Elizabethans, in particular

Leviathan, title-page, 1651. Hobbes conceived the State as a monstrous giant composed of innumerable people.

Endymion Porter, by William Dobson, 'the most excellent painter that England hath yet bred.' ▶
(Compare page 152.)

of Ben Jonson, whose admirer he was. Herrick was untouched by the eccentricities of the metaphysicals, but up in Yorkshire, at Appleton House, Andrew Marvell applied their fanciful imagery to the praise of gardens:

> Annihilating all that's made
> To a green Thought in a green Shade.

He also wrote of love, *To His Coy Mistress* being his masterpiece, and if he had written more of the quality of this and of *The Description of Love*, *Bermudas*, and the *Horatian Ode to Cromwell* he would be among the greatest of English poets.

It is a pity that there was no painter to record the rural life of the Commonwealth period celebrated by these writers in such different ways, but it was still an age of portraits, not of landscapes. When Van Dyck died just before the Civil War his place as Court Painter was taken unofficially by William Dobson, 'the most excellent painter that England hath yet bred', as his contemporary, John Aubrey, described him. A greater vigour and naturalism, as well as erudition, distinguish his work from the elegance and later affectations of Van Dyck, with whose portrait of Endymion Porter, patron of painters,

Dobson's may be compared. Robert Walker, the corresponding figure on the side of Parliament, was much more derivative; we should expect his portraits to reflect the sternness of that puritanical age, yet these armoured Roundheads awkwardly assume the courtly postures of Van Dyck's silken Cavaliers. Dobson died in poverty and Walker in obscurity, but Samuel Cooper had an international reputation, and his miniatures were eagerly bought by both Royalists and Roundheads. His was not the delicate imaginative art of Hilliard, but a development of the more mundane limnings of Isaac Oliver, realistic portraiture in little. Of their kind, however, they are admirable, and his unfinished miniature of Cromwell should be compared with Walker's idealization of the same subject.

The Civil War closed the theatres, killed the poetic drama, and put an end to Court patronage of painting and sculpture, as well as to Inigo Jones's plans for the rebuilding of Whitehall Palace, of which the Banqueting House would have been only the first unit. Musicians also suffered, for many of them were dependent on royal patronage, and some of them were killed in the King's cause, among them Henry Lawes's younger brother William, who wrote the setting for Herrick's 'Gather ye rosebuds'. The average Puritan had no objection to music; like his father, Milton was a musician, loving the art almost as much

Oliver Cromwell, idealized by Robert Walker.

Oliver Cromwell, 'warts and all'.
A miniature by Samuel Cooper.

as he loved poetry, and he wrote a sonnet to Henry Lawes *On the Publishing his Airs*:

> Harry, whose tuneful and well-measured song
> First taught our English music how to span
> Words with just note and accent . . .

Bunyan consoled himself in prison with a self-made flute, Cromwell moved the organ from Magdalen, Oxford, to his Palace of Hampton Court, and under the Commonwealth secular music and its publication continued to flourish. What the Puritans did object to, however, was the elaborate music of the Anglican ritual, and the organ was reduced to an instrument for the accompaniment of hymn-singing. But the government could not control the fanatics who would not even tolerate an organ, or any form of ecclesiastical ornament; the Protestants of the Reformation a hundred years before had ruined much of the art of the Catholic Church, and now the zealots and philistines among the Puritans destroyed the greater part of the remaining medieval glass, sculptures, and painted rood-screens.

Nor could the government control all the entertainments in the provinces, and at fairs and other rural junketings 'drolls' were surreptitiously performed, extracts from the forbidden drama such as *The Merry Conceited Humours of Bottom the Weaver*, and *The Bouncing Knight* (Falstaff), and even *The Gravemakers* from *Hamlet*. Then, the Royalist dramatist Sir William Davenant conceived an ingenious plan for dramatic performances in London. He had seen Italian opera in Paris, and as the government had no objection to music, he got permission to stage a performance of his *Siege of Rhodes*, the words to be sung 'in recitative music'. Thus, the first English opera was performed at Rutland House in 1656. As Inigo Jones had died in 1652, his pupil John Webb designed the setting, in the manner of the Court masques: an architectural proscenium, behind which were painted canvas side-wings, and at the back of the stage sliding shutters for a change of scene: a view of Rhodes, and Solyman's pavilion. The music, which has been lost, was mainly by Henry Lawes, the man who understood recitative, the art of composing musical dialogue, 'how to span words with just note and accent'. John Evelyn made no mention of the performance in his *Diary*, but at the beginning of 1659 he went to see Davenant's elevating *Cruelty of the Spaniards in Peru*, 'a new opera after the Italian way, in recitative music and scenes, much inferior to the Italian composure and magnificence'. Evelyn was a much-travelled man, and might have made allowances; it was as astonishing as it was ironical that the last years of the Puritan Commonwealth should have produced opera, a theatre with changeable scenery – and actresses, the first appearance of women on the public stage.

The first English opera: Davenant's *Siege of Rhodes*, 'the Story sung in *Recitative* Musick', 1656. A back-shutter which slid across the stage to change the scene, a device invented by Inigo Jones.

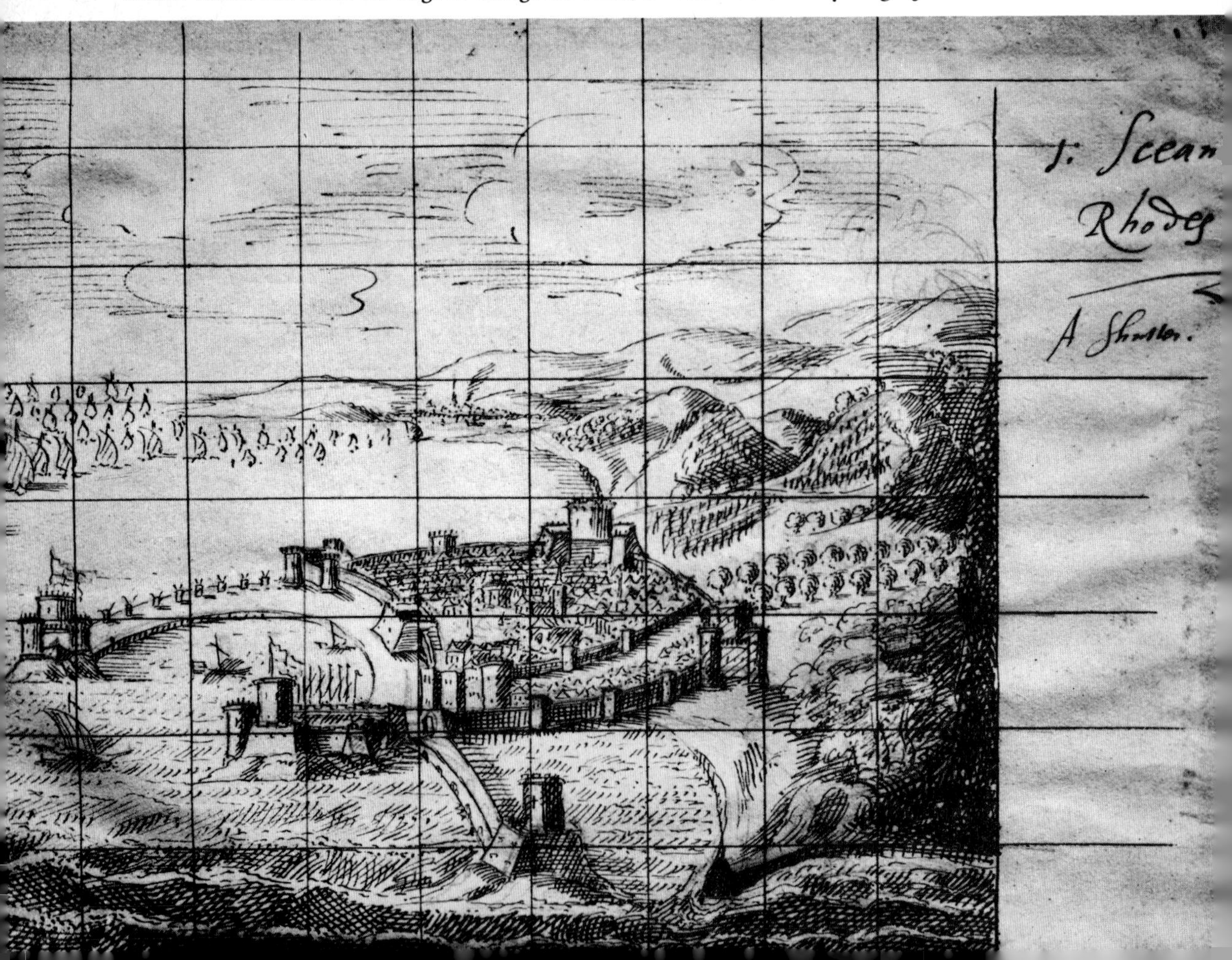

10 *The Later Seventeenth Century 1660–1714*

After the austerities of the Puritan Commonwealth, and the Restoration of Charles II in 1660, a violent reaction was inevitable. In *Hudibras*, a long satirical poem, Samuel Butler ridiculed the 'Sect whose chief devotion lies In odd perverse antipathies', while the poetry of Sedley and Rochester, and prose of the new comedy of manners reflected the licentiousness of the Court. Moreover, Charles was half French and had lived half his thirty years in exile, in either France or Holland, accompanied by supporters, some of whom had wandered farther afield and in Italy discovered the art of contemporary Rome, notably the baroque architecture and sculpture of Bernini.

Like the art of ancient Rome which inspired it, that of the Early Italian Renaissance had been one of serenity and repose, but by the seventeenth century it had become restless, agitated, and theatrical, extravagant variations on classical themes, almost a romantic classicism. The new fashion spread to the France of Louis XIV, and it was a knowledge of this baroque art that Royalist exiles, dilettanti, and wealthy young men who made the Grand Tour brought back to England. Thus, John Evelyn was in Rome in 1644, and much impressed by the 'vastness and magnificence' of the high altar in St Peter's, 'the work of Bernini'. The English have never been given to extremes in art or anything else, but after the Restoration they could scarcely avoid the influence of Baroque, which so perfectly expressed the Royalist revolt against the former enforced asceticism. It is to be found in the architecture of Wren and Vanbrugh, sculpture of Bushnell and Gibbons, painting of Thornhill, music of Purcell, in the poetry of Dryden and even of Milton.

Two Restoration diarists: John Evelyn, 1620–1706. Samuel Pepys, holding the score of his *Beauty retire*, 'and do almost break my neck looking over my shoulder to make the posture for him to work by.' Painted by John Hales, 1666.

It was an extraordinary age, an age that prided itself on its enlightenment and elegance, its emergence from the barbarities of Gothick and absurdities of the Elizabethans, yet coarse and cynical, callous and corrupt, which nevertheless produced some of the greatest men in the history of English art, philosophy, and science. At the Restoration Milton was fifty-two, Dryden twenty-nine, Wren and John Locke twenty-eight, Newton eighteen, and Purcell one. Fortunately, two other men of more than common talents were there to record events in their diaries; the elder was the Royalist country gentleman John Evelyn, a great lover of gardens and the visual arts, the other young Samuel Pepys of the Navy Office, an amateur of music, who had been with the fleet that brought Charles back to England in May 1660.

On 1 January he had begun his *Diary*, an account in cipher of all his daily doings, however mean, and on 8 July he noted: 'Lord's Day. To White Hall chapel . . . Here I heard very good music, the first time that I ever remember to have heard the organs and singing-men in surplices in my life.' The Anglican service, as new to the boy choristers and most of the men as it was to Pepys, had been restored, though the music was no longer the horizontal polyphony of Tallis, Byrd, and Gibbons, but the vertical harmony of chords for orchestra and organ, as developed in masque and opera. The new Master of the Children of the Chapel Royal was Henry Cooke, a Royalist soldier still known by his title of Captain, who had sung in *The Siege of Rhodes* and composed some of the music: 'Captain Cooke,' wrote Evelyn, 'esteemed the best singer after the Italian manner [i.e. operatic] of any in England.' Although Charles was no great patron of the arts, Henry Lawes, who died two years later, was one of his Court musicians, as was Matthew Locke, composer of the music for Charles's progress through the City. In the same year John Wilson, probably the singer of 'Sigh no more, ladies' in an early production of *Much Ado about Nothing*, and now Professor of Music at Oxford, published his *Cheerful Ayres . . . set for three Voices*, the first book of catches to appear. They had become very popular, and no doubt Pepys had Wilson's song-book when on 21 July he 'dined at a club, where we had three voices to sing catches'.

Pepys was just twenty-seven when Charles was restored, only nine therefore when the theatres had been closed in 1642, and had never seen a play performed.

His first visit to a theatre appears to have been to see Fletcher's *Loyal Subject* in August 1660, the month in which Charles authorized two companies of players, one under Thomas Killigrew at the Cockpit in Drury Lane, the other under Davenant in Lincoln's Inn Fields at the 'Opera', so called because of his operatic ventures. Both were 'private' theatres, that is roofed, unlike the 'public' Elizabethan playhouses, the audiences composed largely of courtiers, and Davenant was fortunate in finding young Thomas Betterton, whom Pepys saw in 1661: 'To the Opera, and there saw *Hamlet*, done with scenes very well, but above all, Betterton did the Prince's part beyond imagination.' There were now actresses as well as scenery in the theatre. Evelyn also saw the play, but wrote sadly, 'the old plays begin to disgust this refined age, since his Majesty's being so long abroad'. Pepys was among the refined ones, and for him *Twelfth Night* was merely silly, *A Midsummer Night's Dream* insipid and ridiculous, and *Romeo and Juliet* even worse. If Shakespeare was to be profitable he had to be refined, and Davenant set to work, running together *Measure for Measure* and *Much Ado about Nothing* to make the comedy of *The Law Against Lovers*, enlivened with song, dance, quartet, and chorus. *Macbeth* he purged of its vulgarity and rewrote the scenes of the witches, who flew over the stage singing the music of Locke. In the same year, 1664, Dryden's tragedy *The Indian Queen* drew the town to the rival theatre to see its sumptuous scenery, flying and singing spirits, and real Indian dress of feathers. Davenant, therefore, enlisted Dryden's aid, and together they transformed *The Tempest* into a spectacular and smutty comic opera with music by Bannister. Shakespeare refined! But at least the first stage direction is interesting: 'The front of the stage is opened, and the band of twenty-four violins, with the harpsicals and theorbos which accompany the voices, are played between the pit and the stage.' Violin had ousted viol, and the orchestra, a large one, had been moved from above to the front of the stage.

A Restoration theatre: Elkanah Settle's *Empress of Morocco* at the Duke's, 1673.

Restoration Baroque: stock pose, fluttering hands and drapery. The Countess of Northumberland, by Sir Peter Lely.

It was at about this time that Pepys had his wife's portrait painted by John Hales. He liked it mightily, and was delighted when he saw Lely painting the Duchess of York, with 'nothing near so much resemblance of her face . . . as there was of my wife's . . . the lines not being in proportion'. Little is known about Hales, but his work must have been considerably cheaper than that of Lely, who charged twenty-five pounds for a half-length. Peter Lely was a Dutchman who had come to England at the beginning of the Civil War, when he was about twenty-five. His early work was his most original, for he painted a number of subject pictures and established the convention of a landscape background to his portraits, but when Charles appointed him Principal Painter in 1661 he had time, or inclination, only for portraits, mainly of Court ladies, all of whom have a family resemblance. If they all looked alike there had to be differences in pose, and Lely invented a series of postures which he numbered and used on appropriate occasions, restless postures with fluttering hands in the fashionable baroque manner. He was a fine and conscientious painter, but not a great artist, and his best portraits are those of men, in which character is more important than flattery, as in the series of admirals, or 'Flagmen', at Greenwich, which Pepys so much admired.

Lely's main rival was Michael Wright, a Roman Catholic and apparently a Scot, who spent several years in Rome before coming to London in 1659. Pepys visited his studio after seeing Lely's, 'But Lord! the difference that is between their two works!' There was, but not all to Wright's disadvantage. Wright could not, or would not, flatter Court ladies like Lely, but went his own way and painted, for example, the actor John Lacy in three of his roles, so creating the genre that was to become popular in the next century. Evelyn considered the Lacy portraits to be among Wright's best work, but he does not say what he thought of Lacy's transformation of *The Taming of the Shrew* into *Sauny the Scot*, one of the coarsest refinements of that paradoxical age.

An important post to be filled at the Restoration was that of Surveyor-General of the King's Works. John Webb, Inigo Jones's former pupil and assistant, was the obvious choice, but the office went to the King's loyal supporter, Sir John Denham, a minor poet still remembered for his *Cooper's Hill*, but only an amateur architect. A more distinguished amateur was Sir Roger Pratt, builder of Coleshill House, Berkshire, remarkable for two important new features: its division into a 'double pile' by a long central corridor, and conversion of the medieval dining-hall into an entrance hall with a double flight of stairs sweeping up to the first floor in the baroque manner that Pratt had seen in Italy. Another influential house was Eltham Lodge, Kent, built by the new Paymaster of the Works, Hugh May, whose inspiration was the simpler Palladian style that he brought back from Holland: a rectangular brick house with four stone pilasters supporting a pediment over the central bays, which served as a model for innumerable medium-sized houses, and also influenced Wren.

Medieval dining-hall becomes Restoration entrance hall. Coleshill House, Berkshire, by Sir Roger Pratt.

The Sheldonian Theatre, Oxford, built by Wren, 1662–3, when only thirty.

At the Restoration Wren was Gresham Professor of Astronomy and inventor of numerous ingenious devices. Evelyn had met him in 1654 when he was still little more than a boy at Oxford – 'that miracle of a youth . . . that prodigious young scholar' – but did not hear his lecture at Gresham College in 1660, which led to the foundation of the Royal Society two years later. By that time Wren was back at Oxford as Savilian Professor of Astronomy and, presumably because of his mathematical ability, designing a building for university ceremonies. This was the Sheldonian Theatre, in plan resembling a Roman theatre, and he solved the problem of spanning the formidable width by adding a trussed roof from which to hang his ceiling. This was covered by Robert Streeter with a baroque allegorical painting of the heavens, in which Truth is surrounded by the Arts and Sciences. Streeter, Serjeant Painter to the King, tried his hand at many forms of painting: his were the 'very glorious scenes and perspectives' for Dryden's celebrated 'heroic' play, *The Conquest of Granada*, and his *View of Boscobel House*, though not pure landscape, is among the first paintings of a country-house and its setting.

Wren next turned his attention to Cambridge, where he designed Pembroke College Chapel, the west end of which, with giant Ionic pilasters and pediment, resembles the central feature of Eltham Lodge, and then in the summer of 1665, perhaps because the Great Plague had begun, he went to Paris. It was a memorable visit, for in addition to seeing the northern châteaux, including Fontainebleau and Versailles, he met many of the architects and artists engaged on new work, Mansard perhaps, and certainly the great master of Italian Baroque, Bernini. 'Bernini's Design of the Louvre,' he wrote, 'I would have given my Skin for, but the old reserv'd Italian gave me but a few Minutes View.' He was back in England by the spring of 1666, when he would see the beginning of a palace at Greenwich, Webb's 'King Charles' Block', a long building in the manner of Inigo Jones, with an attic storey at each end, though

Two paintings
by Robert Streeter:
Baroque explosion on the
ceiling of the
Sheldonian Theatre.

Boscobel House,
Shropshire, where Charles II
hid in 1651.
The beginning of English
landscape painting.

(*Below*) First unit of a new
Greenwich Palace:
King Charles' Block,
by John Webb, 1665.

the groups of giant pillars and pilasters gave it a touch of Baroque. Wren was to incorporate it later in his great design for Greenwich Hospital, but more urgently he had to advise on the repair of St Paul's Cathedral, the central tower of which was in danger of collapse. Fresh from his French visit, he recommended its replacement by a dome, 'a form of church-building not as yet known in England, but of wonderful grace', Evelyn wrote approvingly. That was on 27 August. Then on 2 September: 'This fatal night, about ten, began the deplorable fire near Fish Street in London.' Thirteen thousand houses and eighty-seven churches were destroyed by the Great Fire in the City. Old St Paul's also perished, though Evelyn regretted less the loss of the Gothic fabric than that of the 'beautiful portico . . . comparable to any in Europe', the classical west front that Inigo Jones had built thirty years before.

Dryden was writing a poem on the Dutch War, and added a section on the 'prodigious fire', which finished with a prophetic vision of 'a city of more precious mould' rising 'from this chemic flame':

> More great than human now, and more august,
> Now deified she from her fires does rise:
> Her widening streets on new foundations trust,
> And opening into larger parts she flies.

Annus Mirabilis is not a great poem, but 1666–7 was a wonderful year. First came *Grace Abounding*, the spiritual autobiography of a young Puritan, John Bunyan, thrown into prison at the Restoration, written in the simplest prose, the language of everyday life modified by the rhythms of the Bible and imagery of a poet. It was followed by the profounder theme of another Puritan, *Paradise Lost*, a sonorous blank-verse epic which, though lacking the easy flow of Shakespearean counterpoint, is a marvel of sustained and formal orchestration.

◀ The end of medieval St Paul's Cathedral, 1666. (Note the Inigo Jones classical portico.)

John Dryden (1631–1700) by Sir Godfrey Kneller.

(*Below*) From the 1688 edition of *Paradise Lost*:
John Milton, 1608–74.
Raphael, at the request of Adam, relates how and wherefore this world was first created.

He, with his consorted Eve,
The story heard attentive.

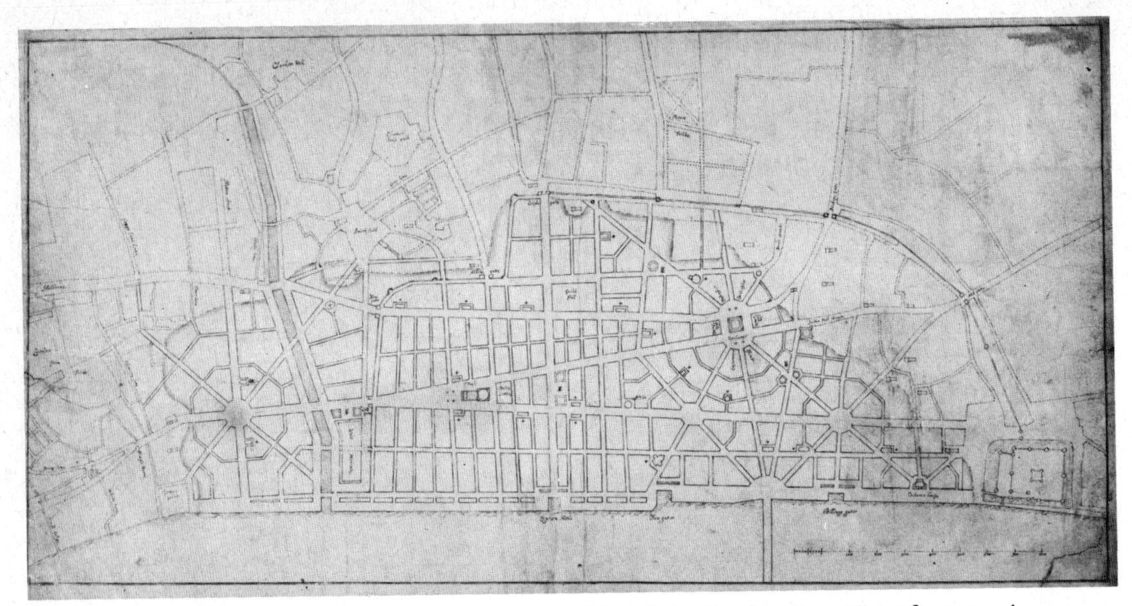

Wren's design for rebuilding the City of London after the Great Fire of 1666: piazzas, long vistas and terraces by the river.

A few years later came the sequel, *Paradise Regained*, though Milton found salvation less inspiring than damnation, and *Samson Agonistes* is at once a classical tragedy and an allegory of his own blindness and struggle against his enemies.

Milton wrote in blank verse because he had come to consider rhyme 'the invention of a barbarous age, to set off wretched matter and lame metre'. This may have been a hit at Dryden, who had recently written that 'the advantages that rhyme has over blank verse are so many that it were lost time to name them', and in his *Essay of Dramatic Poesy*, 1668, maintained that rhyme, by which he meant the heroic couplet, was the proper medium for English tragedy, and to prove, or try to prove, his point, wrote a number of 'heroic' plays, baroque inflations of elevating nonsense about love and honour, culminating in *Aurengzebe*. He also tried his hand at comedy, but his wit was often merely coarseness, and even Pepys complained that his *Evening's Love* was 'very smutty', while Evelyn was 'afflicted to see how the stage was degenerated and polluted by the licentious times'.

Evelyn was probably thinking of the comedies of George Etherege, the first to strike the right Restoration note in the comedy of manners: of heartless wit and amorous intrigue in an amoral society. His first play was produced in 1664, his last and best, *The Man of Mode*, in 1676, but shortly before that four plays of William Wycherley had appeared in rapid succession, the most brilliantly indecent being *The Country Wife*, in which the young rake Horner secures his prey by affecting 'the foppish distemper'. Equally cynical, and called

Three of the City Churches rebuilt by Wren, 1670–*c.* 1686:
a dome: St Stephen Walbrook, and two steeples: St Bride's and St Mary-le-Bow.

by Voltaire the wittiest comedy of all time, was *The Plain Dealer* of 1674, the year of Milton's death.

Meanwhile, the new London was rising from its ashes, not, however, according to the plan that Wren submitted, a city of long straight streets and piazzas, for as the owners of ruined shops and houses had to pay for their rebuilding they were allowed to use their old sites, subject to certain conditions. The greater part of the cost of replacing public buildings was borne by the City and its Companies, and that of the churches by a tax on coal. Wren was appointed Surveyor-General, and under his direction work began on the reconstruction of fifty-five churches, though obviously he had to leave much of the detail to assistants. Scarcely any churches had been built in England in the century since the Reformation, and as the Anglican service differed from the Roman, notably in its emphasis on the sermon, Wren's churches were essentially halls, often with a gallery, in which everyone could see the preacher and hear the service, so that the chancel became vestigial. When the rebuilding began in 1670 Wren was planning a new St Paul's Cathedral, and it is not surprising to find him experimenting with a central dome at St Stephen Walbrook, where the framework of wood and plaster is carried, not by the outer walls, but by eight Corinthian columns. To find a classical equivalent for a Gothic spire, by which he set great store, was another problem, brilliantly solved in a number of ways: at St Bride's with a slender cone of diminishing octagons, at St Mary-le-Bow with receding stages of encircling pillars united by inverted consoles.

Baroque heroics in sculpture, the visual equivalent of the Heroic Play:
(*Left*) Charles II, by John Bushnell.
(*Right*) *Charles II succouring the City of London*, by C.G. Cibber, 1674. ▶

While the ruined cathedral was being demolished, Wren's Temple Bar and Edward Jerman's new Royal Exchange were completed, for both of which statues of the Stuart kings were carved by John Bushnell, a sculptor who had spent some time in Italy, and the influence of Bernini and Baroque is obvious enough in the heroics of Charles II in Roman armour, and the theatrical pose and agitated drapery of his father. The Restoration produced no sculptors of the calibre of Wren, though it did produce a sculpture that was worthy of him: Edward Pierce's portrait bust of the great architect himself, with visionary eyes and wide generous mouth, apparently carved in 1673 to celebrate his

Sir Christopher Wren, *c.* 1673, by Edward Pierce.

Wren's Library at Trinity College, Cambridge, 1676–84. ▶

knighthood. At this time Caius Gabriel Cibber, a Dane recently arrived in London, was carving a large relief for the Monument erected on the site where the Great Fire began: a baroque allegory, extravagant as Dryden's eulogies, of Charles II instructing Architecture and Science to restore the fainting figure of London. A few years later Cibber carved the statues of Divinity, Law, Physics, and Mathematics for the parapet of Trinity College Library, Cambridge, one of Wren's masterpieces and the culmination of his earlier, simpler style: on one side a Doric loggia supporting an Ionic colonnade, and an even simpler façade facing the river.

On 18 January 1671 Evelyn entered in his *Diary*: 'This day I first acquainted his Majesty with that incomparable young man, Gibbons, whom I had lately met with in an obscure place by mere accident. . . . I found him shut in, but, looking in at the window I perceived him carving that large cartoon, or crucifix, of Tintoretto, a copy of which I had myself brought from Venice.' Evelyn hoped that the Catholic Queen would buy the carving, but 'a French peddling woman' intervened, and he had to be content with Wren's promise to employ his young protégé.

Wren had completed his first design for St Paul's, but he was dissatisfied and made another, the Great Model of 1673, a design of splendid simplicity, with a portico of giant columns, and inward curving walls that emphasized the convexity of the dome. Perhaps it looked more like a monument than a cathedral, and it lacked the traditional drama of a long nave vista closed by the altar, or perhaps it was too original and simple. Whatever the cause, the model was rejected and Wren prepared the Warrant Design, a Latin cross in plan with a bizarre oriental-looking dome and spire, which was accepted. He kept fairly closely to the plan, but modified the elevation as work proceeded, raising the outer walls of the aisles to screen and support the flying buttresses that braced the nave vault. It was 1697 before the dome, very different from the Warrant Design, was begun: a drum supporting the interior dome as well as a cone of masonry, which in turn supported the lantern and leaden shell of the outer dome that concealed it. The cathedral as built was more elaborately dramatic than the Great Model, the triumph of Wren's moderate exploitation of Baroque, and finest of all buildings by a single British architect.

Stages in the designing of St Paul's Cathedral:
The Great Model, 1673. The Warrant Design, 1675. As completed, *c.* 1709.

'A Curious Perspective View of the inside of St Paul's Cathedral,' soon after its completion.

St Paul's Cathedral: the choir stalls, by Grinling Gibbons, who was also responsible for some of the stone ornaments on the exterior walls.

The Conversion of St Paul, carved by Francis Bird on the west pediment of St Paul's Cathedral, 1706.

Among the sculptors whom Wren employed were Pierce, who worked on the south side of the cathedral, and Cibber, carver of the keystones of the dome arches. Gibbons also carved some of the exterior stone ornament, but his finest work was inside in wood: the choir stalls, organ-case, and bishop's throne. 'There is no instance before him,' Horace Walpole was to write a century later, 'of a man who gave to wood the loose and airy lightness of flowers', an art that seems to derive from Dutch still-life painting. Yet, though Gibbons was appointed Master Sculptor to the Crown in 1684, and made the fine bronze statue of James II, now outside the National Gallery, it was not to him that Wren turned to complete the sculptures for St Paul's after Cibber's death, but to Francis Bird, a young man who had worked in both Flanders and Rome, and it was he who carved the sensational *Conversion of St Paul* on the great west pediment.

Sir Peter Lely – for like Van Dyck he had been knighted – died in 1680, and the post of Principal Painter was vacant. John Riley was a possible choice had he not suffered from two disabilities: he was an Englishman, and sometimes painted humbler and more genuine portraits than those of Court beauties; and in an age when it had become fashionable to cover the walls of houses with frescoes, the Italian Antonio Verrio was preferred. Evelyn first saw his work in 1679 at Windsor Castle, which 'will celebrate his name as long as those walls last', and never tired of praising his luscious fantasies, even those for the 'Popish services' in James II's Whitehall Chapel. But when James was overthrown in 1688 Verrio was replaced by the Protestants Riley and Godfrey Kneller, who held the office jointly. Riley died in 1691, and for the next thirty years Kneller, a German who had come to England in 1674, dominated painting and continued the portrait tradition of Lely, and even the same factory-like division of labour in his studio, where assistants filled in background and costumes. There was a difference, however, a greater virility of style, and whereas Lely's characteristic portraits are those of voluptuous ladies, Kneller's are those of men, often of men remarkable not for their birth but their genius, such as Wren, Dryden, and Purcell.

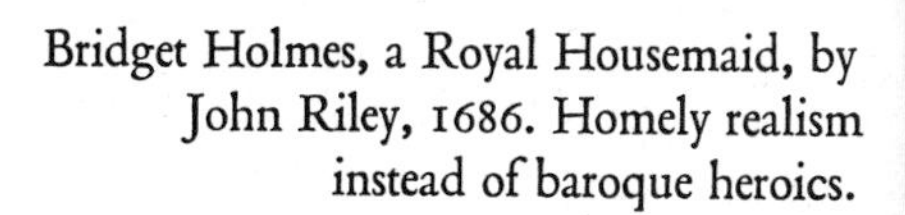

Bridget Holmes, a Royal Housemaid, by John Riley, 1686. Homely realism instead of baroque heroics.

In 1680, at the age of twenty-one, Purcell succeeded John Blow as organist at Westminster Abbey, the year in which he composed his fantasies for strings, somewhat old-fashioned essays in polyphony for old-fashioned instruments, a chest of viols. He was, however, essentially an innovator, and in his sonatas, which were really quartets, he wrote for harpsichord, bass viol (or cello), and two violins, the new instrument of which Dryden wrote:

> Sharp violins proclaim
> Their jealous pangs and desperation,
> Fury, frantic indignation,
> Depth of pains and height of passion
> For the fair, disdainful dame.

The lines come from his *Song for St Cecilia's Day*, one of the odes that Purcell set to celebrate the patron saint of music, reputed inventor of the organ, most baroque of musical instruments, and favourite of the age:

> Orpheus could lead the savage race,
> And trees uprooted left their place,
> Sequacious of the lyre:
> But bright Cecilia raised the wonder higher;
> When to her organ vocal breath was given,
> An angel heard, and straight appeared,
> Mistaking earth for heaven.

Purcell had already written the music for some of Dryden's plays, including *Aurengzebe* and his version of *The Tempest*, and in 1691 collaborated with him in *King Arthur*, a musical drama rather than an opera, and in the following year with Betterton in *The Fairy Queen*, an adaptation of the fairy scenes in *A Midsummer Night's Dream*. That was the year in which Nahum Tate succeeded Thomas Shadwell as Poet Laureate, Dryden having been deprived of the office at the Revolution of 1688 for having turned Catholic. Among Tate's major

(*Far left*) The opening bars of Purcell's 'Golden Sonata', one of the 'Sonatas of Four Parts'.
(*Left*) Henry Purcell (1658–95), the last English composer of international fame for two centuries.

'As I walked through the wilderness of this world I lighted on a certain place where was a den, and laid me down in that place to sleep.'

follies was his refinement of *King Lear*, in which Cordelia marries Edgar and all ends happily, a version that held the stage, with Dr Johnson's approval, until early Victorian times. He also wrote the libretto of an opera *Dido and Aeneas* for a boarding-school for young ladies, and Purcell wrote the music. The words were worthless, but the music was triumphant, and one of Purcell's greatest achievements; yet he wrote no more opera, though there is an operatic element in his Church music, in his anthems, with their choruses and solo declamation. A master of every musical form, and one of the very greatest English composers, probably the greatest of his age anywhere in Europe, he died in 1695, aged only thirty-six, and was buried under the organ in Westminster Abbey.

The Commonwealth Puritans had been indirectly responsible for the birth of English opera, and, even more ironically, for musical entertainment in taverns, whose owners bought the organs banished from churches to attract customers who chanted their 'bestial bacchanalias' to the sacred instrument of St Cecilia. Until the Restoration, however, there were no public concerts, and the first were those given daily in John Banister's house in Whitefriars, admission one shilling. They lasted only six years, but then Thomas Britton converted a loft over his Clerkenwell coalhouse into a music-room with small organ and virginal, and after this concert halls became fairly common, particularly in the Covent Garden area.

These diversions, with others less innocent in the Restoration Court and theatre, formed the Vanity Fair of Bunyan's *Pilgrim's Progress*, the two parts of which appeared in 1678 and 1684. Written in a purified colloquial English, with white-hot passion and imagination, it is a morality novel, as *Everyman* is a morality play, its characters so lifelike, its situations so vividly described, that for some two centuries it remained one of the most widely read and influential books in the language. Although there is satire in the allegory, it is very different from the deadly thrusts and ripostes of the couplets that Dryden had sharpened in his heroic plays. The Duke of Buckingham had ridiculed their pretentious

Nature and Nature's laws lay hid in night;
God said, Let Newton be! and all was light. Pope.

bombast in his comedy *The Rehearsal*, but Dryden had his revenge in *Absalom and Achitophel*, where Buckingham is Zimri, 'everything by starts and nothing long . . . chemist, fiddler, statesman and buffoon'. Then there was the wretched Shadwell, who had dared to attack him and was annihilated in *MacFlecknoe*:

> The rest to some faint meaning make pretence,
> But Shadwell never deviates into sense.

Though not great poetry, Dryden's satires are at least great verse, but in 1678 he abandoned the couplet in his tragedy of *All for Love*, a version of the Antony and Cleopatra story, professing in his style 'to imitate the divine Shakespeare'. It is his finest play, though it would be truer to say that in his blank verse he imitated the very mortal Fletcher, as did Thomas Otway in his *Venice Preserved* of 1682, a last attempt to revive the glories of Jacobean tragedy.

These were the memorable years in which Newton was formulating his Universal Principle of Gravitation, which developed Galileo's First Law of Motion, that a moving body will continue uniformly in a straight line unless affected by another force, a principle that accounted not only for the fall of an apple, but also for the movement of the earth round the sun and of the moon

John Locke (1632–1704), apostle of toleration.

round the earth, and the rise and fall of tides. It was a triumph for naturalism over supernaturalism, for there could now be no distinction between the laws that govern the heavens and those of earth. Yet Newton's *Principia* was followed in 1690 by *An Essay Concerning Human Understanding*, in which Locke concluded that man cannot know the real essence of anything, and that a science of physical bodies is beyond his powers. Nevertheless, scientific discovery encouraged the acceptance of naturalism, and young George Berkeley attempted to counter the growing materialism of the age by formulating a philosophy in which ideas and spiritual beings, not material objects, were the only reality. Locke was the philosopher of the Revolution of 1688. Society, he agreed with Hooker, is natural to man, and there is therefore no need of a Hobbesian absolutism to hold it together. The people themselves are sovereign, and can limit the power of any government they may establish. Moreover, as man's understanding is so limited, he has no right to impose his beliefs on others, and Locke's philosophy was largely responsible for the religious toleration of the eighteenth century.

In the theatre the last decade of the century was that of William Congreve, whose first play, *The Old Bachelor*, appeared when he was only twenty-three, and

Royal Naval College, Greenwich: 'the most stately procession of buildings we possess'. The medieval Greenwich House was demolished by Charles II, for whom John Webb began a new

the comedy of intrigue reached its brilliant climax in 1700 with *The Way of the World*. Congreve was a master of prose dialogue, and there is more genuine fun in this play than in most of its kind, as when Millamant affects to forget why she is so late, and asks her maid:

> *Mincing*. O mem, your laship stayed to peruse a packet of letters.
> *Millamant*. O ay, letters – I had letters – I am persecuted with letters – I hate letters – nobody knows how to write letters; and yet one has 'em, one does not know why – they serve one to pin up one's hair.
> *Witwoud*. Is that the way? Pray, madam, do you pin up your hair with all your letters? I find I must keep copies.
> *Millamant*. Only with those in verse, Mr Witwoud. I never pin up my hair with prose. I think I tried once, Mincing?
> *Mincing*. O mem, I shall never forget it.
> *Millamant*. Ay, poor Mincing tift and tift all the morning.
> *Mincing*. Till I had the cramp in my fingers, I'll vow, mem. And all to no purpose. But when your laship pins it up with poetry, it sits so pleasant the next day as anything, and is so pure and so crips.

Congreve's main rival was another young man, John Vanbrugh, whose first comedies, *The Relapse*, with its inimitable Lord Foppington, and *The Provoked Wife*, were great successes in 1696–7, though they were not to pass without criticism.

palace (p. 171), but William and Mary preferred Hampton Court, and Wren completed the Greenwich building as a Naval Hospital. In 1873 it became the Royal Naval College.

Vanbrugh was a versatile man, and just before the end of the century, when about thirty-five, turned architect. Wren was then nearly seventy, and by that time delegating the drawing and perhaps even the designing of some of his work to assistants, one of whom was Nicholas Hawksmoor. The City churches were finished by 1686, but meanwhile Wren had built the upper part of Tom Tower at Christ Church, Oxford, capping late ogival Gothic with an ogival dome. This he followed with the grand Chelsea Hospital for army pensioners, the barrack-like austerity of which he relieved with a central cupola and pediment supported by giant Doric columns. Then, after the Revolution of 1688 and accession of William and Mary, he added the south and east wings to Hampton Court before converting the palace begun by Webb for Charles II into Greenwich Hospital, the naval counterpart of Chelsea and, after St Paul's, his most distinguished building. Begun in 1696, it incorporated Webb's block, and eventually became two successive courtyards leading from the river, the second narrower than the first, each flanked by buildings, with a domed chapel and hall, the vista closing with Inigo Jones's Queen's House.

It was now that Vanbrugh turned architect and, helped by Hawksmoor, designed Castle Howard in Yorkshire. Vanbrugh was a dramatist of the age of Dryden, and Castle Howard is the architectural equivalent of the heroic play, theatrical, grandiose, a dramatic grouping of restless masses with little reference to function: the first truly baroque building in England. Blenheim

Palace, which Vanbrugh built for the Duke of Marlborough as a present from Queen Anne, was an even more massive and monumental essay in Baroque, but most theatrical of all his houses was Seaton Delaval, where the rustication of the façade was repeated in the shafts of the giant Doric columns.

Although Hawksmoor, a modest man, was overshadowed by his partner, his was the knowledge and experience that gave form to Vanbrugh's essential romanticism and made possible this brief period of English Baroque at the beginning of the eighteenth century, and we can see his own more restrained work in the churches that he built after 1711, baroque variations on themes of his master, Wren: St Anne, Limehouse, St Mary Woolnoth, the classical and sombre inspiration of romantic Seaton Delaval, and St George, Bloomsbury, which, however, with its Palladian portico, leads into the next age. In the western towers of Westminster Abbey he tried, not very successfully, to build in the Gothic style, and far finer is the simple and classically severe Mausoleum at Castle Howard.

There was no lack of artists, most of them foreigners, to cover the walls of these palaces, hospitals, and houses built by Wren, Vanbrugh, and Hawksmoor. At Chelsea Hospital the Venetian Sebastiano Ricci splendidly painted *The Resurrection* in the chapel apse, and Verrio less splendidly a complex allegory in the hall. Verrio's too was the painting of the great staircase at Hampton Court, where Cibber carved the *Triumph of Hercules over Envy* (of William III over Louis XIV) on the pediment of the garden front, Gibbons the woodwork in the royal apartments, and John Nost, a Fleming, the chimneypieces. Vanbrugh employed another Venetian painter, Pellegrini, at Castle Howard, and the French Louis Laguerre at Blenheim, but more important was the work of Sir James Thornhill in the hall of Greenwich Hospital.

Queen Anne Baroque: (*Below*) Blenheim Palace, by Sir John Vanbrugh. The formal gardens are typical of the period; the park was 'landscaped' later by 'Capability' Brown. (*Right*) Sir James Thornhill's painted ceiling at Greenwich Naval Hospital. ►

Thornhill, a Devonshire man, was the greatest English master of baroque painting, and his allegorical figures explode and pour out of the central oval of the ceiling, while the *Landing of William III* is represented in the Grand Manner of the heroic play, 'as it should have been, rather than as it was'. Whatever Wren may have thought of Thornhill's work in his Greenwich hall, he did not want it in his cathedral, but he was overruled, and Thornhill began the eight vast grisaille paintings of the life of St Paul inside the dome.

The reign of Anne (1702–14) was a period of violent political contention during which Whig politicians, painters, and writers formed the Kit-Cat Club, of whose members, including Marlborough, Walpole, Vanbrugh, Congreve, Addison, and Steele, Kneller painted a series of portraits. They were all of the same size, 36 by 28 inches, to fit into their clubroom in the house of their secretary, the publisher Jacob Tonson: the Kit-Cat size, which just allowed room for a half-length and one hand. Apart from their historical value, these portraits contain most of Kneller's best work, with a greater liveliness than the customary heaviness of his more commercial painting. In 1711 Kneller became Governor of the first Academy of Painting to be established in England, where, under Thornhill who succeeded him, young William Hogarth occasionally studied.

By 1700, when Dryden's death marked the end of an epoch, taste was changing, a change that is first to be detected in literature. There had been some forty years of Restoration comedy, and society was tiring of its interminable variations on the same themes and types: seduction, adultery, and dowry hunting; rakes, fops, cuckolds, and swindlers. *The Way of the World* was condemned when first produced, partly because in 1698 Jeremy Collier had published his *Short View of the Immorality and Profaneness of the English Stage*, in which he cited Dryden, Congreve, and Vanbrugh as examples. Dryden admitted the justice of his strictures, but Congreve replied angrily and wrote no more for the stage, Vanbrugh little more, and it is significant that *The Confederacy* of 1705 is a comedy not of aristocratic London drawing-rooms but of middle-class life. Restoration drama may be said to have ended with the death of George Farquhar at the age of thirty in 1707, the year of his *Beaux' Stratagem*, a racy comedy of adventurers and highwaymen, the scene of which is Lichfield (where Samuel Johnson was to be born two years later), and which has more in common with the novels of Fielding than with classical Restoration comedy. At the same time eighteenth-century sentimental comedy began with the plays of Richard Steele, from *The Funeral* to *The Conscious Lovers*, of which Fielding was to remark that it was 'as good as a sermon'.

As good as sermons also were Steele's genial, intimate essays, almost letters to his readers, in the periodicals that he published from 1709 to 1712, *The Tatler* and *The Spectator*. His friend Joseph Addison contributed, and developed the character sketched by Steele into the eccentric and lovable Sir Roger de Coverley. He also wrote the libretto for *Rosamond*, a comic opera, at

Two Kit-Cat Club portraits by Sir Godfrey Kneller:
(*Left*) William Congreve (1670–1729). (*Right*) Joseph Addison (1672–1719).

least one assumes it to be a comic opera, for it is very funny, but, with a score by one Thomas Clayton, it was a disastrous failure, and Addison revenged himself by attacking opera in *The Spectator*. His tragedy of *Cato* was little better, its emotions as false as its blank verse undistinguished, though it was beautifully constructed in the classical manner of Racine and rapturously received as a political play by both Whigs and Tories.

It was not only against Restoration indecency that the new writers revolted, but also, perhaps unconsciously, against the florid inflation, foreign to the English genius, of baroque art as a whole, from heroic drama and Italian opera to the buildings of Vanbrugh and paintings of Thornhill. Addison's style may lack colour and warmth, but it has the classical virtues of clarity and restraint, and so has that of one of the very greatest masters of plain English prose, Jonathan Swift, whose *Tale of a Tub* of 1704 begins:

> Once upon a time, there was a man who had three sons by one wife, and all at a birth; neither could the midwife tell certainly which was the eldest. Their father died while they were young, and upon his death-bed, calling the lads to him, spoke thus . . .

Nothing could be simpler than that, nor any prose more effective as a medium for his satirical account of the quarrels of Catholics, Anglicans, and Dissenters.

Then in 1711 came *The Essay on Criticism* by the twenty-three-year-old genius, Alexander Pope:

> 'Tis more to guide than spur the Muse's steed;
> Restrain his fury, than provoke his speed . . .
> Avoid extremes . . .

By 1714 St Paul's was finished – it is a strange irony that the building of the cathedral and City churches coincided with Restoration comedy – Pope was twenty-six, Hogarth seventeen, Handel twenty-five, and his patron, the Elector of Hanover, was George I of England.

Si monumentum requiris, circumspice. Wren's legacy: the rebuilt City of London in 1714.

11 The Eighteenth Century 1714–1789

The eighteenth century may be said to have begun in 1714 with the death of Queen Anne, last of the Stuarts, and accession of the Hanoverian George I. Up to 1750 the century is that of Pope, Swift, Defoe, and Fielding, in painting of Hogarth, in music of Handel, in sculpture of Rysbrack, Scheemakers, and Roubiliac, in architecture of Burlington and the Palladians, in politics of Walpole and the Whigs, who placed and kept the Hanoverians on the throne. It was a period of rationalism and materialism, when any form of 'enthusiasm' was suspect, and imagination subordinated to good sense. Pope was the poet of this cult of reason, of the curbing of emotion by the conscious mind – ''Tis more to guide than spur the Muse's steed' – so that in his work we shall find no eagle flights of imagination; yet he is the most perfect, which is not at all the same thing as greatest, of English poets, and the mock-heroic *Rape of the Lock*, exquisite as porcelain, is the most perfect of his poems. In his hands the heroic couplet developed by Dryden became the sinewy medium of his aphorisms, 'What oft was thought, but ne'er so well expressed,' and at the same time the rapier on which he spitted his opponents, as in *The Dunciad*, most brilliant of his satires. His translation of Homer's *Iliad*, though far removed from the majesty of the original, was to influence the neoclassical movement later in the century, and the classical simplicity and clarity of his style inevitably meant that he opposed contemporary Baroque. 'Avoid extremes,' he wrote in his *Essay on Criticism*, and 'follow Nature,' for 'Nature and Homer were the same.' The rules of the ancients are like Nature, by which he meant the laws of Nature, which we break at our peril, and, restraining enthusiasm and our own feelings, we should admire what we know to be correct. Criticism, in short, should be objective, not subjective. Pope has some sour things to say about Vanbrugh's Blenheim Palace, and in his *Moral Essays* makes sport of

Canons, Lord Chandos's new house, which 'brings all Brobdingnag before your thought', the first literary allusion to Gulliver's land of the giants:

> Lo, what huge heaps of littleness around!
> The whole a laboured quarry above ground . . .
> On painted ceilings you devoutly stare,
> Where sprawl the saints of Verrio or Laguerre.

Canons was mainly the work of James Gibbs, a Tory Scot and possibly a Catholic Jacobite to boot, scarcely acceptable, therefore, to the victorious Whig aristocracy. Having studied in Rome, he admired the baroque element in Wren, and continued the tradition of the great master, the church of St Mary-le-Strand being inspired both by the City churches of Wren and by those of seventeenth-century Rome, though the steeple rising above the pediment, a Gothic device dwarfing a classical façade, offended the purists. Wren's steeples never competed in this way with the body of the building, but Gibbs triumphantly repeated the solecism at St Martin-in-the-Fields, where the steeple and great Corinthian portico are reconciled. The Fellows' Building at King's College, Cambridge, was in an appropriately restrained academic style, but in the Tory stronghold of Oxford he returned to Wren and Roman Baroque in the splendid cylindrical and domed Radcliffe Camera. Meanwhile, in 1728, he had published his *Book of Architecture*, which was to influence building throughout the century, not only in England but also in America.

The influence of Wren. Two buildings by James Gibbs:
(*Left*) St Martin-in-the-Fields, London, 1721–6. (*Right*) The Radcliffe Camera, Oxford, 1739–49.

The return to the simpler style of Palladio and Inigo Jones. Burlington's Chiswick Villa, *c.* 1730, with the earlier house on the right.

Gibbs's influence on the main stream of architecture, however, was slight. He was a conservative disciple of Wren, and the current had set in another, and Whiggish, direction. Shaftesbury, 'The first Whig', had written: 'Hardly . . . should we bear to see . . . even a new Cathedral like St Paul's', and Pope's *Moral Essay*, Epistle IV, already quoted, was addressed to the young Whig Earl of Burlington, whom he adjured:

> You, too, proceed! make falling arts your care,
> Erect new wonders, and the old repair;
> Jones and Palladio to themselves restore,
> And be whate'er Vitruvius was before.

Like poetry, architecture should follow the ancient rules, as established by the old Roman Vitruvius, codified by the sixteenth-century Italian Palladio, and practised by the English Inigo Jones. Away then with Vanbrugh, Hawksmoor, and even Wren, and back to the classical simplicity of Jones. Colen Campbell, another Scottish architect and Gibbs's rival, had said the same thing in his *Vitruvius Britannicus* of 1715, and under the banner of the old triumvirate the new Palladian triumvirate of Campbell, Burlington, and Kent entered the lists. Campbell was first, with Wanstead House and its six-columned Palladian portico, and Houghton Hall for Sir Robert Walpole, the stone hall of which derived from Jones's Queen's House and was adorned with classical busts by Rysbrack. Better known is Mereworth, a square house with hexastyle porticoes attached to each side and uneasily surmounted by a dome: a variation of Palladio's Villa Rotonda near Vicenza. More successful and original was Burlington's exercise on the same theme at Chiswick Villa, where there are only two porticoes, the main one approached by elaborate Italian flights of steps, and the drum of the dome articulated with the central hexagonal hall.

Holkham Hall, Norfolk, *c.* 1734–53, designed by William Kent and Lord Burlington. Built of a local brick, the severe south front is a contrast to the grandeur of the entrance hall (*below*).

With the interior decoration Burlington was helped by William Kent, a painter whom he had recently brought from Rome while on his Grand Tour. Kent also laid out the grounds, and began a revolution in landscape gardening by introducing a touch of wildness into fashionable Restoration formality, and in sympathy country-houses became less domineering, more a part of their natural surroundings.

It may be that Kent was partly responsible for Burlington's Assembly Room at York, a copy of a Vitruvian-Palladian basilica, by which time, 1730, thanks to the patronage and tuition of Burlington, he was Deputy Surveyor, and the two continued their collaboration at Holkham Hall in Norfolk. The exterior is classically austere, as befitted a great Whig house, for the Whigs liked to identify themselves with antique Romans, and at the same time characteristically Kent-Burlington, the roof-line broken and defined by pediments and gables. Kent's interior is a complete contrast, and the apsidal and colonnaded hall with classical frieze and coffered ceiling is a splendid exhibition of Palladian grandeur. In London, Kent's Horse Guards is a repetition of the Holkham façade, with cupola instead of portico, the Whitehall front of which is illustrated on page 149.

Town planning ►
spreads to the provinces.
Bath in the eighteenth century.

The beginning of town planning in England. Lincoln's Inn Fields in the later seventeenth century.

Town planning and modern, as distinct from medieval, town-houses had begun in 1630 with the piazza at Covent Garden, for which Inigo Jones was partly responsible, and shortly afterwards rows of regularly designed houses were built in Lincoln's Inn Fields and the neighbouring Great Queen Street. Nearly a hundred years later came the Palladian row of town-houses, which was to remain the standard for another century: normally three storeys with an attic, the lowest being defined by rustication or a band, while the other two might be linked by pilasters. Then, about 1730, two sides of Grosvenor Square were built, each in the manner of a single great mansion, the central house being emphasized on one side by a pediment, on the other by a portico. The Palladian house soon spread to the bigger provincial towns, and was carried to Bath by John Wood, who built Queen Square and, remembering the glories of Roman Bath, the magnificent Circus. He died in 1754, shortly after the Circus was begun, but his work was carried on by his son, John Wood the Younger, who built the great Crescent and made Bath into one of the finest towns in Europe.

Many of these Palladian houses were adorned with sculptures, for the Academy established under the directorship of Kneller in 1711 contained casts

of classical statues which stimulated an interest in the art, and the end of the long French wars led to a flood of young gentlemen visiting Italy, where they acquired a taste for the antique and returned with copies or forgeries of classical works. They could not import ancient portraits of themselves, but they did the next best thing by commissioning their funeral monuments in Roman dress and portrait busts in the antique manner. English painting had been confined mainly to portraits, but when Kneller died in 1723 (as did Wren) patrons had to wait twenty years for the appearance of a great portrait painter, Allan Ramsay, and another ten for Joshua Reynolds, born in the year of Kneller's death, and they turned to portrait busts rather than paintings. The sculptors, mainly foreigners, were soon there to supply them. Young Michael Rysbrack arrived from Antwerp *c.* 1720, when he was employed by Kent in the redecoration of Kensington Palace. Soon afterwards he was commissioned to make Kneller's monument, but more historic was the portrait bust of the Earl of Nottingham, the first representation of an English aristocrat as an ancient Roman. There followed a long series of busts, that of Pope being one of the finest: a hauntingly melancholy face, the intellect and sensuality of which are symbolically repeated in the classical modelling of the head and baroque treatment of the dress. There is a similar combination of styles in the Newton monument in Westminster Abbey, but the equestrian bronze of William III at Bristol is Baroque at its best.

Rysbrack's contemporary and compatriot was Peter Scheemakers, who was in London soon after 1720. His work, however, lacked the ease and grace of his rival's, and it was only in 1740 that his statue of Shakespeare brought him a comparable fame. It was designed by Kent, but Scheemakers artfully contrived to give it the aura of sentimental reverence that Garrick was just beginning to exploit: the Bard leans cross-legged and negligently on a pile of folios, his Van Dyckian head, resembling no contemporary likeness, supported by his right hand, his left pointing to a characteristically mangled version of Prospero's famous speech from *The Tempest*. It is ludicrous by modern standards, but a good example of the dramatic element that had invaded the non-dramatic arts.

For the English drama was moribund, and no plays of any consequence were written during the reigns of the first two Georges, between 1714 and 1760, though Lillo's melodramatic *George Barnwell* is significant as a play that reduces its hero to an apprentice, and introduces a new note of realism, as well as sentimentality. This lack of new material for the stage accounts for the popularity and continued 'improvement' of Shakespeare's plays by Colley Cibber, Garrick, and others, and partly for the sentimental cult of 'Avonian Willy', and it seems probable that it was in compensation that sculpture, painting, and music assumed more dramatic, or theatrical, roles. It also accounts for the rise of the novel: the transference of drama from the stage to the study and boudoir.

The way had been prepared by *The Pilgrim's Progress* and essays of Addison and Steele, but the one was an allegory, and the others little more than anecdotes.

Gulliver's Travels of 1726 approached the novel form, and the first two adventures at least have generally been read as delightfully imaginative stories, few readers being aware of Swift's ferocious satire: that the Lilliputians represent the pettiness of man, the Brobdingnagians his grossness, though none could fail to understand the meaning of the Yahoos. Swift gave an air of authenticity to his narrative by writing in the first person with a variety of realistic detail, the method adopted by Defoe in *Robinson Crusoe*, 1719, a brilliantly written but rambling story of adventure interspersed with moral reflections. It was so successful that he followed it with *Captain Singleton*, in which the scene shifts to Africa, *Moll Flanders*, and *A Journal of the Plague Year*, a reconstruction of the Great Plague of 1665, again written in the first person, although he was only five in that year. Fascinating and entertaining as these books were, and still are, they are romances rather than novels, dependent for their interest almost entirely on what happened, relatively formless successions of events with little consideration of character and motivation.

Jonathan Swift (1667–1745), by Charles Jervas.

The eighteenth-century conception of Shakespeare. Statue by Peter Scheemakers, 1740.

These elements came into prose fiction almost by accident, when Samuel Richardson thought he might inculcate virtue by writing a series of improving letters exchanged by imaginary characters. *Pamela: or Virtue Rewarded* appeared in 1740, the story of a servant-girl who, by resisting the improper advances of her mistress's son, succeeds in marrying him. It is the first true English novel, for here in addition to the story, to what happened, is why it happened and a corresponding revelation of character and motive. It was a singularly humourless novel, and Henry Fielding at once began a parody, *The Adventures of Joseph Andrews*, in which the virtuous footman Joseph, Pamela's brother, resists the improper advances of his mistress, runs away and eventually succeeds in marrying his beloved Fanny. Yet Fielding almost forgot parody in the excitement of creating Parson Adams, and the main interest of the novel – for as *Pamela* is the first, so *Joseph Andrews* is the second – lies in the character and fortunes of that innocent and gullible giant. Fielding was no fugitive and cloistered moralist, his robust and magnanimous humanity was revolted by hypocrisy and any form of humbug, and the adventures of Joseph and the Parson among alehouses and chamber-pots were very different from those that befell Pamela. Richardson, however, was unperturbed, and wrote another epistolary novel, *Clarissa*, this time the moral tragedy of a young lady who falls a prey to a libertine and dies of a broken heart. In 1749 Fielding replied with the story of a

Joseph Highmore finds inspiration in the first true English novel. 'Pamela tells a Nursery Story': a scene from Richardson's *Pamela*.

Dr Arne playing 'Rule, Britannia!', from James Thomson's masque *Alfred*, for which Arne wrote the music.

scapegrace, though an impetuous and generous young man after his own heart, *Tom Jones*, the first really great novel in English, or in any language, a novel that made ample amends for the deplorable quality of the contemporary drama, except perhaps for his own contribution, the burlesque 'tragedy of tragedies', *Tom Thumb.*

One of Fielding's butts was James Thomson, a Scot, whose tragedy *Sophonisba* contained the memorable line, 'O Sophonisba, Sophonisba, O!', immortalized in the parody, 'O Jemmy Thomson, Jemmy Thomson, O!' Yet Thomson was the only other considerable poet of the age of Pope, though a very different one. Although he looked back to ancient masters, to Milton in *The Seasons*, to Spenser in *The Castle of Indolence*, he was a nature poet who escaped from the tyranny of the heroic couplet and poetry of the town, a precursor of the Romantic movement, of Wordsworth and Keats, and in *Liberty* may be said to be the prophet of Neoclassicism when he describes the beauties of Roman and Greek sculpture: the *Dying Gladiator, Apollo of The Belvedere*, and that 'utmost Masterpiece' *Laocoön.* He was thinking of the plaster casts in the Academy, and was of his age in preferring his Greek art late, and sculptures that tell a story.

Thomson also wrote a masque, *Alfred*, with music by Thomas Arne, the most distinguished English composer of the century, but a work remembered now only because of the song, 'Rule, Britannia!' That was in 1740, and Arne was only eighteen when *The Beggar's Opera* took the town by storm in 1728: a play about harlots and highwaymen by John Gay, interspersed with his lyrics set to popular tunes by Dr Pepusch, the first and much the best of the ballad-operas that had such a vogue in the 1730s. Primarily an attack on the corruption of Walpole and the Whigs, it also made fun of Italian opera, and of the scratches recently exchanged by two Italian prima donnas during a performance of Bononcini's *Astyanax.* Like other forms of art, music had to be dramatic to be fashionably acceptable, and on his arrival in England Handel, always an opportunist, had put together some of his old music to form the score of *Rinaldo*, the first of innumerable Italian operas that he wrote in the next thirty years: that is, operas in the Italian manner with endless arias sung in Italian by Italian castrati and prima donnas.

Messiah: 'I know that my Redeemer liveth.' Handel's autograph.

Handel: from the first edition of the score of *Alexander's Feast*, 1738.

No wonder the ordinary English music-lover revolted, and applauded Richard Leveridge's burlesque Italian opera of *Pyramus and Thisbe*, and *The Beggar's Opera* broke all records with a run of sixty-three nights. Then in 1732 Arne wrote a new score for Addison's *Rosamond*, an English opera that the public could understand, half-way between the esoteric Italian and popular ballad forms. Meanwhile, the Three Choirs Festival had been formed in 1724, whereby for charitable purposes the cathedral choirs of Gloucester, Worcester, and Hereford were to give annual performances in each city by turn. English musicians were beginning to assert themselves, Italian opera was beginning to totter, partly because there was a split in its ranks when the Prince of Wales supported a rival company, and Handel had a nervous breakdown.

Not that that great master of baroque music, now a naturalized Englishman, composed only opera: in addition to vocal chamber music and anthems, he wrote for the harpsichord, orchestra, and organ, and some forty sonatas for various instruments. He was no great innovator, however, but followed the taste of the age for dramatic art, and in the year of Arne's *Rosamond* tried his hand at a modified form of English opera, setting Gay's *Acis and Galatea* as a cantata to be sung without action, following this with a setting of Dryden's *Alexander's Feast*. It was only a step to oratorio, opera without action, on a sacred theme, and a longer version of an earlier work was performed in 1733. Gradually the chorus encroached on the solos until *Israel in Egypt* was almost entirely choral, to the disgust of the virtuosi who wanted trills and cadenzas to show their skill, and of opera-goers who wanted to hear them. Then in 1742, the year of *Joseph Andrews*, the *Messiah* was performed in Dublin, followed by a triumphant London performance when the audience, led by George II, rose to its feet at the beginning of the 'Hallelujah Chorus'. Yet by 1750 English music was in a poor condition: Handel was failing, Italian opera was almost dead, Church music was merely insipid, oratorios were not for every day, or every-body, and Arne's attempt to revive the masque, as in Thomson's *Alfred*, was a confession of creative failure.

The Beggar's Opera was important not only as a musical event but also because the thirty-year-old Hogarth painted a number of versions of one of its scenes, and in them first displayed his genius and originality, for they were something quite new in British art. The 'conversation piece', a family or group of friends, had recently come into fashion, but Hogarth, in the baroque manner that had been expelled from poetry and architecture, dramatized it, as Handel dramatized music. Very English, insular even, like Fielding he satirized dilettante Italianate Englishmen who would look at nothing but foreign works of art, and offered them subjects other than fashionable portraits. These paintings, however, were only illustrations, opera in paint, and he soon went a stage further by inventing his own drama in the six pictures, *The Harlot's Progress*, followed by a similar series, *The Rake's Progress*, and some ten years later by his masterpiece of satirical observation, *Marriage à la Mode*. His object, he wrote,

Drama in paint: Hogarth illustrates Gay's *Beggar's Opera* of 1728, a political satire and parody of the fashionable Italian opera of Handel. A scene in Newgate Prison (*see* p. 220).

The Shrimp Girl, by Hogarth. A brilliant sketch, very different from the dramatic stories in paint with which he tried to 'improve the mind'.

Mr and Mrs Robert Andrews, by Gainsborough, *c.* 1748. An early, and splendid painting, that combines his genius for landscape with that of portraiture. ▶

was to paint 'modern moral subjects . . . similar to representations on the stage . . . subjects which will both entertain and improve the mind.' In this, therefore, he anticipated Richardson and *Pamela*, though he more closely resembled Fielding in the robustness of his satire and moral teaching. In his youth he had been a silver-plate engraver, and in 1724 published his first engraving, in which he satirized Italian opera-singers and William Kent and the Palladians, so that naturally he engraved what he called his 'dumb shows', beginning with *The Harlot's Progress*. These were avidly bought by the people, but most of the original paintings remained unsold: modern British pictures were not for the recently formed aristocratic Society of Dilettanti.

Hogarth was never a fashionable portrait painter like his inferior contemporary, Thomas Hudson, teacher of Reynolds, yet that he was one of the greatest of all English masters of the art can be seen from the brilliant sketch, the *Shrimp Girl*, and the seated figure, *Captain Coram*, radiant with the goodness of the little seaman who established the Foundling Hospital, and the sympathetically painted heads of his servants. All these were revolutionary works: portraits of humble people, painted not for money but for the sheer joy of painting those whom he found interesting or admired. He had his followers: one of his friends, Joseph Highmore, painted scenes from *Pamela*, and another, Francis Hayman, conversation pieces of middle-class life, and also designed the illustrations, engraved by Gravelot, for Hanmer's sumptuous and fantastic edition of Shakespeare. But Hogarth was the supreme painter of the first half of the eighteenth century, and from him we can learn more about London life of the period than from any other source.

At the same time Samuel Scott was painting views of London and the Thames, as was, from 1746 to 1756, the great Venetian Canaletto. It was essentially the age of the town, of London in particular, but shortly before 1750 Thomas Gainsborough painted his *Mr and Mrs Andrews*, a conversation piece in which the figures are wonderfully blended with an English landscape. Gainsborough was little more than twenty when he painted this masterpiece.

The mid-eighteenth-century oriental influence: 'Chinese Chippendale'.

Hogarth lived until 1764, but his best work was done by 1750, by which time, or soon after, most of the masters of the first half-century were dead, Pope, Fielding, and the Palladians; a new generation filled the scene, and the next forty years were those of Johnson, Reynolds, Chambers, and Adam. New ideas were already in the air. John Wesley had begun his great evangelical work, and was travelling about Britain preaching a 'vital practical religion' to the poor, so neglected by a dormant Church. Yet at the same time the seeds of scepticism were being sown. In 1748 David Hume had published his *Enquiry Concerning Human Understanding*, one of the most influential books of the century. He agreed with Berkeley that there is insufficient evidence for the reality of the material world, but neither is there sufficient evidence for Berkeley's world of ideas and spirits. 'The new philosophy calls all in doubt': miracles, the immortality of the soul, and the existence of God. Although a Scot, Hume wrote the first scholarly, though prejudiced, *History of England*, and affected with his scepticism an even greater historian, Edward Gibbon. This growing interest in history and archaeology was partly responsible for the Neoclassicism of the period, a return to ancient Rome and Greece rather than to the Italian Renaissance. In Italy Piranesi was nostalgically publishing illustrations of Roman ruins as well as fantastic architectural drawings, and in the 1750s Englishmen explored classical sites and published books on *The Ruins of Palmyra*, *The Ruins of Balbec*, *The Antiquities of Athens* and – the work of Robert Adam – *The Ruins of the Palace of Diocletian at Spalato*, while in Germany Winckelmann was preaching that Greek art was superior to Roman, and its appreciation subjective not objective, a matter of feeling not rules. This was precisely the opposite of the aesthetic theory of Pope and the Palladians, and Neoclassicism was in part an escape from rules into a greater freedom and eclecticism.

The Pagoda at Kew, by Sir William Chambers.

In 1748 Horace Walpole had begun the whimsical transformation of his Twickenham villa, Strawberry Hill, into a 'Gothick' house, and a few years later Sir William Chambers, who had been to China and published *Designs of Chinese Buildings*, built the Pagoda at Kew. These, of course, were anything but classical, but they were symptomatic of the liberation from rules and, incidentally, had their influence on Chippendale's furniture. Chambers, one of the founders in 1768 of the Royal Academy, of which he became Treasurer, was too conservative to be a great innovator, and his most important work, the new Somerset House, a huge, dignified public building, is neoclassical only in the greater freedom of its detail.

Robert Adam was much more adventurous, his style being a modified compound of many others, so that he and his brother James could write in their *Works of Architecture* of 1773, 'we have been able to seize, with some degree of success, the beautiful spirit of antiquity, and to transpose it, with novelty and variety'. Thus, from Palladianism they took the broken façade, which gave, they claimed, a sense of 'movement' comparable to that of landscape; they even returned to the drama of Baroque, though in a much lighter form, and borrowed from all the classical sites they knew, including Spalato and Athens, as well as from the French and Italian Renaissance. Adam was essentially a domestic architect, as much interested in the interior as exterior, designing everything from ceilings to furniture and door-knobs, re-creating, as he thought, the interior decoration of a Roman house, very different from the monumental Palladian imitation of temple interiors, and inventing the 'Etruscan style', which is really derived from the painting on Greek vases, then thought to be Etruscan, as at Osterley Park House. A good example of an Adam exterior is the south front of Kedleston Hall, which is a variation on a Roman triumphal arch, and one

The imperial theme: Kedleston Hall, Derbyshire, inspired by a Roman triumphal arch, and built by Robert Adam *c.* 1760, when the British Empire was rapidly expanding.

(*Left*) Adam interior elegance. Syon House, Middlesex: the hall, 1762–3. As at Kedleston, the columns are merely pedestals for the statues.

has only to compare the hall of Syon House with that of Holkham to see the difference between the grace of Adam's style and the grandeur of Kent's Palladianism. The biggest venture of the Adam brothers was the Adelphi, a long terrace of houses built over Roman arches and vaults facing the Thames, recalling the Spalato ruins. The desirable 'movement' was given by the projection of pedimented houses at each end, and characteristic interior decoration was applied in terracotta to the outside. The elegant and delicate Adam style, freed from the 'massive entablature' and heavier elements of Roman architecture, was immensely influential, and led to the neoclassic design of the great potter Josiah Wedgwood in his Etruscan ware. It also influenced Adam's young rival, James Wyatt, who in 1770 began the celebrated Pantheon in Oxford Street, a neoclassical combination of S. Sophia and the Roman Pantheon, though with a wooden dome.

'Adelphi . . . Being so contrived as to keep the Access to the Houses . . . distinct from the traffic of the Wharfs.' Begun in 1768 by the brothers (Greek *adelphoi*) Robert and James Adam.

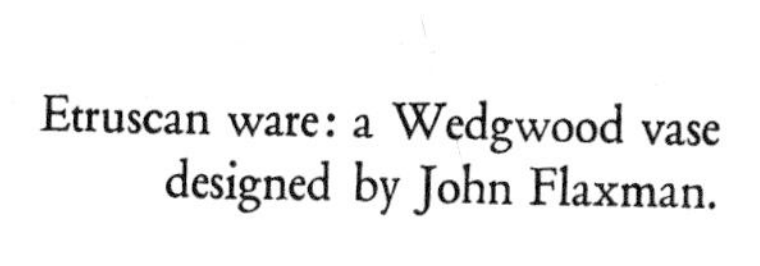

Etruscan ware: a Wedgwood vase designed by John Flaxman.

The Pantheon was sometimes used for concerts. There was no lack of performers, many of them foreigners, but no British composer of more than mediocre talent, a dismal state of affairs that was to last another hundred years. There was Arne, who in the 1760s wrote unpretentious operas, the more ambitious *Artaxerxes*, the oratorio *Judith*, the music of Garrick's preposterous *Ode* for the Stratford Jubilee, and settings for some of Shakespeare's songs. There was his exact contemporary William Boyce, an organist who also wrote for the stage, but is best remembered as the compiler of *English Cathedral Music*, though his own century had little that merited inclusion; and at Bath was Thomas Linley, father-in-law of Sheridan, for whose *Duenna* he arranged the music. Then there was Johann Christian Bach, youngest son of the great composer, who in 1762 settled in London, where his concerts with his countryman Karl Friedrich Abel became fashionable public entertainments. 'The English Bach' is of some importance as the first writer of symphonies in Britain, and the first composer to prefer the newly invented pianoforte, on which the strings were struck instead of plucked and, unlike the harpsichord, could be played softly or loudly on a single keyboard. The new instrument encouraged a proliferation of pianist-composers, mainly interested in displaying their virtuosity, though one of them, Muzio Clementi, has claims to be considered the first serious composer for the pianoforte. He had been an infant prodigy, and it was an age that delighted in prodigies: in 1764 the eight-year-old Mozart was

David Garrick, the great actor, and proprietor of Drury Lane, 1747–76.

This, 1763, was the year in which Boswell (*right*) met Johnson (*left*). 'I found that I had a very perfect idea of Johnson's figure, from the portrait painted of him by Sir Joshua Reynolds . . . sitting in his easy chair in deep meditation.'

◀ (*Left*) Riot at Drury Lane Theatre during a performance of Arne's opera *Artaxerxes*, 1763.

brought to England to give performances on the harpsichord, but even Mozart was bettered by William Crotch who in 1779, at the age of four, gave daily recitals on the organ. Music simply was not treated seriously by the English public: Italian opera had become an esoteric and snobbish cult, Lord Chesterfield dismissed musicians as 'fiddlers, pipers . . . unbecoming company for a man of fashion', and original native music was largely that of rollicking songs, catches, and glees that were sung at the Catch Club, Glee Club, and other convivial gatherings.

However, at least two men took music seriously: Sir John Hawkins, who published his *History of Music* in 1776, and Dr Burney, whose first volume of his *General History of Music* appeared in the same year, as did that of Adam Smith's *Wealth of Nations*, the first volume of Gibbon's *Decline and Fall of the Roman Empire*, and the American Declaration of Independence. Burney's history is the more readable, but he thought of music as a gradual ascent to the perfection of his own day, ridiculing Hawkins's opinion that the finest period was the sixteenth and early seventeenth centuries. He had no use for 'ruin-diggers', among whom, if he was consistent, he must have included Robert Adam.

Hawkins and Burney were members of the Literary Club founded by Johnson and Reynolds in 1764, the year after Johnson's auspicious meeting with young James Boswell. By that time Johnson was fifty-four, in comfortable circumstances, having just received a pension from George III, and the literary lion of his age, famous principally for his *Dictionary*, which gave precision of usage and meaning to the English language. His life had been a struggle, and in his early poem, *London*, he had written bitterly:

> This mournful truth is everywhere confessed:
> 'Slow rises worth by poverty depressed.'

Ever a conservative, he also wrote *The Vanity of Human Wishes* in the heroic couplets of Dryden and Pope, whom he so much admired. He tried his hand at tragedy in *Irene*, the novel in *Rasselas*, the essay in his periodicals *The Rambler* and *The Idler*, not very successfully, for his style was ponderous and his tone magisterial, and his best work is in the Preface to his edition of Shakespeare, 1765, and *The Lives of the Poets*, 1779–81. He seems to have been deaf to the poetry of Shakespeare, and it is worth remarking some of his pronouncements on the other arts, as recorded by Boswell: 'Ornamental architecture . . . consumes labour disproportionate to its utility.' 'The value of statuary is owing to its difficulty.' 'Had I learned to fiddle, I should have done nothing else . . . a man would never undertake great things, could he be amused with small.' 'Painting, Sir, can illustrate, but cannot inform.' As for archaeology: 'We can know no more than what the old writers have told us.' Prejudiced, obstinate, pompous, he had no ear for music, no eye for nature or art, and would rarely confess ignorance, yet within his limits no man's judgement has ever been sounder or more generous, and as a talker he has probably never been surpassed. This was the man who dominated the literary scene from the publication of his *Dictionary* in 1755 to his death in 1784.

The 1760s saw the triumph of Johnson's younger contemporary and friend, Oliver Goldsmith, from his *Citizen of the World* to *The Deserted Village*, one of the last great poems in the classical tradition, yet in its humour and nostalgia tinged with romanticism. It was an age of prose rather than poetry, of reason rather than imagination, and it may be significant that two of its best, though very unequal, poets were afflicted with periods of insanity: William Collins, author of the exquisite *Dirge in 'Cymbeline'* and the unrhymed *Ode to Evening*, reminiscent of the early Milton; and Christopher Smart, whose *Song to David* curiously recalls Marvell and anticipates Blake. Better known is Gray's *Elegy*, published in 1750, for the melancholy music of its platitudes has become part of the English heritage. All these poets were trying to escape from the rules and rationalism of the Augustan Age – as were the neoclassical architects, who, in their enthusiasm for the ruins of Rome and Greece, were also neoromantics – and so was 'the marvellous boy' Thomas Chatterton, who wrote poetry that he claimed was by a medieval monk, and in 1770 poisoned himself in desperation. Also symptomatic of the new romanticism was Bishop Percy's collection of old ballads, *Reliques of English Poetry*, published in 1765, the same year as *The Castle of Otranto*, a fantastic medieval romance by Horace Walpole, who was still tinkering with Gothick at Strawberry Hill.

Edmund Burke's youthful essay *On the Sublime and Beautiful*, published in 1756, was having its effect. An extraordinary book for its time, it was essentially a plea for emotional freedom, for all emotion is pleasurable, and the greater the emotion the greater the pleasure, provided we are not ourselves involved in suffering, as we are not when watching tragedy or reading poetry. In this form, terror may be more enjoyable than mere beauty, for beauty is associated with smallness and delicacy, but terror with grandeur, immensity, and mystery: in short, with the Sublime. It was a remarkable anticipation of romanticism, though Burke being an Englishman, or rather Irishman, was concerned only with literature; but his book was to have a powerful influence on visual art later in the century.

Meanwhile, Tobias Smollett, a Scottish ship's surgeon, was writing his salty, picaresque novels, from *Roderick Random* to *Humphrey Clinker*, and in 1760 came the first part of Laurence Sterne's brilliantly eccentric *Tristram Shandy*, a series of digressions – during one of which the hero is born – that illustrate the illogical working of man's unconscious mind, another protest, perhaps itself unconscious, against the current rule of reason. 'Nothing odd will do long,' Johnson pronounced in 1776, '*Tristram Shandy* did not last.' He was wrong: 'my Uncle Toby', Corporal Trim, and Dr Slop have not yet been forgotten. Nor has Goldsmith's *Vicar of Wakefield*, most innocent of novels, written with an Irish charm very different from what Goldsmith himself called the 'great whale' manner of Johnson.

Strawberry Hill: the Twickenham villa bought by the young dilettante Horace Walpole in 1747, and gradually converted into a 'Gothick' castle. His medieval romance, *The Castle of Otranto*, was printed here.

Two self-portraits of the 1770s:
(*Above*) Allan Ramsay (1713–84), aged 63.

(*Right*) Sir Joshua Reynolds (1723–92), aged 50.

The years 1740 to 1770 had seen the birth and rapid development of the modern novel, but the next decade was that of a brief revival of the drama, beginning with Goldsmith's *The Good Natured Man* and the equally good-natured *She Stoops to Conquer*. Then in swift succession came the comedies of Sheridan, who in 1776, when only twenty-five, bought Garrick's share in Drury Lane Theatre, and in the next year presented *The Rivals*, with the immortal Mrs Malaprop, *A Trip to Scarborough*, and *The School for Scandal*, a return to the Restoration comedy of manners without its indecency, followed in 1779 by *The Critic*, containing a hilarious parody of an Elizabethan play. Goldsmith had died in 1774, Sheridan wrote little more, and after this brilliant interlude, darkness, or at least twilight, again enveloped the English stage for another hundred years.

Johnson wrote a noble epitaph on Goldsmith, in Latin, for 'he would never consent to disgrace the walls of Westminster Abbey with an English inscription'. So long as Johnson lived, so did the classical Grand Style; and what Johnson was to literature, Reynolds was to painting. Reynolds, however, did not introduce the Grand Style, for when he returned from Italy, aged thirty, in 1753, after three years' study of the Italian masters, he found that he had been anticipated by the Scotsman, Allan Ramsay, who had supplanted Hudson as the most fashionable portrait painter in London. Reynolds at once challenged him by painting *Commodore Keppel* in the same pose as Ramsay's *Norman MacLeod*. There is no mistaking the greater vigour and dramatic intensity of the Keppel portrait; with it Reynolds made his reputation, and Ramsay developed a more delicate style, as seen in the famous portrait of his wife. By 1768 Reynolds was first President of the Royal Academy, for which he shamelessly painted 'Exhibition pictures' that would be noticed, and delivered an annual *Discourse*. The following extract is typical: 'On the sight of the Capella Sistina, he [Raphael] immediately from a dry, Gothick and even insipid manner, which attends to the minute accidental discriminations of particular and individual objects, assumed that grand style of painting which improves partial representation by the general and invariable ideas of nature.' 'I think I might as well have said this myself', remarked Johnson, and indeed he very nearly did in *Rasselas*: 'The business of a poet is to examine, not the individual but the species; to remark general properties and large appearances. He . . . must neglect the minuter discriminations . . . for those characteristics which are alike obvious to vigilance and carelessness.' And compare Blake's comment on Reynolds: 'All Sublimity is founded on Minute Discrimination.' Here is the difference, or one major difference, between classical and romantic art. Reynolds painted from the head, and his portraits are types as well as individuals: the 'Roscius of the age' is not only Garrick but an actor, the 'Great Lexicographer' not only Johnson but a man of letters.

Ramsay challenged by Reynolds:
(*Left*) *Norman MacLeod*, painted by Ramsay, 1748. (*Right*) *Commodore Keppel*, painted by Reynolds, 1753.

The monumental Mediterranean manner of Reynolds was very different from that of Gainsborough, who never went to Italy. Reynolds was a townsman, Gainsborough a countryman whose heart was in landscape and who turned to portraiture from necessity, working in fashionable Bath from 1759 to 1774, while John Wood was building the Royal Crescent. An experimenter with no academic training, he was more interested in the transient and accidental than in the solidity of Reynolds's forms; Reynolds is an epic painter, Gainsborough lyrical in his delicacy and lightness, both in portraits and landscape. George Romney, their slightly younger contemporary, had a neo-classical simplicity of contour and a profitable flair for idealization that made him their rival in the fashionable world.

This was the age of the grandiose 'history' painting, of the 'sublime', the vast and awe-inspiring, as propounded by Burke, of James Barry and Benjamin West, whose *Death of Wolfe* was revolutionary in depicting a contemporary event in contemporary, instead of classical, costume. The subject-matter of painting was expanding; Zoffany extended the range of the conversation piece from stage to royal palace; Joseph Wright of Derby painted scenes of the early

(*Left above*) The Grand Style (7 feet by 6 feet): *The Death of Wolfe*, by Benjamin West, 1770.

The renewed appreciation of nature:
(*Left*) *Mares and Foals*, by George Stubbs, *c.* 1760. (*Right*) *Snowdon*, by Richard Wilson, *c.* 1770.

Industrial Revolution as revealed by artificial light; George Stubbs, author and illustrator of *The Anatomy of the Horse*, lovingly depicted every form of nature, but as horses were his passion he inspired the English genre of sporting picture. Richard Wilson was originally a portrait painter, but when he went to Italy in 1750 he became the first dedicated British painter of landscape; he was born before his time, however, for there was no demand for his pictures of the English scene, and he returned to his native Wales, where he painted what is perhaps his masterpiece, *Snowdon*. He died in 1782, when Constable and Wordsworth were small boys. All these were painters in oils, but the last half of the century saw the beginning of water-colour in the art of Paul Sandby, first to paint the English landscape as it really is, instead of an idealized version, and that of Alexander Cozens and his son John Robert, employed by William Beckford to make a pictorial record of his journey into Switzerland and Italy.

In 1780 Reynolds delivered a Royal Academy *Discourse on Sculpture*. The theme was again the Grand Style: sculpture must be austerely formal and symmetrically balanced, must avoid the Picturesque, and must not, of course, disgrace the walls of Westminster Abbey, or St Paul's, with English costume. No doubt he was glancing at the so undesirable baroque elements in the work of Rysbrack and Scheemakers, and the milder Rococo of Louis-François Roubiliac, who by 1750 had become their rival. With Roubiliac drama enters the realm of monumental sculpture on the grand scale, with the deceased as protagonist in the action. The Westminster Abbey memorial to Lady Elizabeth Nightingale shows her husband trying to protect the fainting lady from the dart that Death is about to hurl, while the theme of that to General Hargrave is no less than the End of the World itself. The Handel memorial of 1761 more modestly represents the great composer, surrounded by organs and trumpets, holding the score of the *Messiah*, a variation on the theme of the Scheemakers *Shakespeare*, which it faces in the Abbey. There was less scope for drama in his portrait busts, and his statue of Newton in Trinity College Chapel, Cambridge, was to be immortalized by Wordsworth. Joseph Wilton emulated Roubiliac in his Wolfe monument, though his general, unlike Benjamin West's, dies without his clothes.

Henry Fuseli's translation of Winckelmann's famous *Gedanken* appeared in 1765 as *Reflections on the Painting and Sculpture of the Greeks*, and his neoclassical doctrine of simplicity and clarity of contour, of feeling and sentiment, affected the art of Joseph Nollekens, notably in his statues of alluring goddesses, and, unhappily, that of John Bacon (apparently the inventor of the artificial Coade stone) for his monument to Thomas Guy in contemporary costume is one of the best sculptures of the century, while his later tribute to Dr Johnson as a Grecian sage, although it does not disgrace, scarcely graces the walls of St Paul's. The first truly neoclassical sculptor was Fuseli's friend, Thomas Banks, whose *Death of Germanicus*, 1776, exhibits all the desirable qualities, from contour to sentiment.

Rococo and neoclassical:
(*Above left*) The Handel monument in Westminster Abbey, by L.-F. Roubiliac, 1761.
(*Above right*) Thomas Guy, founder of Guy's Hospital, by John Bacon, 1779.
(*Below*) *The Death of Germanicus*, by Thomas Banks, 1776.

This new classicism was further advanced by architects a generation younger than the conservative Chambers and adventurous Adam, over-adventurous for much contemporary taste. In 1769 George Dance the Younger began Newgate Prison, the severity of which, and particularly the superimposed rows of arched openings, recalled the Colosseum, and Henry Holland employed the Greek Ionic order for the screen of the Prince of Wales's Carlton House, and even the Doric – anathema to Chambers – in the hall of Dover House, Whitehall. From this eclectic classicism, which admitted so many styles of ancient Greece and Rome, and looked nostalgically at their vanished glories, the step to a romantic appreciation of Gothic was easy, and one that Wyatt, ever ready to exploit current feeling, was soon to take.

For the 1780s formed the transition between the Classical and Romantic ages. The Industrial Revolution was beginning, and one by one the great men of the old tradition were going: Johnson, Gainsborough, Reynolds, Adam, Chambers. In 1785 William Cowper published *The Task*, a long conversational blank-verse poem, with a genuine feeling for nature that anticipated Wordsworth, while his *Castaway*, written in fear of returning madness, is one of the most deeply moving poems in the language, far removed from the restraint of the Augustans. In 1788 came the last three volumes of Gibbon's monumental *Decline and Fall of the Roman Empire*, the lapidary prose of which was, apart from Boswell's *Life of Johnson*, the last great contribution to the Age of Reason. Then in 1789, while crowds were gaping at the pictures in Alderman Boydell's Shakespeare Gallery, others singing catches and glees, or listening to 'Tom Bowling' and other sea-songs of Charles Dibdin, Blake published his *Songs of Innocence* and the Paris mob stormed the Bastille.

Newgate Prison, begun 1769, by the younger George Dance. In this grim, fortress-like front, Pope's advice to 'restrain the Muse's steed' is carried to its extreme.

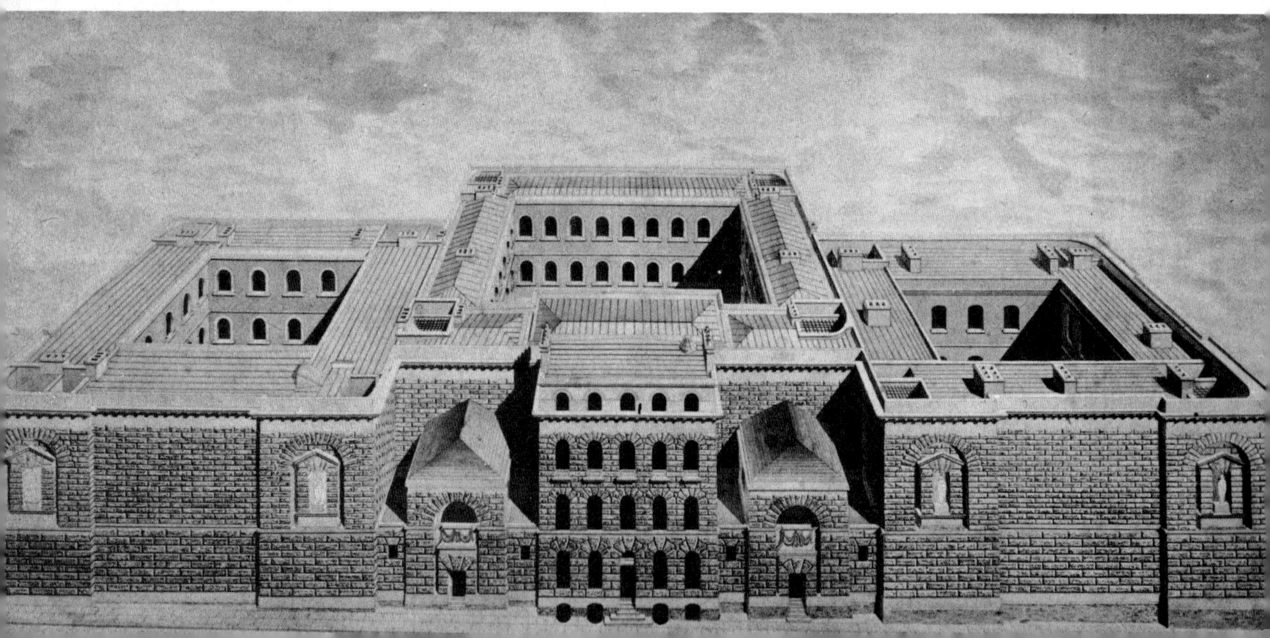

12 The Romantics 1789–1837

William Blake was born in 1757, though no man could have been less characteristic of the eighteenth century. An individualist, he belonged to no school and, rejecting the cult of reason, pursued the visions of his own mythology in both poetry and painting. Much of his later *Prophetic Books* is written almost in a private language, and his best work is in short and simple poems like the matchless *Sunflower* and *The Tiger*, a poem that nobody but he could have written. In his painting he revolted against the Royal Academy, Reynolds, and realism, and, as oil-colours were symbolic of all three, he used water-colour to depict the visions inspired by the Bible, Milton, Dante, and the Middle Ages, and was of his own age only in the neoclassical clarity of his contour. Robert Burns, two years younger than Blake, was another poet out of sympathy with his century, though for different reasons. A liberal thinker, liver, and lover, he satirized hypocrisy in poems such as *Holy Willie's Prayer* and wrote a century of lyrics in Scottish dialect and a number of racy, humorously improper stories like *Tam O'Shanter*. Such lines as,

> Fast by an ingle bleezin' finely,
> Wi' reamin' swats that drank divinely,

would scarcely have won the approbation of Dr Johnson.

Burns died in 1796, by which time England had been at war with Revolutionary France for three years and, apart from one short break, the war was to last until the final victory of Waterloo in 1815: two decades that were also those of the first phase of the Romantic Movement. This was a revolt precipitated by the French Revolution, against the rule of reason and the restraints of Classicism, for the glorification of freedom, imagination, and emotion, the rediscovery of wonder, a retreat from the town to the country, to medieval romance, the mysterious, irrational, and supernatural. The movement had been foreshadowed in the nature poetry of Thomson and Cowper, the landscapes of Gainsborough, rustic scenes of George Morland, and architectural cult of the Picturesque, the kind of building that might have come out of a picture, from a landscape painting by Claude or Poussin. Strawberry Hill was picturesque in its irregularity, but it was also Gothick, and it was a short step from the picturesque to the medievally romantic. In 1795 John Carter published his *Ancient Architecture of England*, and in the same year Wyatt began the building of Fonthill Abbey, a vast Gothick mansion in Wiltshire resembling a cathedral, with a soaring central octagonal tower.

Fonthill was built for the wealthy William Beckford, who emulated not only Walpole's Strawberry Hill but also his *Castle of Otranto*, and wrote *Vathek*, a fantastic oriental story of black magic. This return to fourteenth-century romance produced a crop of similar novels of mystery and terror in the 1790s, the most famous being Mrs Radcliffe's *Mysteries of Udolpho* and Matthew Lewis's *The Monk*. Then in 1798 came *The Rime of the Ancyent Marinere*.

This was Coleridge's main contribution to the *Lyrical Ballads*, the remainder of the poems being by his friend, the twenty-eight-year-old Wordsworth. In his *Biographia Literaria* Coleridge was to write that it was his object to make the supernatural appear credible, whereas Wordsworth's was 'to give the charm of novelty to things of every day, and to excite a feeling analogous to the supernatural, by awakening the mind's attention from the lethargy of custom, and directing it to the loveliness and the wonders of the world before us.' Wordsworth said much the same thing in a second edition of the *Lyrical Ballads*, a Preface that was the manifesto of the Romantic Movement. And so, at the very end of the eighteenth century, English poetry escaped from the restraints and conventions, the metrical forms and poetic diction of the classical age, into a new freedom of matter and manner, 'a selection of language really used by men', as Wordsworth claimed. Coleridge was a romantic in his return to the ballad form and supernatural in *The Ancient Mariner*, to the medieval in *Christabel*, and he anticipated the extreme romanticism of the Surrealists in the dream-poem of *Kubla Khan*. But Wordsworth proved the more influential poet, and today, when industry and uninformed town-dwellers in motor-cars are destroying both countryside and coast, the message of *The Prelude*, *Tintern Abbey*, and his lyrics has never been more important: the benign influence of nature on man, its formative, consolatory and healing power. Like Coleridge's, most of Wordsworth's finest poetry, the work that makes him one of the greatest of English poets, was written by 1815, as were the immensely popular verse romances, *The Lay of the Last Minstrel* and *Marmion*, of their contemporary Sir Walter Scott.

The second phase of the Romantic Movement may be said to have begun after Waterloo, though it was during the last years of the war that young Lord Byron recorded his Mediterranean travels in *Childe Harold*, the first two cantos of which appeared in 1812. A supreme egotist, he was the hero of all his poems, and his strength lies in description, satire, mockery, ingenious rhyming, and humorous bathos, above all in *Don Juan*, though some of his lyrics are among the

Fonthill Abbey, Wiltshire: the Gothick house built, 1795–1807, by James Wyatt for the romantic millionaire William Beckford, author of the oriental fantasy *Vathek*.

best of his age. He created the image of the romantic 'Byronic' figure, and the romance of Greece, yet he disliked the poetry of Wordsworth as much as he admired Pope, as well as George Crabbe, who went on writing, in classical couplets, grim realistic stories like *Peter Grimes* into the age of Shelley and Keats. Like Byron, Shelley was the champion of liberty, but he had none of Byron's cynicism, levity, and worldliness; an idealist, he wrote of man's liberation in the lyrical allegory *Prometheus Unbound*, though man is little more than a spirit in his poetry of air and ocean, he himself little more than a prophetic voice in the wind with which he identified himself: 'Be thou me, impetuous one!' He was the ethereal poet of night and the moon, of shadows and the intangible, but Keats was the poet of earth and the sun, of autumnal richness and sensuous beauty, identifying himself not with the wind but with the sparrow pecking among the gravel outside his window. He is the arch-romantic, for whom the rule-bound school of Pope 'blasphemed the bright Lyrist in his face', and for whom 'poetry should surprise by a fine excess'. That is certainly true of his own work, and though it is sometimes over-lush for modern taste, he is the nearest to Shakespeare in the haunting beauty of his phrase and remote reverberations of his

The first generation of romantic poets: Coleridge, 1772–1834; Wordsworth, 1770–1850; Scott, 1771–1834.

imagery. He died of consumption in Rome in 1821, aged twenty-five, and Shelley wrote his elegy, *Adonais*, concluding:

> The breath whose might I have invoked in song
> Descends on me; my spirit's bark is driven
> Far from the shore, far from the trembling throng
> Whose sails were never to the tempest given;
> The massy earth and sphered skies are riven!
> I am borne darkly, fearfully, afar;
> Whilst burning through the inmost veil of Heaven,
> The soul of Adonais, like a star,
> Beacons from the abode where the eternal are.

It was prophetic as well as valedictory, for in the following year Shelley, aged thirty, was drowned while sailing in the Gulf of Spezia. Byron was the longest lived of the three, dying in Greece in 1824, aged thirty-six.

The first quarter of the nineteenth century rivals the age of Shakespeare in the splendour of its poetry, and all five of the great romantic poets tried to revive the Elizabethan poetic drama, but their tragedies remain plays for the study rather than the stage, though Shelley's *Cenci* might have been successful had it not been for the theme of incest. Scott proved a greater dramatist than any of them, though he chose the form of the novel, and from *Waverley* in 1814 to *Woodstock* in 1827 created characters with almost Shakespearean ease and prodigality. Few people read his novels now; they are too prolix and their medievalism is as false as Fonthill Abbey, yet *Guy Mannering*, *The Antiquary*, and *The Heart of Midlothian* are among the great things in the literature of Britain. Very different were the novels of Jane Austen, all six of which appeared between 1811 and 1817. For her the medieval and romantic were equally a joke, satirized in *Northanger Abbey*, and the most sensational event in her work is a mild case of concussion at Lyme Regis; yet a trivial incident in these perfectly

The second generation: Byron, 1788–1824; Shelley, 1792–1822; Keats, 1795–1821.

constructed domestic comedies – whether it will snow or the carriage be late – may be more fraught with suspense than the horrors of Mary Shelley's *Frankenstein* which appeared in 1818, the year after Jane Austen's death. It was also the year of the *Nightmare Abbey* of Shelley's friend, Thomas Love Peacock, and fully to savour the Romantic period Peacock's novels, or at least *Nightmare Abbey* and *Crotchet Castle*, are essential reading. Both Abbey and Castle are

The Romantic Movement in painting: nature and medieval ruins. *Kirkstall Abbey*: a water-colour by Thomas Girtin, *c.* 1800.

'castellated' Regency houses, in which forgather a number of men who talk, like Ben Jonson's characters, each 'in his humour'. Here we meet gentle caricatures of Shelley, Byron, Malthus, and Coleridge, 'the transcendental philosopher', with Mr Chainmail the medievalist, Mr Trillo the opera-goer, the Hon. Mr Listless and his valet, apparently the originals of Bertie Wooster and Jeeves. And Peacock, as the Rev. Dr Folliott, humorously mocks the fashionable foibles: the March of Mind, Political Economy, the Picturesque, Romanticism, Neoclassicism, and Benthamism.

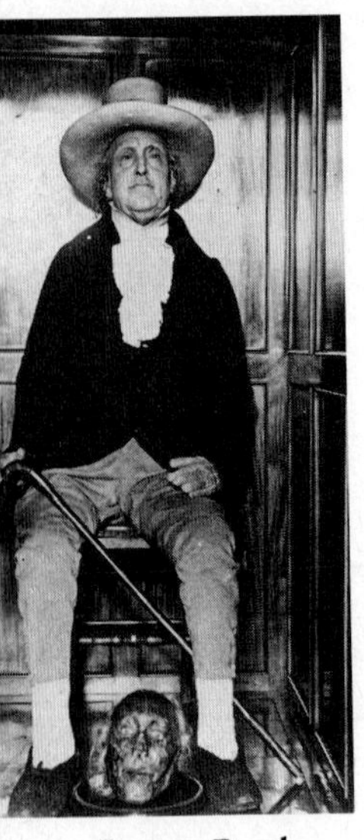

Jeremy Bentham, Utilitarian, 1748–1832.

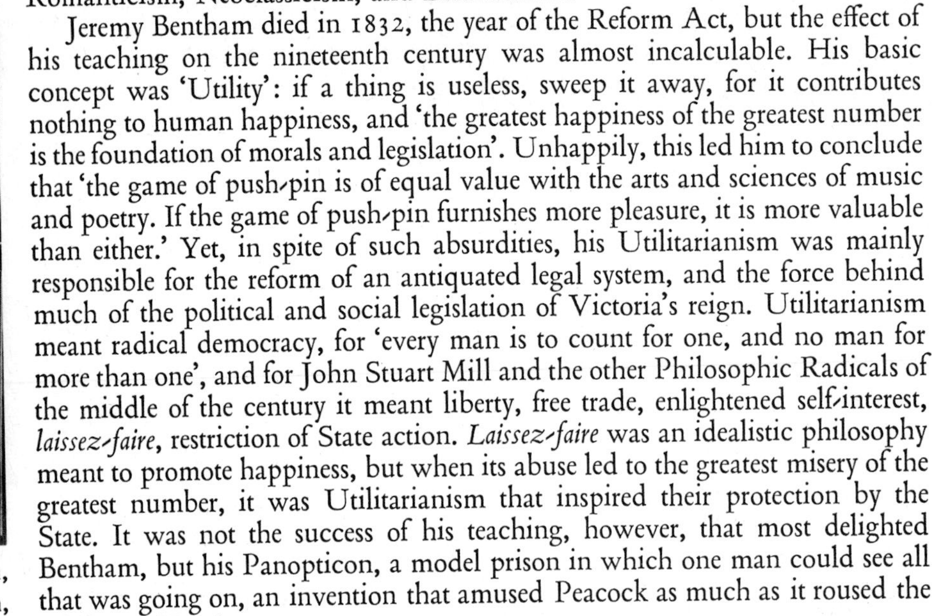

Jeremy Bentham died in 1832, the year of the Reform Act, but the effect of his teaching on the nineteenth century was almost incalculable. His basic concept was 'Utility': if a thing is useless, sweep it away, for it contributes nothing to human happiness, and 'the greatest happiness of the greatest number is the foundation of morals and legislation'. Unhappily, this led him to conclude that 'the game of push-pin is of equal value with the arts and sciences of music and poetry. If the game of push-pin furnishes more pleasure, it is more valuable than either.' Yet, in spite of such absurdities, his Utilitarianism was mainly responsible for the reform of an antiquated legal system, and the force behind much of the political and social legislation of Victoria's reign. Utilitarianism meant radical democracy, for 'every man is to count for one, and no man for more than one', and for John Stuart Mill and the other Philosophic Radicals of the middle of the century it meant liberty, free trade, enlightened self-interest, *laissez-faire*, restriction of State action. *Laissez-faire* was an idealistic philosophy meant to promote happiness, but when its abuse led to the greatest misery of the greatest number, it was Utilitarianism that inspired their protection by the State. It was not the success of his teaching, however, that most delighted Bentham, but his Panopticon, a model prison in which one man could see all that was going on, an invention that amused Peacock as much as it roused the derision of Pugin.

In the years between Waterloo and the accession of Queen Victoria, Charles Lamb was writing his whimsical essays 'for antiquity', de Quincey the dream prose of *An English Opium Eater*, Cobbett his breezy, indignant survey of a changing England, *Rural Rides*, and Hazlitt his penetrating criticism of the works of his contemporaries and Shakespeare. Coleridge too, most inspired of critics, was demolishing the classical conception of Shakespeare as 'a wild irregular genius' and substituting that of a poet whose judgement was equal to his genius. Somewhat apart from these was Walter Savage Landor, whose chiselled verse and marmoreal prose of the *Imaginary Conversations* were the equivalent of Flaxman's neoclassical reliefs.

Like Wordsworth, John Flaxman was full of high moral purpose: the business of sculpture, and of all the arts, was to elevate the mind, and he set himself to do for the Protestant Church what Michelangelo and the other Italians had done for the Catholic. It was the age of Bowdler, whose expurgated *Family Shakespeare* appeared in 1818, and the decencies were preserved:

although naked gentlemen were allowable, there are no naked ladies in his work, most of his females being heavily draped and mourning over funerary urns or, like his men, improving their minds, or those of others, with a book. Patriotism was one of the higher virtues, which he tried to instil in monuments such as his *Lord Howe* and *Nelson* in St Paul's. 'He had', as his friend Allan Cunningham mildly remarked, 'a serious leaning towards allegory, and dealt largely in British Lions, Victories and Britannias.' Freed from these encumbrances, his reliefs are better, for his talent was for line rather than form.

Flaxman's *Howe* was one of the first monuments to be erected in St Paul's, to commemorate the heroes of the French war. The State was beginning to take over the patronage of sculpture, and a Committee of National Monuments, formed in 1802, was empowered to commission memorials according to a sliding scale: the higher the rank of the subject the higher the reward. Thus Richard Westmacott would receive six thousand guineas for his *General Abercromby*, a not very subtle exercise in diagonals, the central feature of which is a horse's head, the expiring general being half hidden by the back view of a supporting Highlander. Westmacott was fond of backs, and even more remarkable is his *Pitt* over the west door of Westminster Abbey, with History at his feet recording his oration. Statues of public men were overflowing into public places: Westmacott's *Canning* was erected in Parliament Square, and *Nelsons* were soon to be seen in the squares of many provincial cities, though not yet in London.

Neoclassicism in St Paul's Cathedral: Lord Howe's monument, by John Flaxman, 1803–11. 'He had a serious leaning towards allegory, and dealt largely in British Lions, Victories and Britannias.'

With the end of the war and renewal of contact with continental Europe, the 'voluptuous' work of the Italian Canova was much admired in Britain, though more important was the revelation of the Elgin Marbles, the Parthenon sculptures, which were bought for the nation in 1816. Their influence is most obvious in John Henning's friezes on Decimus Burton's Arch at Hyde Park Corner and the Athenaeum Club, but it can also be seen in the reliefs of Westmacott and his slightly younger contemporary, Francis Chantrey. Chantrey, however, was primarily a sculptor in the round, and, impatient of fashionable allegory, carved realistic statues like the seated figure of James Watt at Birmingham, and busts, of which the best known is that of Scott, made in 1820 when the novelist was writing *Kenilworth*. Chantrey was a better sculptor than Flaxman and Westmacott, but he was over-fond of death-bed scenes and mothers and children, and his new naturalism was the beginning of Victorian sentimentality.

Idealism and the Elgin Marbles:
The frieze at Hyde Park Corner, London: by John Henning, 1828.

Sir Henry Bishop (1786–1855), composer of 'Home, sweet home', and the first musician to be knighted.

The Romantic Age produced no British sculpture comparable to its literature, nor did it inspire any new music worthy of that great period of poetry. In this it differed from the Elizabethan Age, when music was the peer of poetry, and the descent from Tallis, Byrd, Morley, and Dowland to the Romantic composers is mere bathos. Among the pupils of the Italian-born Clementi was the German-born pianist Johann Cramer, an infant prodigy who began to play in public in 1781 at the age of ten, and like his master combined the writing of sonatas, long forgotten, with piano manufacture. John Field, an Irishman, was another prodigy pupil of Clementi, for whom he sold pianos and with whom he travelled abroad giving recitals. His piano compositions are of some historical importance, for he devised the nocturne, a form that was soon to be developed by Chopin. It is some measure of the decline of English music that the most famous musician of the period was Henry Bishop, composer of forgotten operas and incidental music for the trivialities of the stage. In 1806, when only twenty, he wrote the music for *Tamerlan et Bajazet*, a ballet, and had the distinction of being the first Englishman to write for this form of art imported from France, where it had been developed from the masque, and was to have a great vogue in London after the arrival of the dancer Marie Taglioni in the 1820s. Bishop made his name with the opera *The Maniac*, and when the Philharmonic Society was formed in 1813 he was appointed one of the directors, sometimes taking the place of the ageing Clementi as conductor. The Waverley Novels were a godsend to a composer in search of librettos, and there followed what can only be called the Waverley Operas, from *Guy Mannering* to *Kenilworth*, though many of them were merely dramatized versions with incidental music. His opera *Aladdin*, written for the New Drury Lane Theatre to forestall the production of Weber's *Oberon* at the rival Covent Garden, was a failure, and he turned to more academic pursuits, becoming successively Professor of

Music at Edinburgh and Oxford. He was knighted by Queen Victoria soon after her accession, the first musician to be so honoured, perhaps because he was the composer of 'Home, sweet home', the theme-song of his *Clari: the Maid of Milan.*

Scott was not the only writer whose work was set to music. In this age of romantic love-lyrics, Isaac Nathan made Byron's *Hebrew Melodies* into songs with piano accompaniment, and John Stevenson did the same for Tom Moore's *Irish Melodies.* It was, indeed, Stevenson's settings, many of them adapted from national airs, that led to Moore's immense popularity and the success of his oriental verse romance of *Lalla Rookh,* which was made into an opera by Charles Horn, better known as the composer of the setting for Herrick's *Cherry Ripe.* Moore was himself a charming singer, and wrote many of his lyrics to fit old Irish tunes, 'The harp that once through Tara's halls', for example, and Burns did a similar service for Scotland. In this they were encouraged by George Thomson, who in 1793 published a collection of Scottish, Irish, and Welsh folk-music – though not English, for England was then thought to have no folk-music. In fact, apart from old folk-tunes, new ones were even then being created by sailors as they worked at the capstan or halliards, the shanty man singing the solo part and the others joining in the chorus. 'Blow the man down' and 'Lowlands away' are good examples of the sea-shanty, which died out when steam replaced sail about 1870.

In the eighteenth century, concerts were in the main confined to subscribers drawn from fashionable society, though at Vauxhall and Ranelagh Gardens music could be heard by bigger and more varied audiences. Ranelagh was closed in 1803, but Vauxhall survived until 1859, and in *Vanity Fair* there is an unforgettable description of an evening there shortly before Waterloo, by which time it had become a more popular resort, the fare more varied: 'The fiddlers in cocked hats, who played ravishing melodies under the gilded cockle-shell in the midst of the Gardens; the singers, both of comic and sentimental ballads; the country dances, formed by bouncing cockneys and cockneyesses . . . the signal which announced that Madame Saqui was about to mount skyward on a slack-rope . . . while Mrs Salmon performed the Battle of Borodino (a savage cantata against the Corsican upstart).'

Opera was confined to London, but not concerts, and when Haydn visited England in 1791 his Symphony in G major was christened the 'Oxford' when performed in the Sheldonian Theatre on the occasion of his receiving an honorary degree. It was Salomon, the German violinist, who persuaded him to visit England and compose the last twelve of his century of symphonies for performance there, Haydn himself conducting at the keyboard, as the fashion then was, while Salomon led the violins. While German literature and philosophy were influencing Coleridge and Carlyle, German music was beginning to compete with Italian and French, particularly after the formation of the Philharmonic Society, who, in their new quarters in Regent Street,

UNDER THE IMMEDIATE PATRONAGE OF

His Royal Highness the Prince Regent.

PHILHARMONIC SOCIETY.

First Concert, MONDAY, March 8th, 1813.

PART I.

Overture to Anacreon - - - - - *Cherubini.*
Quartetto, two Violins, Viola and Violoncello, Messrs. F. CRAMER, MORALT, SHERRINGTON, and LINDLEY - - - - - - - *Mozart.*
Quartetto & Chorus, Nell' orror, Mrs. MORALT, Messrs. HAWES, P. A. CORRI, and KELLNER *Sacchini.*
Serenade, Wind Instruments, Messrs. MAHON, OLIVER, HOLMES, TULLY, and the PETRIDES *Mozart.*
Symphony - - - - - - - - *Beethoven.*

PART II.

Symphony - - - - - - - - - *Haydn.*
Chorus, Placido e' il mar, Mrs. MORALT, Miss HUGHES, Messrs. P. A. CORRI, C. SMITH, &c. *Mozart.*
Quintetto, two Violins, Viola, and two Violoncellos, Messrs. SALOMON, CUDMORE, SHERRINGTON, LINDLEY, and C. ASHLEY - - *Boccherini.*
Chaconne, Jomelle, and March - - - *Haydn.*

Leader, Mr. SALOMON.—Piano-Forte, Mr. CLEMENTI.

The Second will take place on Monday next, the 15th March.

Reynell, Printer, 21, Piccadilly, London.

The inaugural concert of the Philharmonic Society, 1813.

(*Left*) 'Vanity Fair': Vauxhall Gardens in 1809.

played the strange music of the new man, Beethoven. In 1826 Weber, composer of the romantic German (not Italian) opera, *Der Freischütz*, arrived in England to conduct his *Oberon*, commissioned by Kemble for Covent Garden, where scenery such as a 'Perforated Cavern on the Beach' was more of an attraction than music. The venture proved too much for Weber, who died in London soon after conducting twelve performances. Three years later the young Mendelssohn paid the first of his many visits to London, where his *Midsummer Night's Dream* overture was given its first English performance, while a journey to Scotland inspired his *Scottish Symphony* and the overture *Fingal's Cave*.

Thus, though there was good music to be heard in England during the Romantic period, it was mainly composed and performed by foreigners. English Church music, too, was still in the doldrums, though Samuel Wesley – another prodigy, who composed an oratorio at the age of eight – was a brilliant organist who wrote a memorable eight-part motet, *In exitu Israel*, and was largely responsible for introducing the work of Bach to English organists before his death in 1837.

Not music but painting was the peer of poetry in the Romantic Age; never before had Britain had such a wealth of great painters, and most of them, whether consciously or not, did for their art what Wordsworth and Coleridge set out to do for theirs: give the charm of novelty to things of every day, and a semblance of truth to 'shadows of imagination'. The visionary art of Blake came nearest to Coleridge's ideal and that of Fuseli illustrates the grotesque and supernatural element in romanticism. Henry Fuseli was a German-Swiss who settled in England about 1780, where he first attracted attention with his *Night-mare*, a more disturbing revelation of the unconscious mind than the dream-poem *Kubla Khan*, as were his Surrealistic interpretations of *A Midsummer Night's Dream* exhibited in the Shakespeare Gallery. The clear-cut neoclassical contour of Fuseli was partly responsible for Blake's flowing linear style and muscular but boneless bodies, and Blake himself influenced the young, idealistic Samuel Palmer, who saw and painted nature with an almost apocalyptic intensity.

Neither Fuseli nor Blake was a Wordsworthian: 'Damn Nature! She always puts me out,' Fuseli would say; and Blake: 'Painting, as well as poetry and music, exists and exults in immortal thoughts,' which is not far from Coleridge's 'Painting is the intermediate somewhat between a thought and a thing.' Most of the other Romantic painters, however, wished to represent nature as they saw it, and as water-colour is the medium with which fleeting and 'picturesque' effects can most easily be captured, this was a great period of water-colour painting. Moreover, as the French war virtually precluded foreign travel until 1815, their pictures of the first half of the period are mainly of the British scene. Thus Girtin, although a Londoner, was attracted by the hills and ruined abbeys of the north, and by the suppression of irrelevant detail gave a new breadth to landscape painting. 'Had Tom Girtin lived, I should have starved,' said his friend Turner. He died aged twenty-six in 1802, the year in which the equally short-lived Richard Bonington was born. Bonington painted mainly in France, where his work, both in water-colour and oils, was better known and appreciated than in England, the luminosity and richness of his colour gaining him a Gold Medal at the Salon of 1824. David Cox, born in 1783, was a Midlander who found his chief inspiration in the romantic scenery of Wales, and delighted in representing the effect of atmosphere on landscape, almost painting the wind, and with his broken touches giving his work something of the brilliance and sparkle of Impressionist painting. On the other hand, his contemporary John Sell Cotman, like his friend Girtin, worked in a broader manner, achieving a serenity that is almost abstract in the interplay of simplified forms, as in the magnificent *Greta Bridge*.

Although Cotman was born in Norwich, his early training was in London, and it was only after Girtin's death that he returned to his native city. There he found John Crome, a humbly born man some twelve years his senior, at the centre of a group of painters who in 1805, Trafalgar year, formed themselves

Nightmare, by Henry Fuseli, 1782: the visual equivalent of the horrific romantic novel, and an anticipation of Surrealism.

Water-colour had been practised by a few painters of the eighteenth century, notably by Paul Sandby, Alexander Cozens and his son John Robert Cozens, and it became a favourite medium when the Romantics rediscovered nature. (*Below*) *Rhyl Sands*, 'painting the wind', by David Cox (1783–1859). *Greta Bridge*, a study in serenity, by John Sell Cotman (1782–1842).

into the Norwich Society of Artists, the beginning of the 'Norwich school', the first provincial school of art since medieval times. There had always been a close cultural and commercial relationship between East Anglia and the Netherlands, the flat landscapes of which are similar, and Crome was much influenced by the Dutch landscape painters of the seventeenth century, notably Hobbema. So while Wordsworth at Grasmere was composing *The Excursion*, Byron making fun of it – 'a drowsy frowsy poem' – in *Don Juan*, and Keats writing his *Odes* at Hampstead, Crome was painting his beloved Norfolk countryside, its heaths, slow rivers, boats, and trees, as simplified forms under wide luminous skies.

The greatest and most original of these East Anglian painters, however, was a Suffolk man, John Constable, who did for the region of his birthplace on the River Stour what Crome did for the neighbourhood of Norwich. His early patron, Sir George Beaumont, an amateur painter of the old school,

Mousehold Heath, by John Crome (1769–1821). John Crome, often called 'Old' Crome, to distinguish him from his son, was born at Norwich, where he was a house-painter before becoming a drawing-master and founder of the Norwich School. Asked why he painted this picture, he replied, 'For air and space.'

assured him that 'a good picture, like a good fiddle, should be brown', but Constable had other ideas, for, like Wordsworth, he really looked at nature, saw nature with his own eyes, not through those of other painters, however much he admired them. 'When I sit down to make a sketch from nature,' he said, 'the first thing I try to do is to forget that I have ever seen a picture.' And this was why the French Romantic painter, Delacroix, wrote that 'The Englishmen' – particularly 'that admirable man, Constable' – 'seem to be pursuing nature, while we are merely occupied in imitating pictures.' It was the new brilliance, greenness, freshness, instead of conventional colouring, that was so revolutionary in his art, best seen in the preliminary studies made from nature, like those for *The Hay Wain* and *Leaping Horse*, and the exhilarating sketch of *Brighton Beach with Colliers*, all painted in the early 1820s. Although Constable did not copy, but represented, interpreted nature, no other painter has so faithfully reproduced the atmosphere, the feeling of the English countryside.

The Hay Wain, by John Constable, *c.* 1821. Constable's work was much admired by his contemporary Delacroix, the French romantic painter: 'That admirable man, Constable, is one of the glories of England. He and Turner are real reformers. They have got clear of the rut of the old landscape painters.'

Yet, even after half a century of Romantic art, England was not ready to accept pure landscape. Richard Wilson had been neglected, Gainsborough was compelled to abandon landscape for portrait painting, Cotman had to support himself by teaching, and Constable's genius was unrecognized in England until after his death in 1837. The English are an incurably literary people: they like their art to tell a story or point a moral, and all that these East Anglian painters offered was views of their unsensational countryside. Yet the greatest of all English landscape painters, J. M. W. Turner, was more fortunate in every sense of the word, and for a number of reasons. Born in 1775, the year before Constable, he made a name for himself in the acceptable art of topographical water-colour, and early oil-paintings, such as *Calais Pier*, are in the highest degree dramatic: a torn white sail against louring clouds, a heaving sea and groups of straining men. Then, to the elemental drama of his later paintings he would often add a nominal human one, calling a mountain

Two paintings by J. M. W. Turner (1775–1851):
(*Left*) *Petworth Park*, in his later style, *c.* 1830, when his palette became much brighter. A sketch for the paintings at Petworth House, Sussex, where he was a frequent visitor.
(*Below*) *Hannibal and his Army Crossing the Alps*, a romantic painting of 1811, in which history is merely the pretext for the portrayal of elemental grandeur.

snowstorm *Hannibal and his Army Crossing the Alps*. Again, his travels in France, Germany, Switzerland, and Italy gave him an enormous range of subjects, and finally, he was a Romantic poet whose medium was paint. It was of his first sketching tour of the southern English coast that his great apologist, Ruskin, was to write how he discovered the real nature of the sea: 'now striking like a steel gauntlet, and now becoming a cloud, and vanishing, no eye could tell whither; one moment a flint cave, the next a marble pillar, the next a mere white fleece thickening the thundery rain. He never forgot those facts; never afterwards was able to recover the idea of positive distinction between sea and sky, or sea and land.' His later paintings are an interpenetration of the elements: land, sea, air, and fire, substance dissolving into light in swirling near-abstract patterns of grey, blue, white, lemon, and crimson. Never before had nature in all its moods been painted with such passionate intensity and understanding, and when Ruskin claimed him as the greatest of all painters he may well have been right.

Despite the Romantic revolution, the classical tradition of British portraiture in the manner of Reynolds survived, and while Scott was writing at Abbotsford, Henry Raeburn was happily painting in Edinburgh his vigorous full-length portraits of its citizens. In London the boy prodigy from Bath, Thomas Lawrence, was the darling of society, in preference to Hoppner and Opie, 'the Cornish wonder', and in 1792, at the age of twenty-three, he succeeded Reynolds as Principal Portrait Painter to George III. Successful as he was agreeable, he painted the royalty and nobility of Europe as well as of England, but success corrupted his genius, and his natural liveliness too often descended into a flattering artificiality. Lawrence's prosperity must have been gall to Benjamin Robert Haydon, whose megalomania was to paint more 'sublime', bigger and better 'history pictures' than Benjamin West, the new President of the Royal Academy and unhappy butt of 'Peter Pindar'. Keats admired his work and wrote him a sonnet, but his humble scenes of contemporary life mean far more than such grandiose work as the *Entry of Christ into Jerusalem*. Poor Haydon shot himself, but his less aspiring contemporaries, David Wilkie, William Etty, and William Mulready were honoured among Academicians. Etty was also a 'history' painter on the scale of canvases a hundred feet square, but with a fine Venetian feeling for colour, which he applied to his popular paintings of the nude. The vogue of the huge 'history' picture was almost over, though revived by David Wilkie in his frescoes for the Palace of Westminster, and Wilkie might almost be said to be the complement of Constable, an observer, not of nature, but of human nature, a recorder of scenes of ordinary life, its humour and pathos, as were William Frith and so many other Victorian painters.

When in 1797 Wordsworth described how a thrush's song transformed Cheapside and Lothbury into river valleys of his native Westmorland, this area of the City was being less lyrically transformed by John Soane, Surveyor of the Bank of England, which in the course of the next thirty years he rebuilt.

Classical dignity and romantic prettiness: (*Left*) Sir John Sinclair, by Sir Henry Raeburn (1756–1823). (*Above*) Lady Blessington, by Sir Thomas Lawrence (1769–1830).

It was a difficult task, for the long low walls had to be proof against possible mob violence, but he relieved a compulsory austerity by converting the acute, yet principal corner of the building into a segmental temple of Vesta, surmounted by a Greek sarcophagus, a good example of his eclecticism. His real originality, however, was in his interiors. The Bank, with windowless walls, had to be lighted from above, its Roman arches and groined vaults pierced by lunettes and domes of glass, but similar overhead lighting is characteristic of all his work, of the Dulwich Picture Gallery, where it is also functional, and of

Arch, dome and medallion: the unmistakable style of Sir John Soane. Bank of England, Dividend Office, 1818–23.

his own house, No. 13 Lincoln's Inn Fields, where it is not. Shelley must have known the house when staying with his cousins, the Groves, in Lincoln's Inn Fields, and remembered it when writing *Adonais*:

> Life, like a dome of many-coloured glass,
> Stains the white radiance of Eternity.

Scholarly and fastidious, Soane selected what he wanted from the whole range of architecture, from Greek to the Picturesque, combining and modifying their elements to form his wholly personal and unmistakable style, epitomized in the house that is now the Soane Museum.

His exact contemporary, John Nash, was also his exact contrary. Unscholarly and unfastidious, he was an enthusiastic extrovert, concerned with exteriors not interiors, and with doing for London's streets what his friend Humphrey Repton was doing for the grounds of country-houses, converting them into the Picturesque. He had already designed picturesque villas and castellated mansions as far afield as Caerhays in Cornwall, but in 1810, at the beginning of the Regency period, his chance came to develop the Crown farmlands north of Marylebone Road. His plan was to make them into a new Regent's Park for fifty villas cunningly concealed from one another, and a summer palace for the Prince. To make the site worthy of this royal residence, never erected, the palatial Cumberland Terrace was built down the east side of the Park, and Park Crescent at the top of Portland Place. This was the northern entry to the great street that was to connect the Regent's Park with the Regent's Carlton House a mile and a half to the south, the royal route running through Langham Place, with a new All Souls Church, where it became the

The Regency Style: Regent's Quadrant and part of Regent Street, London, by John Nash, 1819–20.

new Regent Street, expanding into Oxford Circus, sweeping in a colonnaded quadrant into Piccadilly Circus, and then turning into the more formal approach of Waterloo Place. When the Regent became King in 1820, Carlton House was demolished, and in its place Nash built Carlton Terrace, and began a disastrous conversion of old Buckingham House into Buckingham Palace. He was dismissed when George IV died in 1830, and followed his patron five years later, aged eighty-three.

John Nash: Cumberland Terrace, 1827, built to look like a palace, facing the proposed royal palace in Regent's Park.

The classical Regency style was largely Nash's creation, with stucco façades, pilasters, caryatids, balconies, and comfortably rounded corners, domestic variations on the theme of Soane's Tivoli temple at the Bank. It soon spread to the provinces, notably Brighton and Cheltenham, which retired military men and 'nabobs' like Jos Sedley (it was to Cheltenham that he retreated after the affair at Vauxhall Gardens) were beginning to make fashionable. There, in the 1820s, John Papworth built the Montpellier Pump Room, John Forbes the rival Pittville, and the great rows of houses in Pittville and the Promenade were inspired by Nash's Cumberland Terrace at Regent's Park.

This was by no means the only style, however, for antiquarianism and the Elgin Marbles encouraged the 'revival' of both Greek and Gothic, though nobody at this time, save perhaps A. C. Pugin, understood the principles of Gothic construction. Moreover, architects obligingly offered to build in either

The Greek Revival: Downing College, Cambridge, built by William Wilkins, using the Greek Ionic order, 1806–11.

Greek Doric and frieze: the new Covent Garden Theatre, built by Robert Smirke, 1808–9. In the battle of the styles – Classical versus Gothic – Smirke, like Wilkins, was prepared to support either side.

manner; Nash himself, and even Soane converted Port Eliot into a castellated mansion. In the early 1800s James Wyatt, creator of the Pantheon and Fonthill Abbey, and destroyer of genuine Gothic and Renaissance work in cathedrals, submitted a design for Downing College, Cambridge, but it was young William Wilkins who built it in severely Greek Ionic, following it a few years later with the Gothic gateway and screen at King's. The even younger Robert Smirke was his somewhat pedestrian rival, rebuilding Covent Garden Theatre in Greek Doric, complete with frieze, at the same time designing Eastnor Castle, then in 1823 turning classical again and beginning the British Museum with its interminable rows of giant Ionic pillars. Neoclassical eclecticism had led to architectural eccentricity and confusion. Not only was there a building of stucco Gothic and Greek churches, Tudor and Italian villas, but at Kew was a Turkish mosque in addition to the Chinese pagoda; Sezincote in the Cotswolds was inspired by the Taj Mahal, Nash's Brighton Pavilion by Sezincote, and even at Penzance there was an Egyptian house. The oriental and exotic were not serious competitors, however; the battle of styles had been essentially that between Roman and the now victorious Greek, though it was broadening into one between Classical, whether Greek or Roman, and Gothic, despite the foundation of the Royal Institute of British Architects in 1834.

By the time the young Princess Victoria became Queen in 1837 the Romantic fury had spent itself: the visions of Blake and nightmares of Fuseli, the immensities of John Martin's mountains and violence of John Ward's bulls, the ferocious caricatures of Gillray and grotesqueries of Rowlandson, the grandiosity of West and posturing of Lawrence, and though Turner was still painting snowstorm and fire at sea, his real subject was light. The horrific in literature had reached its climax with Mary Shelley's *Frankenstein* and Maturin's *Melmoth the Wanderer* in 1820, and the early years of the next decade carried off most of the remaining great writers of the Romantic Age: Scott, Coleridge, Hazlitt, Lamb. Wordsworth remained, a conservative Distributor of Stamps in the Lake District, Landseer had arrived, and in music there were the early operas of Balfe. The fury was spent, and the word 'romantic' was assuming a less sensational connotation.

The confusion brought about by Romanticism. Most bizarre of Regency buildings, the Royal Pavilion, Brighton, designed by Nash for the Prince Regent in the Indian style, 1815–21.

13 The Victorians 1837–1901

The Romantic Age had also been one of industrial and social revolution: by 1837 new manufacturing towns were rapidly expanding on the northern coal-fields, a system of trunk roads and canals linked the principal ports, and the railway age was beginning. These things inevitably affected the arts: new functional forms had to be devised for factories and aqueducts, bridges and railway stations, architectural-engineering forms that inspired painters such as Cotman, Turner, and Frith. Then, a new middle class had arisen, factory-owners and merchants who had gained the right to vote and to govern their own municipalities, many of them self-made men of little education and taste, the new patrons of the arts, who demanded civic buildings, houses, pictures, furnishings, and the domestic comforts that machinery now made possible. At the other extreme were the new poor, agricultural and industrial labourers, for whom great barrack-like workhouses were going up, grim contrasts to the new middle-class public schools, or 'colleges', Cheltenham, Marlborough, Radley, Lancing, Epsom, and the rest.

Charles Dickens in 1836.

It was as a protest against these workhouses and the harsh treatment of the poor that Dickens, then only twenty-five, wrote *Oliver Twist* in 1837. *Pickwick Papers* was appearing in monthly parts at the same time, and for the next thirty years, the first half of Victoria's reign, the great sequence of novels poured from his pen in a racy effortless prose of irresistible momentum, from *Nicholas Nickleby* and *Martin Chuzzlewit* to *David Copperfield*, *Great Expectations*, and the unfinished *Mystery of Edwin Drood*. Nowhere outside Shakespeare is there such a gallery of memorable characters, though they are mostly men, eccentrics drawn from the middle and lower ranks of society. There are no tragic heroines, nor even tragic heroes, partly because his readers preferred sentiment and pathos, but as a compound of high spirits, comedy, satire, indignation, compassion, and brilliant story-telling the novels are among the best things in the language.

Dickens was by no means the only great novelist of his age. Thackeray was his contemporary, and in a sense his complement, for his strength lay in depicting the middle and upper classes, from *Vanity Fair* in 1847–8 to *The Newcomes* and *Denis Duval*, left unfinished at his death in 1863. Like Dickens, he was frustrated by the prudery of his age; he belonged spiritually to that of the Regency, and had he written at the beginning instead of in the middle of the century might have been an even finer novelist. The work of the three astonishing

Brontë sisters in a remote Yorkshire parsonage all belongs to half a dozen years in the middle of the century. Charlotte's disquieting *Jane Eyre* appeared in 1847, the same year as Emily's passionate, most un-Victorian and unladylike outburst, *Wuthering Heights*, a novel of genius, but then Emily Brontë was also a poet. She was only thirty when she died in 1848, but George Eliot (Mary Ann Evans) was forty when she published her first full-length novel, *Adam Bede*, in 1859. This was something new, a story of humble rural life, in which tragedy is lightened by descriptive writing and humorous observation of character. *The Mill on the Floss*, partly autobiographical, has similar qualities, but *Middlemarch* of 1871, a much more complex work, is probably her masterpiece. Very different were the six Barchester Novels of Anthony Trollope, written between 1855 and 1867, unpretentious, entertaining stories of life in a cathedral city, which anticipate the technique of the popular television serials of today. Other writers who made the age of Dickens such a memorable period for the novel were Bulwer-Lytton, Disraeli, George Borrow, Mrs Gaskell, Charles Kingsley, Charles Reade, and George Meredith, whose first important novel, *Richard Feverel*, appeared in 1859.

It is odd that Britain has produced no great woman dramatist yet so many great women novelists, and equally odd that during this classic period of the novel the drama remained in such a deplorable condition; the actors were there, the Keans and Kembles, but where were the plays? It is true that in 1837 Macready staged young Robert Browning's tragedy *Strafford*, but Browning preferred the study to the theatre, and developed a dramatic form of poem, *Pippa Passes* for example, and a dramatic monologue that was peculiarly his own, as in *Andrea del Sarto*. Much of his best work was inspired by Italy, where he lived with his wife, Elizabeth Barrett, also a poet, from 1846 to 1861, and *The Ring and the Book* is eleven versions of a Roman murder case, an attempt to find the truth by illumination from every side. Browning broke away from 'poetical' conventions into harsher rhythms, grotesque rhymes, colloquialisms, and often into obscurity, and ever an optimist, was convinced that 'God's in His heaven, all's right with the world'. Tennyson, whose *Poems* of 1842 brought him fame, was less sure, though he did his best to convince himself, the Queen, and Victorian England that 'all is well'. He had a faultless ear and is at his best in lyric and descriptive writing where the words, in Pope's phrase, 'seem an echo to the sense', as in the splendid *Song* in *The Lotos-Eaters*. *In Memoriam*, an elegy on the death of his friend Arthur Hallam, is also a record of his struggle to reconcile the revelations of religion with those of science. It was published in 1850, the year in which he succeeded Wordsworth as Poet Laureate, after which he declined, with occasional recovery, into the 'Lawn Tennyson' of the *Idylls of the King*. It was during these years, 1850–70, that Matthew Arnold published his best work, his nostalgic, elegiac poetry, and the essays in which he contrasted the sweetness and light of ancient Greece with the sick hurry and divided aim of the Philistines and Barbarians of Victorian England, very different from the

The Brontë Sisters: Anne, Charlotte and Emily, painted by their brother Branwell, *c.* 1838.

Pathos on pathos: *The Old Shepherd's Chief Mourner*, by Sir Edwin Landseer (1802–73). A fine painter, Landseer succumbed to Victorian sentimentality. ▼

The Houses of Parliament, rebuilt 1837–67 in the Tudor Gothic style by Charles Barry, knighted in 1852 when the Queen opened the House of Commons. A.W.N. Pugin designed all the detail.

exuberant confidence of Macaulay's essays and his *History of England*, published during the 1850s.

It was an age of historians, particularly historians of England, though Thomas Carlyle's first history was his *French Revolution* of 1837. One of the most influential writers of the century, in spite of, or because of, his eccentric Teutonic style, Carlyle glorified the great man, the hero, and like one of his heroes, Shakespeare, made history live. *Heroes and Hero-Worship* appeared in 1841 and *Past and Present* – significant title – in 1843. The eminent Victorians were looking back from the mess and misery of their industrial age: Arnold to Greece, Carlyle and Ruskin to the Middle Ages, as the two schools of architecture, Greek and Gothic, were also looking back. In the same year, 1843, came the first volume of *Modern Painters*, in which young John Ruskin, sickened by Early Victorian sentimentalism and the declension of an artist like Landseer from a painter of noble landscape into one of the pathetic fallacy of stags at bay and canine dignity and impudence, propounded his doctrine that painting is valuable only as a vehicle of thought. He underrated Constable, overrated Clarkson Stanfield, and worshipped Turner, whose late paintings were beyond the understanding of the new patrons. It was the year in which

Peel's government, conscious of the 'elevating influence of the fine arts' in this decade of the 'Hungry Forties' and threatened revolution, organized a fresco competition in Westminster Hall under the presidency of the Prince Consort, the scenes to be from British history or the works of the major British poets. Among the prize-winners was the young G. F. Watts.

The real occasion for the competition was to select painters to decorate the walls of the new Houses of Parliament. Old Westminster Palace had been destroyed by fire in 1834, and in 1837 rebuilding had begun. The architect was Charles Barry, and the style what he called 'late medieval and Tudor', Gothic being considered the true national style, and Tudor that of the century of England's greatest glory. Barry had built the Regency Gothic St Peter's Church in Brighton, but his later work had been in the manner of the Italian Renaissance, as at the Travellers' and neighbouring Reform Club in Pall Mall, and the new Houses of Parliament were a compromise in their decoration; classical in their symmetry and construction, but Gothic in appearance. This was largely the work of A. W. N. Pugin, a recent convert to Catholicism, who maintained that Gothic was essentially the style of the Roman Catholic Church, and in 1836, seven years before Carlyle's *Past and Present*, published

From Pugin's *Contrasts*, 1841, showing the transformation of a medieval town into an industrial city. Instead of Gothic stone and steeples, cast iron, mill chimneys and 'classical' gas works. The prison in the foreground is Robert Owen's Panopticon.

Contrasts, an illustrated and satirical 'Parallel between the noble edifices of the Middle Ages and corresponding buildings of the present day, shewing the decline of taste.' He followed this in 1841 with *The True Principles of Pointed or Christian Architecture*, these being that there should be no features in a building which are not necessary for 'convenience, construction or propriety', and that ornament should be confined to the essential structure. Unlike the earlier dabblers whose Gothic was merely a veneer, Pugin really understood its structural principles, and put his exemplary precepts into practice at St Chad's in Birmingham and his own Church of St Augustine at Ramsgate, both with stained glass by the Birmingham firm of the Catholic Hardman family.

Pugin had joined the Roman Catholic Church largely because of his devotion to Gothic architecture, ten years before John Henry Newman followed him for very different reasons. In 1833 the Oxford Movement, an attempt to revive the High Church ideals of the early seventeenth century, began with John Keble's celebrated sermon on 'National Apostasy', and in the 1830s there followed a series of *Tracts for the Times*, many of them by Newman, who by 1845 found his position as an Anglican untenable, and was received into the Roman Catholic Church. It was ironical that a main object of the Oxford Movement had been to prevent such apostasy after the passing of the Roman Catholic Emancipation Act, and after being attacked by Charles Kingsley, Newman wrote his defence in his spiritual autobiography *Apologia pro Vita Sua*, one of the classics of Victorian prose. It was also ironical that not Oxford but Cambridge, through the Camden Society founded in 1839, led the way in promoting the study of ecclesiastical architecture.

By the 1840s Gothic was well on its way to winning the battle of the styles, though the Classical was not yet defeated. For civil purposes, it was argued by those who opposed the neo-Tudor Houses of Parliament, the Greek, Roman, and Italian styles were the most appropriate, and in the early years of Victoria's reign a number of notable classical buildings were completed or begun. Thomas Hamilton's Parthenon-inspired High School at Edinburgh was followed by Harvey Elmes's St George's Hall, Liverpool, where the order was Corinthian, not Doric, and the inspiration apparently the Roman Baths of Caracalla. It was finished by Charles Cockerell, architect of the Ashmolean Museum and Taylor Institution at Oxford, an essay in Ionic. Philip Hardwick's Greek Doric propylaeum at Euston Station celebrated Victoria's accession and, less appropriately perhaps, the beginning of the railway age, and in 1838 the National Gallery of the versatile William Wilkins was opened.

This was the year in which a committee was belatedly formed to organize a competition for a Nelson memorial in front of the new Gallery. It was won by William Railton, a Gothic architect whose design was a Corinthian column, the base of which was to have bas-reliefs of Nelson's victories, and recumbent

St George's Hall, Liverpool: a monumental Classical building celebrating Queen Victoria's accession. The architect, Harvey Elmes, was only thirty-three when he died.

The Nelson Memorial, Trafalgar Square, London: the winning design, by William Railton. Edward Baily's statue of Nelson hauled to the top of the column, November 1843.

lions at the corners. Something was felt to be lacking, and Edward Baily, winner of the second prize, was invited to make a statue of Nelson to crown the column. Trafalgar Square was levelled and terraced in front of the Gallery, and in 1843 the statue was hauled to the top of the column. The bas-reliefs were completed a few years later, but it was 1867 before Landseer's bronze lions took up their position.

Sculpture had not been forgotten by the Committee responsible for the decoration of the Houses of Parliament, and another competition was held in Westminster Hall. Samuel Joseph, leader of the movement from romantic allegory to realism, and sculptor of the brilliantly posed Wilberforce statue in the Abbey, was not among those commended, nor was Baily, Flaxman's pupil, who wavered between his master's Grecian idealism and the new realism, but J.H. Foley was selected to design a marble statue of John Hampden for St Stephen's Hall. He was then a young man, and twenty years later was to design the bronze figure of the Prince for the Albert Memorial. To John Gibson, a

(*Left*) Alfred Tennyson, Poet Laureate. Bust by Thomas Woolner, 1857.
(*Right*) William Wilberforce, anti-slavery crusader. Memorial by Samuel Joseph, 1838.

much older man, resident mainly in Rome, was assigned a statue of the Queen seated between Justice and Mercy, a dignified group of neoclassical Victorian ladies in a medieval niche. Thomas Woolner entered a romantic *Death of Boadicea* for the competition, but a spell of digging for gold in Australia encouraged a more realistic approach, and he turned to portrait busts of his great contemporaries, among them the new Poet Laureate.

Woolner was one of those associated with the revolution in the arts in 1848, the momentous year of political revolution in Europe, from which Britain was saved by Peel's financial reforms. It was in this year that three very young artists were drawn together: the earnest Holman Hunt, John Everett Millais, a precocious painter, and Dante Gabriel Rossetti, a poet who, like Hunt, had a passion for the poetry of Keats. Revolted by the drab colour, 'monkeyana' of Landseer, and sentimental anecdotal painting of the day, they formed themselves into a 'Brotherhood' whose aim was 'truth to nature', the doctrine that Ruskin was preaching in *Modern Painters*, and a return to the simplicity and

The Pre-Raphaelite Brotherhood. *The Girlhood of Mary Virgin,* signed 'Dante Gabriele Rossetti. P.R.B. 1849.' Rossetti's mother sat for St Anne, his sister Christina, the poet, for the Virgin.

sincerity of Italian painting before Raphael – hence the nickname, which they adopted, of the Pre-Raphaelite Brotherhood. In 1849 Rossetti exhibited his first picture, *The Girlhood of Mary Virgin,* a portrait of his sister Christina, the whole painted with scrupulous fidelity under the direction of Hunt, whose *Rienzi* was shown at the Royal Academy, as was the *Lorenzo and Isabella* of Millais. To get the desirable brown – really accumulated grime – of the 'Old Masters' it was customary to paint on a dark canvas, but the young revolutionaries painted on a white ground, so that their colours shone with a quite new brilliance. However, the pictures attracted little attention, but in the following year, when Hunt and Rossetti had visited Belgium and called the work of Rubens and Rembrandt 'filthy slush', the storm broke. The attack was directed mainly at Millais's *Christ in the House of His Parents*; it was called 'a pictorial blasphemy', and according to Dickens in *Household Words,* the boy Christ was a guttersnipe, and his mother looked little better than an ugly prostitute. Their reception in 1851 was no better, but help was at hand; Ruskin defended them in *The Times,* and in his new volume of *Modern Painters* wrote: 'Their works are, in finish of drawing and splendour of colour, the best work in the Royal Academy . . . they may become the foundation of a more earnest and able school of art than we have seen for centuries.'

By 1852, when Millais exhibited *Ophelia* and Hunt *The Hireling Shepherd,* the battle was won and the public prepared to accept the bright colours, lack of chiaroscuro, and deliberate angularities of the new style. Other painters were affected, notably Ford Madox Brown, who had always been sympathetic, and

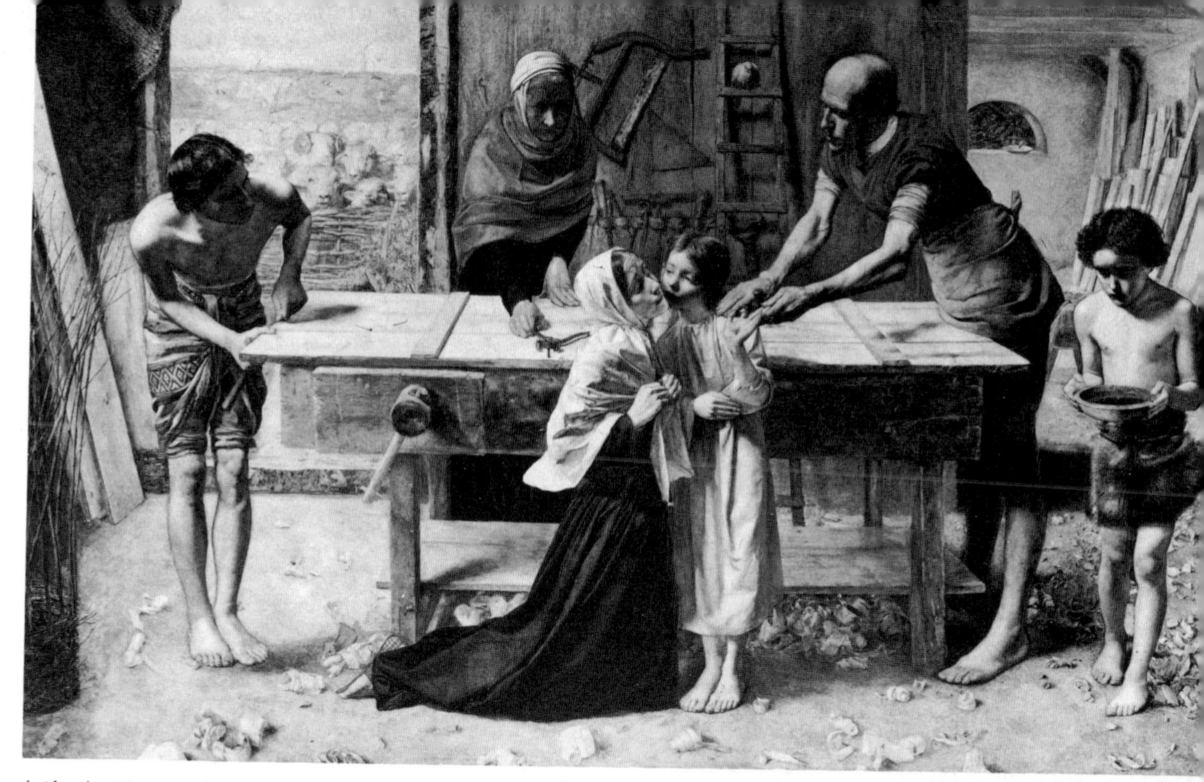

(*Above*) *Christ in the House of His Parents*, by J. E. Millais. The aims of the Pre-Raphaelites were simplicity, sincerity and fidelity, and this picture was bitterly attacked for its realism when shown in the Academy in 1850. (*Below*) 'Truth to nature.' *The Hireling Shepherd*, by Holman Hunt, 1851.

Victorian Gothic: All Saints, Margaret Street, London, *c.* 1851, by William Butterfield.

painted *Work*, illustrating their concern with social reform, and even William Dyce, an established Academician, was affected by Hunt. The 1850s were the heyday of Pre-Raphaelitism, but the Brotherhood was breaking up: Rossetti became more interested in medievalism, water-colours, and poetry, while Millais gradually declined into the successful sentimentalism of such pictures as *Bubbles*, later used to advertise a brand of soap. The serious and dedicated Hunt alone remained to pursue their original aims, painting *The Scapegoat* on the shore of the Dead Sea, and *The Light of the World*, of which Ruskin so unhumorously wrote: 'Unless it had been accompanied with perfectly good nettle painting, and ivy painting, and jewel painting, I should never have praised it.' Compared with the Impressionist Movement in France, Pre-Raphaelitism, with its photographic accuracy and bright pernickety detail, was a provincial affair; but then, Victorian England was provincial, satisfied with its success as the greatest power in the world.

At least Pre-Raphaelitism meant a liberation of colour, and the five middle years of the century, when the Brotherhood was struggling for recognition, were among the most productive in the history of Victorian art. They saw the publication of the first volumes of Macaulay's *History*, of *Dombey and Son* and *David Copperfield*, of Thackeray's historical novel, *Henry Esmond*, and the largely autobiographical *Lavengro* of George Borrow. In poetry there was *In Memoriam* and the first *Poems* of George Meredith, among them the long sweeping lines of *Love in the Valley*. Then in 1850 appeared the four numbers of the Pre-Raphaelite periodical, *The Germ*. Many of Rossetti's early poems are to be found here, including *The Blessed Damozel*, the verse equivalent of his painting of the same year, *The Annunciation*. There were also poems by his sister Christina and Coventry Patmore, and reviews of two volumes of poetry, *The Strayed Reveller* by Matthew Arnold and *The Bothie of Tober-na-vuolich* of Arthur Hugh Clough, whom Arnold was soon to mourn in his great elegy, *Thyrsis*.

In 1849 Ruskin published his *Seven Lamps of Architecture* in praise of Gothic, not only for its beauty but also as the expression of an age of faith. He was thinking of the period about 1300 – Perpendicular was decadent – and in *The Stones of Venice*, which soon followed, his theme was the coloured Venetian Gothic of this period, and he traced the rise and fall of the Venetian Republic in terms of its development of Gothic and its 'decline' into the Renaissance. It was an elaboration of Pugin's doctrine, though Ruskin had little use for that Catholic architect, who died in 1852 aged only forty, and the Gothic cause was taken up by William Butterfield, a High Church Protestant, whom the Cambridge Camden Society commissioned to build All Saints, Margaret Street, Marylebone: dark red brick with blue-black bands and a striped spire, the interior grimly Early English, and walls completely covered with brightly coloured patterns. Not exactly Gothic, but certainly Butterfield, which, in justice, is what he intended.

By 1850, championed by Ruskin, Pugin, Butterfield, and Gilbert Scott, Gothic had triumphed, but the building that housed the Great Exhibition of 1851 was Gothic of a very different kind, a huge greenhouse designed by

The Crystal Palace, 1851, by Joseph Paxton. Some of the structural principles were Gothic, but the materials different: cast-iron pillars and ribs to support the glass walls and vault.

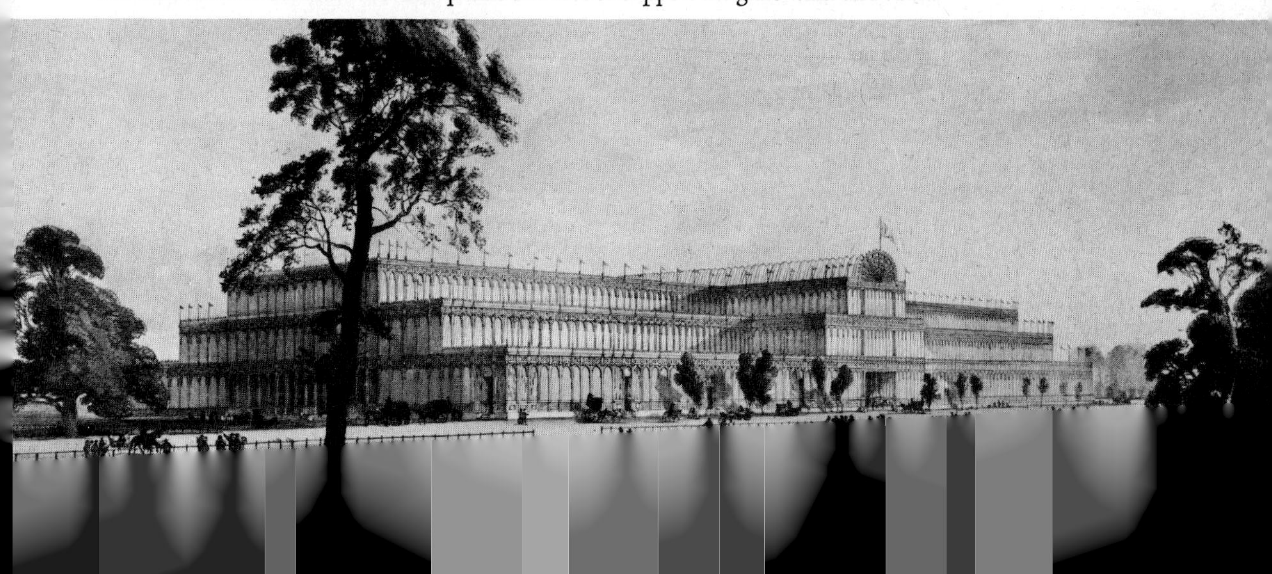

Classical: the Wellington Memorial in St Paul's Cathedral, begun 1856, by Alfred Stevens.

Joseph Paxton, a framework of cast-iron pillars and girders, walled and roofed with glass. Erected in nine months, with a floor space, including galleries, of twenty-three acres, it was a functional forward-looking building of machine-made prefabricated materials. The Exhibition was primarily to display the utilitarian products of British industry, and Tennyson wrote an ode about the 'Shapes and hues of Art divine, All of beauty, all of use', but the fine arts, the useless ones, were not forgotten. There were few pictures, it is true, but the Crystal Palace, as *Punch* called it, was ideal for the exhibition of sculpture, the bigger the better: there were equestrian statues of the Queen and Prince Consort, and Marochetti's *Cœur-de-Lion*, later cast in bronze and erected in front of the House of Lords. The London Corporation was inspired to buy a number of statues for the Egyptian Hall of the Mansion House, the most admired being Foley's *Caractacus*, a favourite Victorian subject.

When the Queen paid her last visit to the Exhibition, she wrote: 'An organ, accompanied by a fine and powerful wind instrument called the sommerophone, was being played, and it nearly upset me.' And there was music in the Crystal Palace when it was re-erected in 1852 at Sydenham, where it became another Vauxhall Gardens. There were organ recitals as well as fireworks, and August Manns conducted a series of Saturday Concerts throughout the second half of the century, doing great service by introducing the public to the classics of the orchestra, as well as to contemporary work of British composers.

Gothic: the Albert Memorial in Kensington Gardens, begun 1864, by Gilbert Scott.

For these concerts George Grove wrote annotated programmes which have themselves become classics, particularly those on the symphonies of Beethoven. It must always be remembered that in the days before gramophone and radio, orchestral music could rarely be heard, just as before photography and colour reproduction a man could have little idea of works of visual art without seeing the originals. Hence the great importance of public concerts and public galleries, most of them dating from the Victorian Age.

Wordsworth died in 1850, Turner in 1851, Wellington in 1852, and a competition was held for a memorial to the Duke in St Paul's. The work was offered to Alfred Stevens, but twenty years passed before its erection, and only in 1912 was his mounted figure of the Duke placed on top. Stevens belonged spiritually to the Italian High Renaissance, and his design was a classical architectural one, worthy of its setting. He was the greatest artist of his age, yet little of his work remains besides the Wellington Memorial, his drawings, and the splendid portrait of Mrs Collmann.

Even in the age of Ruskin a Gothic memorial would scarcely have been acceptable in Wren's cathedral, but ten years later a memorial in Kensington Gardens was another matter. The occasion was the death of the Prince Consort in 1861, the site as close as possible to that of the Great Exhibition for which he had been primarily responsible, the design by Gilbert Scott, the famous Gothic architect and relentless restorer of cathedrals, the sum at his disposal £120,000.

British sculptors, from Nicholas Stone to John Bushnell, on the frieze surrounding the Albert Memorial: the work of H. H. Armstead and J. B. Philip.

Scott's aim was to erect 'a kind of ciborium', an ancient shrine, 'to protect a statue of the Prince . . . These shrines were models of imaginary buildings, and my idea was to realise one of these imaginary structures with its precious metals, its inlaying, its enamels, etc.' One can sympathize with the idea, but the product, like most Victorian Gothic, recalls the ornate clutter of a Victorian drawing-room. Under the canopy supported by granite shafts sits the bronze figure of the Prince by Foley, who was also responsible for the group of Asia at one of the corners, the surrounding frieze of the world's great men, among whom are a surprising number of Victorians, being by Henry Armstead and John Philip. Oddly enough, the Albert Hall which was being built at the same time on the other side of the road was classical in inspiration and simplicity, a huge cylindrical building with a terracotta frieze of the Triumph of the Arts, and a glass and iron dome. But then, the designer was a Royal Engineer, Captain Fowke. Another building of the same decade was Scott's St Pancras, an ingenious combination of Venetian, French, and Flemish Gothic, which legend says was originally the design for Government Offices in Whitehall, until the old-fashioned Palmerston forced Scott to substitute the Italian style. Yet another building of the 1860s was Butterfield's polychromatic Keble College Chapel, Oxford, an all-over pattern of coloured bricks and tiles without, of mosaics within. The Goths were in the ascendant, and everywhere, particularly in the new towns of the north, their buildings, soon to be encrusted with grime, were going up, such as the Venetian Gothic Exchange and Florentine Gothic Town Hall at Bradford, while older towns were beginning to resemble the section of an onion: a medieval church (restored) at the core, surrounded by a layer of Georgian houses and shops, and another of Victorian Gothic, to which was soon to be added a fanciful rind by twentieth-century speculative builders. The classical style was not entirely defeated, however, and for secular buildings such as banks and warehouses the Italian Renaissance might be preferred, its horizontal lines giving a greater feeling of stability and material success than the idealizing verticals of Gothic. Thus, for Halifax and Leeds Charles Barry and Cuthbert Brodrick built classical Town Halls, but Alfred Waterhouse's Manchester Town Hall was exceedingly Gothic, as were the London Law Courts of G. E. Street and, of course, the spiky Truro Cathedral of J. L. Pearson. In spite of the Crystal Palace, there was still no sign of a new style.

Municipal Gothic: Manchester Town Hall, begun 1869, by Alfred Waterhouse.

This was partly owing to the influence of William Morris. In 1859, when only twenty-five, he got Philip Webb to build him the Red House at Bexley Heath in the traditional Kentish style and, sickened by the ugliness of Victorian machine-made products, founded the firm of Morris, Marshall, Faulkner and Company for the making of furniture, wallpaper, tapestry, and stained glass, the last designed largely by his friend Edward Burne-Jones. Morris wished to restore the hand-made crafts of the Middle Ages which he had already idealized in his first volume of poems, *The Defence of Guenevere*. Ten years later in *The Earthly Paradise* he escaped in imagination into the century of Chaucer:

> Forget six counties overhung with smoke,
> Forget the snorting steam and piston stroke,
> Forget the spreading of the hideous town;
> Think rather of the pack-horse on the down,
> And dream of London, small, and white, and clean,

and again ten years later into a medieval twentieth century, in the moving prose fantasy of *News from Nowhere*. Romantic interest in the Middle Ages had become Victorian nostalgia, the desire, conscious or unconscious, of poets, painters, and architects to return to a pre-industrial society. It was a mistake; there could be no going back, and the only course was to try to influence the machine age and find fresh inspiration in it. For example, concrete reinforced with steel could have inspired a new architecture.

The Red House, Bexley Heath, Kent, built by Philip Webb for William Morris in the traditional farmhouse style, 1859–60. Important as the first of its kind.

Sir Charles Hallé (1819–95), German-born Mancunian, pianist, conductor and founder of the Hallé Orchestra in Manchester.

British music was sorely in need of fresh inspiration, for though there were opportunities for most people to hear great music in the age of Dickens, it was not that of contemporary native composers. There were the Three Choirs Festivals in the West Country, long-established festivals at Birmingham and Norwich, a Leeds Festival was established in 1858, and the Handel Festival in the Crystal Palace began in 1857. Most of these were choral, but there were also some good orchestras: the Old Philharmonic Society of 1813 was goaded to fresh effort by the formation of the New Philharmonic in 1851 (Exhibition year, which had a stimulating effect), in 1857 Charles Hallé founded his famous orchestra in Manchester, and in 1858 the Popular Monday Concerts in St James's Hall supplemented the Saturday Concerts of Manns in the Crystal Palace. Many of the world's greatest performers appeared at these 'Monday Pops', the great violinist Joseph Joachim being a frequent visitor, and there was a constant stream of foreign composers and conductors, from Mendelssohn and Berlioz to Wagner and Verdi. Yet the most distinguished British composer of the first half of Victoria's reign was Sterndale Bennett, Professor of Music at Cambridge, who devoted much of his time to teaching, and is perhaps now remembered as the composer of the oratorio *The Woman of Samaria.* It is a measure of the musical poverty of the age that its best-known compositions are the operas, *The Bohemian Girl* and *Maritana*, the one by Michael Balfe the other by Vincent Wallace, both Irishmen, and *The Lily of Killarney* by Julius Benedict, a German-born conductor. There were also the songs of Edward Loder, and, best known of all, 'Annie Laurie', the 'Tipperary' of the Crimean War. The one original British contribution was Sarah Glover's invention of the Tonic Sol-fa method of teaching sight-singing.

At this time, the late 1860s, young Thomas Hardy was singing glees in the office of Arthur Blomfield, the Gothic architect, and in 1870, aged thirty, was sent to St Juliot in Cornwall to make drawings for the restoration of its church. There he met his future wife, and the result was the lyric, *When I set out for Lyonnesse*, and *A Pair of Blue Eyes*, first of the great Wessex Novels. This, the central year of Victoria's reign, was a watershed in many other ways: Germany and Italy emerged as united nations; Darwin was writing his *Descent of Man*, and the champion of his evolutionary theory, T.H. Huxley, coining the word 'agnostic'; it was the year of the death of the early Victorians, Dickens and Balfe, soon to be followed by Landseer and Bennett; the year of the Education Act, which in another decade would mean a new generation of readers; of the photographic snapshot, which could reproduce nature with more than Pre-Raphaelite fidelity. It was the beginning of the Late Victorian Age, greeted by Samuel Butler with *Erewhon*, a satirical exposure of contemporary humbug, and at the same time a vision of a rational society.

In 1870 Rossetti published his *Poems*, including the sonnet sequence of *The House of Life*, very different from the Pre-Raphaelite simplicity of *The Blessed Damozel*, the claustral dream-like poetry of a man in love with Love, with an ideal Beauty at once spiritual and voluptuous:

> Such thrilling pallor of cheek as doth enthral
> The heart; a mouth whose passionate forms imply
> All music and all silence held thereby;
> Deep golden locks, her sovereign coronal;
> A round reared neck, meet column of Love's shrine
> To cling to when the heart takes sanctuary.

It is the idealized woman of his paintings, who with variations is to be found in the work of William Morris (for she was his wife), the stained-glass windows of Burne-Jones, even in the paintings of Whistler, and ultimately in the drawings of Aubrey Beardsley, where, however, the pinched cruel features are those of Swinburne's Dolores, 'Our Lady of Pain':

> Cold eyelids that hide like a jewel
>   Hard eyes that grow soft for an hour;
> The heavy white limbs, and the cruel
>   Red mouth like a venomous flower.

Poems and Ballads, of which *Dolores* was one, appeared in 1866, and the heady rhythms and alliteration of this pagan poetry intoxicated the young Victorians. Swinburne was to write for another forty years, but he rarely recaptured the magic of his early passion, and little remained but the whirling words, lilies and languors, roses and raptures, of his verse, and the superlatives of his prose eulogies of his spiritual ancestor Marlowe and the other Elizabethans.

Incipit secunda pars

NOGHT FER FRO THILKE PALAYS HONURABLE
Theras this markys shoop his mariage,
Ther stood a throop, of site delitable,
In which that povre folk of that village
Hadden hir beestes and hir herbergage,
And of hire labour tooke hir sustenance,
After that the erthe yaf hem habundance.

AMONGES thise povre folk ther dwelte a man
Which that was holden povrest of hem alle;
But hye God som tyme senden kan
His grace into a litel oxes stalle:
Janicula men of that throop hym calle.
A doghter hadde he, fair ynogh to sighte,
And Grisildis this yonge mayden highte.

But for to speke of vertuous beautee,
Thanne was she oon the faireste under sonne;
For povreliche yfostred up was she,
No likerous lust was thurgh hire herte yronne;
Wel ofter of the welle than of the tonne
She drank, and for she wolde vertu plese,
She knew wel labour, but noon ydel ese.

But thogh this mayde tendre were of age,
Yet in the brest of hire virginitee
Ther was enclosed rype and sad corage,
And in greet reverence and charitee
Hir olde povre fader fostred shee;
A fewe sheep, spynnynge, on feeld she kepte,
She wolde noght been ydel til she slepte.

And whan she homward cam, she wolde brynge
Wortes, or other herbes, tymes ofte,

(*Right*) *The Kelmscott Chaucer*. In 1871 William Morris rented Kelmscott Manor on the upper Thames. Twenty years later he set up a printing-press there, and the *Chaucer* appeared in the year of his death, 1896. This is the beginning of the second part of the Clerk of Oxford's Tale, the woodcut by Burne-Jones.

(*Below*) The William Morris Room in the Victoria and Albert Museum, London.

G.F. Watts was little influenced by Pre-Raphaelitism, either in its first or later 'aesthetic' phase, though he had the high seriousness of its original aims. He painted some fine portraits, but after his frescoes, *St George and the Dragon*, in the House of Lords he turned mainly to allegories such as the famous *Hope*, pictures intended 'to suggest great thoughts' and 'appeal to the imagination'. This can scarcely have been the aim of Frederick (Lord) Leighton, Laurence Alma-Tadema, and Albert Moore, whose scantily draped Classical-Victorian ladies left so little to the imagination, as did the 'new realism' of contemporary sculptors, of Harry Bates and Onslow Ford, of Leighton himself, whose *Sluggard* was hailed as another Greek masterpiece, and even Watts contributed a seductive bust of *Clytie*.

The most original and brilliant painter of the Late Victorian Age was the American-born, Paris-trained James McNeill Whistler, who settled in Chelsea near Rossetti in 1863. Much influenced by Japanese colour-prints and their restricted range of colour, and contemptuous of Victorian anecdote, illustration, and allegory, he insisted that painting was essentially an aesthetically satisfying arrangement of colour and form, like music, a harmony in a certain key, and called the portrait of his mother *Arrangement in Grey and Black*, his *Little White Girl* of 1870 *Symphony in White, No. II.* Criticism was unfavourable, but it was his series of 'Nocturnes', paintings of the Thames 'when the evening mist clothes the riverside with poetry', that brought the bitterest attacks, notably from Ruskin of all men, defender of Turner's near-abstractions, who called him 'a coxcomb . . . flinging a pot of paint in the public's face'. Whistler was born before his time; recognized abroad, but in England by only a few percipient

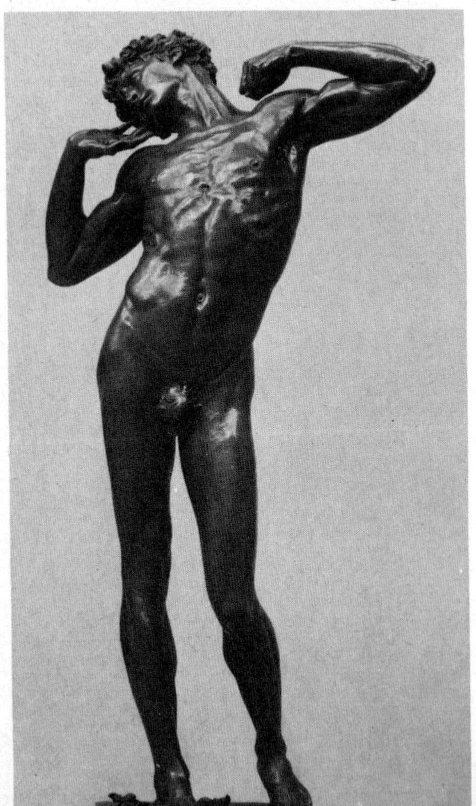

(*Left*) *The Sluggard* by Lord Leighton.

(*Below*) *Clytie* by G.F. Watts.

Nocturne, Blue and Gold: Old Battersea Bridge, by J. A. M. Whistler, *c.* 1865. This was one of the pictures which, when exhibited in 1877, led to Whistler's libel action against Ruskin.

ones, he would have been honoured as leader of a new movement had he been born in the year of his quarrel with Ruskin.

That was in 1878, the year of publication of *Daisy Miller* by his compatriot Henry James. Fascinated by the culture and society of the Old World, James moved to Europe in 1875, when only thirty-two, and finally settled in England. It has been said that there are three Jameses: James I, James II, and James the Old Pretender, and there is some truth in the witticism. The novels of his middle period, beginning with the intensely moving *Daisy Miller* and *Washington Square*, are those by which he is most affectionately remembered, for in his later novels, as in *The Golden Bowl* of 1904, his analysis of motive becomes so minute, his search for the precise phrase so meticulous, his sentences so labyrinthine that the reader is apt to be entangled in the web of words. Yet this minute observation extended the scope, advanced the frontier of the novel.

So did the work of George Meredith, whose *Egoist*, generally considered to be his greatest novel, appeared in 1879. With the wit, but far greater subtlety, of his father-in-law, Peacock, he developed the comic and tragic theme of self-deception, but in prose that became ever more theatrical, a style little to the taste of today. 'We are betrayed by what is false within.' The line comes from *Modern Love*, and it would scarcely be paradoxical to claim this as Meredith's greatest novel, the tragic story of husband, wife, and lover told in eight hundred lines of verse. Certainly Meredith never wrote more greatly than in the last of these fifty sixteen-line 'sonnets':

> Ah, what a dusty answer gets the soul
> When hot for certainties in this our life! –
> In tragic hints here see what evermore
> Moves dark as yonder midnight ocean's force,
> Thundering like ramping hosts of warrior horse,
> To throw that faint thin line upon the shore!

Thomas Hardy in 1893, aged fifty-three.

In his poetry Meredith identified himself with his subject, for all poetry, as distinct from mere verse, is an identification, but as a novelist he was a manipulator. Most novelists and dramatists fall into one or other of these two groups: those who associate themselves with the action, and those who stand outside as observers and controllers, often satirical or didactic writers. Thus Ben Jonson, Congreve, Thackeray, Meredith, and Shaw are manipulators, Shakespeare, Fielding, Dickens, George Eliot, and Hardy are identifiers – Hardy because, even in his prose, he was always a poet. His plots may be clumsily melodramatic, his situations forced, coincidences laughable, but within his range he is unsurpassed. His descriptions of the Wessex countryside are consolatory as Nature herself, and his humble heroes and heroines, Michael Henchard, Tess, and the rest, because of his intense compassion have the dignity and grandeur of Greek tragedy. And half-Greek, half-Shakespearean, is the comic chorus of yokels who comment on the action. *The Return of the Native* was another novel of 1878, and in the next decade came *The Mayor of Casterbridge* and *The Woodlanders*, but after *Tess* in 1891 and *Jude the Obscure* in 1895, Hardy was attacked as an atheist and corrupter of youth, and he abandoned novel-writing for his first love, poetry.

By this time the Education Act had produced its new generation of readers, who demanded shorter novels, romance, and excitement, a demand that was met in the 1880s by Robert Louis Stevenson, beginning with *Treasure Island* and *The New Arabian Nights*, and by Conan Doyle, who in 1887 introduced the public to Sherlock Holmes in *A Study in Scarlet*.

Another production of 1887, Jubilee Year, celebrating Victoria's fifty years as Queen, was *Ruddigore*. The collaboration of Arthur Sullivan with W.S. Gilbert had begun in 1875 with a short piece, *Trial by Jury*, followed by the full-length *Sorcerer* and *H.M.S. Pinafore*, and in almost every year of the 1880s

Gilbert and Sullivan: *The Pirates of Penzance*, produced at the Savoy Theatre, London, 1880. *Patience, or Bunthorne's Bride*, the original production of 1881. Guardsmen turn aesthetes: a skit on the aestheticism of the period.

a new opera was triumphantly produced, from *The Pirates of Penzance* to *The Gondoliers*. Sullivan had made his name in 1862 at the age of twenty, when Manns performed his incidental music for *The Tempest* at the Crystal Palace, and he followed this success with a ballet, the cantata *Kenilworth* and the *Irish Symphony*. Yet, although a serious musician, his real talent was for comedy, for light memorable tunes and amusing rhythms to match Gilbert's racy lyrics, and the operas were immensely popular with the British public, for the most part as incapable of appreciating music without words as of appreciating pictures that did not tell a story. At least they were first-rate entertainment, and did something to educate musical taste; and they were unmistakably English, as provocatively English as *Punch*, in this heyday of jingoism and Empire. The point is of importance, for when in 1882 the Prince of Wales inaugurated the Royal College of Music, he asked, 'Why is it that England has no music recognized as national?' There was a national music, though scarcely recognized at the time: that of the golden age of the sixteenth and seventeenth centuries, from Tallis and Byrd to Dowland and Gibbons, but it had ended with Purcell two centuries before, since when there had been no British music of any importance. Yet in 1882 there were signs of a revival. In 1880 the City of London had founded the Guildhall School of Music, the Royal College opened in 1883 under the directorship of Grove, who had recently published the first volumes of his *Dictionary of Music*, and on his staff as Professor of Composition was Hubert Parry. Though not a greatly inspired composer, Parry revived the Elizabethan art of writing music to fit the words of great English poetry, as in Shelley's *Prometheus Unbound*, Milton's *Blest Pair of Sirens* and, best known of all, Blake's *Jerusalem*. In 1887 Charles Stanford, a thirty-five-year-old Irishman, was appointed Professor of Music at Cambridge, where he had previously been conductor of the Cambridge University Musical Society. The service known as 'Stanford in B flat' had already revolutionized Anglican Church music, and his secular music was equally influential. The interest in folk-music was at this time gathering momentum, and its tunes he sometimes incorporated in his compositions, the *Londonderry Air*, for example, in his first *Irish Rhapsody*, and his *Songs of Old Ireland* are classics of their kind. In the 1880s, therefore, can be traced the beginning of a revived national music, though Stanford's contribution was more Irish than English, and Irish too was the most pungent musical criticism of the decade, that of Bernard Shaw.

It is remarkable how often the Irish have rescued British art, particularly drama, from mediocrity. When the Irish playwright George Farquhar died in 1707, the drama plunged into a dark age from which it was delivered in the decade of the 1770s by Irish Goldsmith and Sheridan before subsiding into another century of gloom. It is true that nearly all the major poets of that century tried to revive the poetic drama, but fine poetry does not make a play and, with the exception of Beddoes, their work bears no more resemblance to the Elizabethans' than Butterfield's Gothic to the real thing, and the dramatic revival began in 1892 with the first plays of two Irishmen born in the same year, 1856, Shaw and Oscar Wilde. Shaw was a devotee of Ibsen and a Socialist, a playwright with a purpose, and in his first plays, *Widowers' Houses* and *Mrs Warren's Profession*, accused society, his audience, of responsibility for the evils of slums and prostitution. *Candida* was another attack on humbug, and these plays, unsentimental, anti-romantic, spiced with wit and paradox, were as bracing as fresh air in the stuffy room of Victorian hypocrisy. Shaw is the arch-manipulator, his characters rarely more than puppets, yet he brought reality, not the same thing as realism, back to the theatre, and if, lacking in compassion and poetry, he did not make men feel, at least he made them think. Wilde, on the other hand, as a dramatist was a mere entertainer: his first play, *Lady Windermere's Fan*, a fashionable melodrama adorned with epigrams, his last, *The Importance of Being Earnest*, the most brilliantly amusing farce in the language. That year, 1895, society attacked him for homosexual practices, and five years later he was dead. It was a theme for Shaw.

Shaw had no sympathy with the aesthetic excesses of Wilde, parodied by Gilbert in *Patience*. This aesthetic movement of the 1890s was the legacy of Rossetti and his peculiar brand of Pre-Raphaelitism, a withdrawal from life into a dream-world of art, a cult that affected the Oxford critic Walter Pater, Whistler, Swinburne, and the accomplished young artist Aubrey Beardsley, whose sinister and erotic drawings illustrated Wilde's French play *Salomé*, and

'Hard eyes . . . and the cruel red mouth.' Aubrey Beardsley illustrates Wilde's *Salomé*. 'The name of Dante Gabriel Rossetti is heard for the first time in the United States of America. Time: 1881. Lecturer: Mr Oscar Wilde.'

the pages of *The Yellow Book*. His thin, sinuous, decorative line is characteristic of Art Nouveau, which in turn derived to some extent from the designs of William Morris and his Arts and Crafts movement founded in the 1860s, not however as art for art's sake, but for life's sake.

Morris also indirectly influenced architecture, particularly domestic architecture, and the Red House built for him by Philip Webb was the forerunner of other modest houses of honest craftsmanship, recalling the simple Tudor style. Norman Shaw was more adventurous, reviving the Queen Anne style, experimenting with Flemish Renaissance and Butterfield stripes, with Scottish baronial at Scotland Yard, and at Bedford Park, Hammmersith, designing the first garden suburb. The work of these men influenced the continental school of Art Nouveau, itself a protest against the machine age and an attempt to create a new style, which as yet, however, was little more than a curvilinear decoration of surface, not structural. Even more influential was C. F. A. Voysey, whose decorative designs and furniture with elongated vertical lines became fashionable in the 1890s, while the cheerful white-stuccoed walls and long window-bands of his houses anticipated the modern idiom. Voysey's houses, however, were free variations of traditional styles, and it was the young Scottish architect Charles Rennie Mackintosh who, opposed to historic revivalism, at the Glasgow School of Art created a style that was both functional and independent of the past. At the end of the century it looked as though Britain was going to be the first country to develop a new architecture.

The 1890s took their toll of the great Victorians – Browning, Tennyson, Ruskin, Morris – and new men with new ideas replaced them. Impressionism was at last beginning to influence British painters, partly through the teaching of Alphonse Legros at the Slade School, partly through the foundation in 1886 of the New English Art Club by a number of young artists with a Paris training. One of these was Wilson Steer, whose early paintings are lively with the broken spectrum colours of the Impressionists. Another early member was Walter Sickert, much influenced by Degas, and fascinated by London music-halls and their audiences, which he painted with a Rembrandtesque richness of chiaroscuro.

A new theme of the 1890s was that of India, celebrated by Rudyard Kipling in the *Jungle Books* and other novels, as well as in the verse of *Barrack Room Ballads*, with their doctrine of the white man's burden and the gulf between East and West, and the vision of the day when all shall work 'for the joy of the working'. A very different vision was that of H. G. Wells, who foresaw the possibilities of science in *The Time Machine*, and the age of space travel in *The War of the Worlds* and *The First Men in the Moon*. In 1896 came A. E. Housman's

Art Nouveau:
Glasgow School of Art,
1896–1909,
by C. R. Mackintosh.

English Impressionism: *The Old Bedford Music Hall*, by Walter Sickert, *c.* 1896.

slim volume of *A Shropshire Lad*, short poems of a classical perfection about the unquietness of man. Housman had no Wordsworthian illusions about Nature, whom he knew to be heartless, as did Hardy, whose first book of verse, *Wessex Poems*, appeared in 1898. As in the novels, his theme is that of man 'slighted and enduring', and in sympathy, the rhythms of his verse are deliberately disturbed, based, as he said, 'on stresses rather than syllables'. Far more daring, however, were the metrical innovations of a Jesuit priest who died in 1889, Gerard Manley Hopkins, as in his sonnet *The Windhover*:

> I caught this morning morning's minion, king-
> dom of daylight's dauphin, dapple-dawn-drawn Falcon, in his riding
> Of the rolling level underneath him steady air, and striding
> High there, how he rung upon the rein of a wimpling wing
> In his ecstasy! . . .

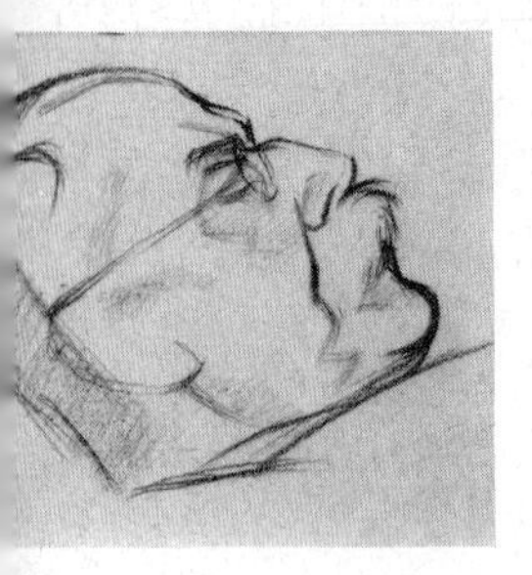

Sir Edward Elgar, 1857–1934.

This 'sprung rhythm', again based on stresses, not syllables, was to be a powerful influence when his poems were published thirty years after his death.

During the 1890s the musical revival begun by Parry and Stanford rose to a climax. A Scottish Orchestra was formed to serve Edinburgh and Glasgow as the Hallé served Manchester and Liverpool. In London the Queen's Hall was opened in 1893, and two years later a series of Promenade Concerts was directed by the young conductor Henry Wood, whose policy it was to introduce new work by promising contemporary composers, such as Ethel Smyth and Edward German. The English Folksong Society was founded; then in 1897, Diamond Jubilee year and that of the opening of the Tate Gallery, two works by Edward Elgar were heard in London. Elgar was then forty, and still little known outside his own West Country, for he had had no academic training, but now London was conquered, and the Victorian Age, which had been introduced by Johann Strauss and the Viennese waltz, and dominated by German musicians, went out triumphantly to the music of the most distinguished English composer since Purcell, to that of the *Enigma Variations* and the oratorio setting of Newman's *Dream of Gerontius*. Yet it was more a salute to the new century than a valediction to the old, the obituary of which was written by Samuel Butler in his satirical novel, *The Way of All Flesh*.

The inaugural concert at the Queen's Hall, 1893. In 1895 the manager Robert Newman engaged Henry Wood to conduct a season of Promenade Concerts.

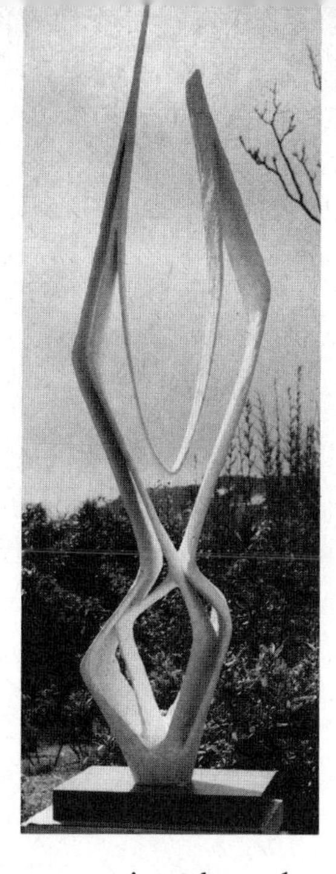

14 *The Twentieth Century*

Fully to appreciate the cultural history of the twentieth century, it must be remembered that technologically the world of 1900 was not so very different from that of 1850, a world of steam, and that electricity, the telephone, gramo-phone, cinema, motor-car, and aeroplane were developed only during the decade before the First World War. In 1900 even H. G. Wells could not foresee the Britain of the 1960s, with its radio and television, computers, nuclear energy, and space travel, the effect of two World Wars, the Russian and Chinese revolutions, and Freud's revelation of man's unconscious mind. Such rapid material progress, extension of knowledge, and political revolution inevitably involved a corresponding revolution in the arts.

Yet there was nothing revolutionary about the arts in Britain during the Edwardian decade of 1901–10. The architecture of Webb, Norman Shaw, Voysey, and Mackintosh had been the most influential in Europe, but still, despite the example of the Crystal Palace fifty years before, there was a failure to adapt new design to new technique and material, to prefabrication, steel, glass, and reinforced concrete, the tensile strength of which allowed cantilevered projections and a plasticity of form hitherto impossible. Architecturally Britain remained a backwater for thirty years, while the new architecture was developed in America by Frank Lloyd Wright, in Germany by Gropius and Mies van der Rohe, in France by Le Corbusier. The Voysey tradition was continued by Edwin Lutyens until called upon to build New Delhi in 1912, while Edwardian taste was reflected in the ornate Neo-Baroque of banks and municipal buildings.

Again, while in France Picasso and Braque were evolving Cubism from the landscapes of Cézanne, the English tradition was maintained in the opulent fashionable portraits of the American-born John Singer Sargent, and those of

the equally accomplished William Orpen. Steer, abandoning his earlier Impressionism, reverted to landscapes in the manner of Constable, while Sickert more gaily found inspiration in the streets of London, and Frank Brangwyn displayed his gift for decorative painting. The most vital painter of the period was Augustus John, another Welshman, who made his name with his early drawings, and in his paintings, brilliant in colour, preferred unconventional types, gipsies and poets, to fashionable society. There was a similar romantic vitality, with signs of greater originality, in the sculptures of the young Jacob Epstein.

Edwardian poetry was dominated by that of the Victorian veteran, Hardy, whose great 'epic-drama' of the Napoleonic Wars, *The Dynasts*, appeared 1904–8. In Shaw's masterpiece of 1903, *Man and Superman*, otherwise Man and Woman, there is no Overworld, as in *The Dynasts*, no Immanent Will

(*Left*)
◀ *A Bloomsbury Family*. The painter Sir William Nicholson, his wife, sister of James Pryde, and their children. The boy on the right is Ben Nicholson, aged twelve. Painted by William Orpen, 1907.

Madame Suggia, an essay in the Grand Style, by Augustus John, *c.* 1923.

'weaving eternal artistries in Circumstance', no Spirit of the Pities, but a Life Force and a brilliantly comic Underworld in which Lucifer persuades his guests to stay by describing the boredom of Heaven, where 'a number of people, mostly English, sit in glory because they think they owe it to their position'. Less concerned with the tragedies and follies of man than the verse of Hardy and prose of Shaw was the somewhat frigid, scholarly poetry of Robert Bridges, the gentle nature poetry of Edward Thomas, the haunting, moonlit poetry of Walter de la Mare, the Irish faery poetry of W. B. Yeats, and John Masefield's more realistic poetry of earth and sea.

Masefield was a sailor, and so was Joseph Conrad, a naturalized Pole, many of whose finest novels, beginning with *Lord Jim*, appeared in this decade: romances told with consummate skill and a profound understanding of man, his courage and cowardice, goodness and evil. There was lighter entertainment in the *Father Brown* stories and paradoxical essays of G.K. Chesterton, and in the humorous novels of Wells, *Kipps* and *The History of Mr Polly*, stories of lower-middle-class life, as were the best novels of Arnold Bennett, whose *Old Wives' Tale*, its scene set in the pottery towns of his native Staffordshire, recalls the realism of Flaubert. There is realism again in John Galsworthy's portrayal of upper-middle-class Edwardian society, with its craving for solidity and security, its possessive instinct, personified by Soames Forsyte in *The Forsyte Saga*. E.M. Forster was concerned with the more sensitive, liberal members of the same class, and the barriers that divide man from man, whether of different nationality, as in his first novel, *Where Angels Fear to Tread* (1905) and his last, *A Passage to India* (1924), or of different social grades, as in *A Room with a View* and *Howards End*. 'Only connect', and the world will be a better and happier place. E.M. Forster, with his gentle irony, humanism, and compassion, is among the great English novelists, and the Edwardian scene closed with the publication of his short stories, *The Celestial Omnibus* – and Max Beerbohm's sophisticated, inimitable burlesque, *Zuleika Dobson*.

Characteristically Edwardian were the lavishly upholstered productions of Shakespeare by Max's half-brother, Beerbohm Tree, but in 1904 J.E. Vedrenne and Granville-Barker set a new standard of production and acting at the Court Theatre, where they presented the plays of Shaw, of Barker himself, notably *Waste*, and of Galsworthy, somewhat heavy-handed treatments of social problems. The success of this enterprise encouraged the formation of the Irish National Theatre, which produced the plays of Yeats and those of J.M. Synge, the tragic *Riders to the Sea* and comic *Playboy of the Western World*, plays that were a revolt against the intellectual drama of Shaw, and written in the poetical prose of Irish peasants. English literature owed much to Ireland at this time: Wilde, Shaw, whose Irish play, *John Bull's Other Island*, was produced at the Court Theatre, Yeats, Synge, and George Moore, a highly self-conscious artist, the first volume of whose autobiographical *Hail and Farewell* appeared in 1911.

George Bernard Shaw, 1856–1950.

Another sign of the Irish renaissance was the formation of the Irish Folksong Society in 1904, and it was now that Cecil Sharp began the collection of English folk-songs by persuading old countrywomen to sing to him, not only in England, but as far afield as the Appalachians, where traditional English tunes still lingered. The young composer Ralph Vaughan Williams was also a collector, for it was his ambition to free English music from German domination, and by returning to folk-song and the Elizabethans to revive the great English tradition. Elgar, now at the height of his powers, had done much for the revival, for his music is as English as it is unmistakably Elgar: his two symphonies, his symphonic poem *Falstaff*, concert overture *Cockaigne*, and the violin concerto, first performed in London by Kreisler in 1910. In the following year the young conductor Thomas Beecham introduced London to the Russian Ballet, the music of Stravinsky and décor of Bakst. The Edwardian era was over, and the Neo-Georgian revolution had begun.

In 1909 the Italian Futurist Manifesto had glorified war, violence, and the machine, the annihilation of all that Morris had stood for. Then came the abstract paintings of Kandinsky, and in 1910 Roger Fry organized the first Post-Impressionist Exhibition, with paintings by Cézanne, Gauguin, Van Gogh, Picasso, Matisse, and the Fauves. Orthodox critics called it 'the negation of civilization', but there was a second exhibition in 1912, as well as a Futurist Exhibition, and in the same year the simplified sculptures of Brancusi were shown in London. After Victorian and Edwardian isolation the sudden revelation of this European art was bewildering. Wyndham Lewis, accepting Cubism and the machine, but considering the Future as remote and sentimental as the Past, that 'the Present is Art', founded Vorticism with its magazine *Blast*, and painted pictures, at first abstract, hard and sharp-edged as metal strips. Essentially a manipulator, he wrote his novel *Tarr* with the same cold metallic quality. Epstein was temporarily affected by Vorticism, representing man as a

Vorticist sculpture. *The Rock Drill*, by Jacob Epstein, 1913–14: the beginning of a new sculpture in England, though its development had to wait for the work of Henry Moore and Barbara Hepworth in the late 1920s.

A Battery Shelled, a painting of the First World War by Wyndham Lewis, founder of Vorticism. Mechanical men, metallic structures and whirling movement.

mechanical monster, and David Bomberg painted *The Mud Bath*, in which the formalized figures of the bathers are welded into a semi-abstract design like a machine in motion. The reaction of the far from revolutionary Sickert was the formation of the Camden Town Group, and the influence of Post-Impressionism can be seen in the colour and impasto of Harold Gilman and Charles Ginner, 'the thickest painters in London', as Sickert called them.

Early in 1914 Clive Bell published *Art*, in which he claimed Cézanne as 'the Christopher Columbus of a new continent of form', and maintained that

The influence of Cubism on British art: *The Mud Bath*, by David Bomberg, *c.* 1912.

'Significant Form', aesthetically moving relations and combinations of lines and colours, 'is the one quality common to all works of visual art'. His friend Roger Fry, in an essay later to be included in *Vision and Design*, commented that now 'the artist is free to choose any degree of representational accuracy which suits the expression of his feeling', and he founded the Omega Workshops to raise the standard of industrial design.

These were the years, 1911–14, in which Granville-Barker was restoring the Elizabethan way of producing Shakespeare, and Hardy writing his most poignant poetry after the death of his wife and revisiting St Juliot. The old Victorian also wrote, as understandably as nostalgically, 'This season's paintings do not please, Like Etty, Mulready, Maclise', and of how 'The bower we shrined to Tennyson is roof-wrecked'. The wreckers were the austere Imagists, and there was nothing revolutionary in the anthologies of *Georgian Poetry* edited by Edward Marsh, in the conventional romanticism of Harold Monro, John Drinkwater, W.H. Davies, and Rupert Brooke, for example, though there were more disturbing poems by a young man, a miner's son, D.H. Lawrence, who published his first important novel in 1913, *Sons and Lovers*. Then in August 1914 came the Great War.

After the Irish Rebellion of Easter 1916 Yeats wrote how all had been changed, 'Transformed utterly: A terrible beauty is born.' The war changed Yeats himself: he realized that 'We had fed the heart on fantasies', his poetry assumed a new strength and authority, and the extent of the change may be judged by comparing the lines about arising and going to Innisfree with those of *Sailing to Byzantium*, one of the great poems of all time. Yeats, 'the last romantic' as he called himself, was not an innovator, but no other poet of the twentieth century has written more memorable lines in the grand manner. An even more terrible beauty was born in Flanders, and this outrageous transformation of nature and man was depicted by the war artists Paul Nash and C.R.W. Nevinson in the premonitory forms of Cubism and Futurism. Then in 1917 T.S. Eliot published his first poems, *Prufrock*:

> Let us go then, you and I,
> When the evening is spread out against the sky
> Like a patient etherised upon a table;
> Let us go, through certain half-deserted streets,
> The muttering retreats
> Of restless nights in one-night cheap hotels
> And sawdust restaurants with oyster-shells.

Clive Bell had written: 'There are things worth expressing that could never have been expressed in traditional forms'; and now the anti-Romantic Eliot: 'The essential advantage of a poet is not to have a beautiful world with which to deal; it is to be able to see the boredom, and the horror, and the glory.' Poetry as well as painting was advancing its frontiers.

T. S. Eliot, 1888–1965.

Rupert Brooke died at the beginning of the war; Wilfred Owen, whose piercing poetry of truth, indignation, and pity was to inspire the poets of the 1930s, was killed a week before its end. Among the survivors were Siegfried Sassoon, Herbert Read, Robert Graves, and Edmund Blunden, but the American-born Eliot emerged as the great post-war poet, and from now on America was to exert a powerful influence on English literature and the other arts: one need only mention Ernest Hemingway, Frank Lloyd Wright, Alexander Calder, Robert Frost, and Jackson Pollock. Eliot himself was influenced by his cosmopolitan countryman Ezra Pound, founder of the Imagist movement in England, whose *Hugh Selwyn Mauberley* appeared in 1920, and there is a similar dramatic form in Eliot's *Waste Land*, which reflected the disillusion of the decade. The abrupt transitions, inspired perhaps by the new art of the cinema, the sudden shifts from banality to splendour, the oblique allusions, echoes, and recondite references made the poem as difficult at the time as for the Jacobeans had been the poetry of Donne, whom Eliot so much admired. And like Donne, Pound, and Eliot, Edith Sitwell felt the need to escape from conventional rhythms, and in 1923 her *Façade*, both flippant and moving, was brilliantly set to music by William Walton.

Walton was only twenty-one, and still had to make his name with his concertos and oratorio *Belshazzar's Feast*, but Vaughan Williams was fifty, an established composer whose experiences during and after the war he expressed in his symphonies, and perhaps in his settings of Housman's *Shropshire Lad*, while such works as the *Fantasia on a Theme by T. Tallis*, the opera *Hugh the Drover* and *Masque of Job* have more obvious affinities with the English tradition. Gustav Holst too, English in spite of his Swedish name, found inspiration in motet, madrigal, and folk-music, though there is, appropriately enough, nothing peculiarly English in *The Planets*, music of the spheres prefiguring the space age.

Other composers who had reached maturity by 1920 were Arnold Bax, whose muse was Celtic rather than Saxon; John Ireland, who made his name with his second *Violin and Piano Sonata* and popular setting of Masefield's *Sea Fever*; and Frank Bridge, whose modest genius was best expressed in chamber music. In music, as in the other arts, the younger men reacted against tradition after the war; Arthur Bliss, another survivor, was only thirty when in 1922 he wrote *A Colour Symphony* with its echoes of Stravinsky, and it is interesting to compare Elgar's serene *Introduction and Allegro for Strings* with the restless, dramatic *Music for Strings* that Bliss wrote soon after Elgar's death in 1934. Constant Lambert, even younger than Walton, and like him a member of the Sitwell circle, wrote for the Russian ballet and varied the rolling rhythms of his *Rio Grande* with jazz, the dance music of the 1920s. Older than any of these was Frederick Delius, whose sinuous music with its surface decoration and tenuous structure has affinities with Art Nouveau. Beecham did his best to make his work known by conducting a Delius Festival in 1929, but his *Requiem* of 1922 had to wait more than forty years for a second performance. Beecham was also responsible for the

'The Lady at the Window.' Scenery by John Armstrong for *Façade*: poems by Edith Sitwell, spoken through a mask and megaphone to the music of William Walton, 1923.

formation in 1922 of the British National Opera Company, which introduced the classics to provincial audiences, and its performance of *The Magic Flute* in 1923 was one of the first broadcasts of the newly formed British Broadcasting Company. Covent Garden, closed during the war, reopened in 1925, the year of the first Dolmetsch Festival at Haslemere, and of the formation of the British Council for the propagation of British art. This was helped by Edward Dent, Professor of Music at Cambridge and President of the International Society for Contemporary Music, while at Edinburgh the scholar-composer Donald Tovey reinterpreted the classics in his books and programme annotations.

While sound radio was bringing good music within the reach of almost every home, and Eliot writing his early poetry, there were significant developments in the art of the novel. Somerset Maugham dispassionately described post-war standards of behaviour, and the young Aldous Huxley, beginning with *Crome Yellow* and *Antic Hay*, mocked the febrile gaiety and despairing vices of the age, and with more serious Swift-like satire fastidiously exposed the grossness of man. Then, in the same year as *The Waste Land*, 1922, came Joyce's monumental *Ulysses*, a day in the life of a Dublin Jew, or rather in his mind, for most of the words are unspoken, some of them indeed, in more senses than one, scarcely speakable, for every detail is recorded and often in a language of Joyce's invention. The nearest precedent to *Ulysses* was *Tristram Shandy*, both of them revolutionary novels, but so original that they could never be repeated, though in *Finnegans Wake* Joyce developed the interior soliloquy to its logical, or illogical, conclusion, for it derives from Freud's explorations of the unconscious mind, and *Ulysses*, despite its realism, is a Surrealist novel. Eliot employed this device of the stream of thought, the unspoken monologue, in his poetry, and so did Virginia Woolf in her novels, though with far greater reticence and delicacy than Joyce – she found *Ulysses* 'underbred, ultimately nauseating' –

James Joyce, 1882–1941.
'Finn, again! Take. Bussoftlhee, mememormee! Till thousendsthee. Lps. The keys to. Given! A way a lone a last a loved a long the'
Last lines of *Finnegans Wake*, 1939.

D.H. Lawrence, 1885–1930.
'My own great religion is a belief in the blood, the flesh, as being wiser than the intellect. We can go wrong in our minds. But what our blood feels and believes and says, is always true.'
From a letter, 1912.

her object being to communicate an impression, a mood, the sensation of living. Perhaps this is why *To the Lighthouse*, 1927, is her most successful novel, for it is a transmutation of her own girlhood experiences in Cornwall.

Virginia Woolf was one of the circle known as the Bloomsbury Group, which included her husband Leonard Woolf, her sister Vanessa, wife of Clive Bell, Roger Fry, E.M. Forster, Maynard Keynes, Lytton Strachey, and Duncan Grant. Most of them were influenced by the philosophy of G.E. Moore, an apostle of common sense with a particular interest in the theory of knowledge and analysis of generally accepted propositions. He found no good reason for belief in God or survival after death, and emphasized the importance of appreciating the good things of this life, personal relationships and the beauty of the world. The background of these Cambridge intellectuals was very different from that of D.H. Lawrence, brought up in the home of a Nottingham miner, and this fiery genius found them cold and emotionally starved. According to Lawrence, modern civilization with its emphasis on reason, science, and the machine, was frustrating the deep, elemental forces of life, and in his novels he preached the gospel of liberating the body's dark unconscious urges. Whatever may be thought of his doctrine, it must be allowed that his novels, though technically conventional and with little claim to style, are the most powerfully impassioned of the century, and he must not be judged by the now notorious *Lady Chatterley's Lover* of 1928, a last despairing attempt to make frankness about sexual relations acceptable; it is as bad a parody of his other novels as *Jude the Obscure* is of Hardy's.

One of the most influential books of the Bloomsbury Group was Roger Fry's *Vision and Design* of 1920, in which he argued that beauty of subject has nothing to do with a work of art, which is 'the expression of an emotion felt by the artist and conveyed to the spectator'. The essential quality was form, though he did not go as far as Clive Bell, who thought 'significant form' might be completely non-representative, and Fry found this form in the art of Giotto, African sculpture, and Cézanne. The other painters of the group, Vanessa Bell and Duncan Grant, were naturally much influenced by Cézanne and Post-Impressionism, as was Matthew Smith by Matisse and the Fauves in his richly

Street Scene, 1962, by L. S. Lowry. A fine example of simplified form: the people breaking away from the centre of the star-shaped crossing.

coloured paintings of the nude. Such work, however, was little more than variations on a now established style, and more original were L. S. Lowry's grey paintings of industrial Lancashire, not unlike Pugin's drawings in *Contrasts*, but more like illustrations of *The Waste Land*, its pathos emphasized by the dark verticals of mill chimneys and isolated human figures. Another essentially English artist, an individualist uninfluenced by new ideas, was Stanley Spencer, who with Pre-Raphaelite realism painted modern-dress versions of New Testament stories, *The Resurrection*, for example, in the churchyard of his native Cookham-on-Thames. The impetus given by Cubism and Futurism appeared to have spent itself. Yet a group of young painters and sculptors had formed the Seven and Five Society, one of whom, Ben Nicholson,

The Wedding at Cana, 1953, by Stanley Spencer (1891–1959). Spencer's paintings have much in common with the visionary art of Blake and Samuel Palmer.

was exhibiting with Christopher Wood, a deceptively naïve painter of Cornish fishing-towns, where they found the untutored sailor Alfred Wallis and his primitive paintings. In 1928 both Henry Moore and Barbara Hepworth had their first London exhibitions, and the stage was set for the revolutionary decade of the 1930s.

It was now, after thirty years of isolation, that the new functional architecture of the Continent, such buildings as Gropius's Bauhaus in Germany, began to influence Britain. The revolution began modestly enough with Charles Holden's designs for London Underground stations and the early work of Owen Williams. Up till this time new factories had been little more than a façade screening old-fashioned works behind, but Williams's factory for Boots near Nottingham was frankly functional reinforced concrete and glass, as was his pioneer Health Centre at Peckham, a community centre as well as a clinic. The new style was applied to domestic architecture by Maxwell Fry in the Sun House, Hampstead, where full use was made of the new materials: flat roof, long window-bands, cantilevered balcony, and in the Ladbroke Grove Flats which incorporated a steel-framed nursery school. The Tecton Group founded by Berthold Lubetkin are perhaps best known for their imaginative Penguin Pool at the London Zoo, but they also built the Highpoint Flats at Highgate, admired as a 'vertical garden city' by Le Corbusier, whose work influenced their Finsbury Health Centre, with its curved and tiled façade, untreated concrete having been found to weather badly in London. One of the first big London stores in the modern idiom was that of Peter Jones by William Crabtree, where steel and glass have the lightness and delicacy of Perpendicular panelling.

International architecture. The Finsbury Health Centre, 1938. The modern style reached England only in the 1930s: functional, stripped of ornament, to emphasize the essential qualities of proportion and relation of parts to one another and the whole.

Abstract art. A *White Relief* of 1935 by Ben Nicholson, which has much in common with modern architecture. The simple geometrical forms are so related to one another that the effect is one of almost planetary serenity.

A number of painters and sculptors were very much in sympathy with this revival of architecture, a structural abstract art of formal relationships, and in 1933 formed another group which included architects, Unit One, their object being, as Paul Nash put it, to give 'structural purpose' to English art. In his paintings of 1931 Ben Nicholson had begun to carve into and incise a gesso ground, but he now began to build in coloured relief, and in 1934 made his first white reliefs, using the geometrical forms of Cubism to construct as it were an architectural façade of asymmetrically related rectangles and circles thrown into relief by recession and shadow. It was also in 1931 that Henry Moore and Barbara Hepworth independently began to pierce their carvings with holes, so adding an architectural dimension to sculpture, the shaping of interior space as well as exterior volume.

Meanwhile, another continental movement was affecting English art, culminating in 1936 with the International Surrealist Exhibition in London,

Reclining Figure, by Henry Moore, 1929. This was inspired by Mexican stone sculpture, in which Moore found an unsurpassed truth to material, power, fertility of form-invention and 'approach to a full three-dimensional conception of form'.

and publication of *Surrealism*, edited by Herbert Read, by now a distinguished critic as well as poet. The very antithesis of Classicism, Surrealism is Romanticism carried to extremes, the unconscious mind being given free play with little or no rational control, so that everyday objects may be equated with the fantastic visions of the dream world. The English, however, are not given to extremes, and though the art of Paul Nash and Henry Moore was affected, it was by little more than 'the addition of strangeness to beauty', which, according to Pater, 'constitutes the romantic character in art'. Moore is not an abstract sculptor; the human figure is his principal interest, though he is not concerned with representing a likeness, but is always aware of correspondences, so that a reclining woman is also mother earth, a landscape fashioned by weather, and similar 'metaphors' animate all his work, giving additional power and vitality to his monumental forms, which have much more in common with primitive Mexican sculpture than with that of classical Greece.

After Hitler's seizure of power in 1933, many foreign artists found refuge in England, among them Gropius, Naum Gabo and Piet Mondrian, an architect, a Constructivist and a painter, and Nicholson's reaction to Surrealism was the editing of *Circle* with Gabo and the architect Leslie Martin, the manifesto of abstract art. The English, with their literary, anecdotal tradition of painting,

Pelagos, by Barbara Hepworth, 1946. 'The colour in the concavities plunged me into the depth of water, caves or shadows. . . . The strings were the tension I felt between myself and the sea, the wind or the hills.'

had little sympathy, and Nicholson pursued his lonely way, his painting becoming little more than a counterpoint of line, shape, and colour, held in a classical repose by the tension of its architectural structure. In the three dimensions of her sculpture Barbara Hepworth pressed along the same path, her work losing its last traces of naturalism as she explored the architectural themes of relationships in space and tensions between forms, and becoming another counterpoint of line and plane, volume and space, light and shadow, a visual music like Nicholson's paintings, the equivalent of a Tallis motet. Many people still fail to understand abstract art, because they confuse 'meaning' with subject, art with nature; yet it should make all art easier to understand, for stripped of all that is merely superficial and ephemeral it reveals those eternal qualities of harmony and proportion that our senses demand.

The British, like most northern people, are temperamentally romantic rather than classical, more subjective than objective in their art, more introvert than extrovert, and Expressionism, a personal interpretation of nature, a less extreme form of Romanticism than Surrealism, was characteristic of much of the art of the 1930s, as it is of that of today. There is an element of Expressionism in the work of Henry Moore, and more still in the emotionally charged and distorted sculptures of Epstein, but because of the colour it is more obvious in paintings of the period. Thus, Ivon Hitchens 'translates' still-life and landscape into semi-abstract forms which by their colour and shape suggest their essential qualities. Graham Sutherland's paintings are almost metaphysical in their imagery: a fallen tree assumes an animal form, a boulder becomes a landscape, and the entrance to a lane a spiral design of leaves, yellow sunlight, and deep shadow. John Piper painted a number of abstract pictures in the middle 1930s, but, essentially a romantic, he turned to landscape and architectural subjects to which he gave his own dramatic interpretations. The imagery of Ceri Richards is more elusive, suggesting music and the sea.

It was inevitable that some artists should react against these extremes of Abstraction and Expressionism, and in 1937 the Euston Road School was founded with the object of restoring the realism of Sickert and his circle. Among the founders were William Coldstream, a distinguished draughtsman and painter of the nude, and Victor Pasmore, a versatile painter of both the indoor and outdoor scene who, however, ten years later was to become a leading exponent of Abstraction.

The decade of the 1930s, which saw the beginnings of a new architecture, of new art forms, and the first significant school of British sculpture since the Middle Ages, was also one of economic and political depression, and these were major themes of the young Oxford poets whose work began to appear in 1930. Thus W.H. Auden:

> Get there if you can and see the land you once were proud to own
> Though the roads have almost vanished and the expresses never run.

Stephen Spender in *Poems*, 1933:

> Oh comrades, let not those who follow after
> – The beautiful generation that shall spring from our sides –
> Let not them wonder how after the failure of banks
> The failure of cathedrals and the declared insanity of our rulers,
> We lacked the Spring-like resources of the tiger.

Cecil Day Lewis in *A Time to Dance*, 1935:

> I sang as one
> Who on a tilting deck sings
> To keep their courage up, though the wave hangs
> That shall cut off their sun.

Louis MacNeice in *Autumn Journal*, 1939:

> Hitler yells on the wireless,
> The night is damp and still
> And I hear dull blows on wood outside my window;
> They are cutting down the trees on Primrose Hill.

Entrance to a Lane, by Graham Sutherland, 1939. 'I found I could express what I felt only by paraphrasing what I saw.'

In 1934 Day Lewis published *A Hope for Poetry*, in which he wrote: 'Post-war poetry was born among the ruins. Its immediate ancestors are Hopkins, Owen and Eliot', and, agreeing with Owen that the poet should warn and be truthful, in clipped colloquial language and contemporary image of machine and war, the new poets exalted 'the vertical man', a legendary explorer, mountaineer, airman, whose example might yet save the world from impending catastrophe. Yet their poems were not all political: Spender is essentially a lyrical poet, Auden more clinical and philosophical, Day Lewis, also a novelist, at his best in narrative, MacNeice in evoking the sensation of living.

Apart from, or opposed to, these 'left-wing intellectuals' were other poets. Robert Graves, an older man, was more concerned with traditional themes and the past, with love, mythology, and history, and published his novel *I, Claudius* as well as his *Collected Poems*. Roy Campbell fought for Franco in the Spanish Civil War, and his poetry reflects the violence of his adventurous life, but better known was John Betjeman, not because he wrote nostalgically of Victoriana and Butterfield churches but because he wrote simply, often with pathos,

A scene from Benjamin Britten's opera *Billy Budd*, 1951. Britten wrote an operetta, *Paul Bunyan*, in 1941, but his first full-length opera was *Peter Grimes* in 1945.

nearly always with humour, about people. His work was a contrast to the esoteric distillations of William Empson, full of deliberate ambiguities, though *Just a Smack at Auden* is as simple as it is genial parody and admirable criticism. As a critic, Empson was influenced by the new 'Cambridge School' of I. A. Richards, who insisted on the meaning rather than the manner of a poem, and F. R. Leavis who, finding much writing superficial, in his books and the periodical *Scrutiny* demanded sincerity and a positive attitude to life.

The novel continued to flourish in the 1930s: there was the robust work of J. B. Priestley both in fiction and the drama, Dickensian in its vitality, the brilliant brittle comedy of Evelyn Waugh's early novels, the realism of Graham Greene's revelations of good and evil, and the prim, sinister conversations, 'something between a novel and a play', of Ivy Compton-Burnett. Other distinguished women novelists active at this time were Rose Macaulay, Rebecca West, Elizabeth Bowen, and Rosamond Lehmann. Then, as might be expected in this troubled decade, there were political novels, inspired mainly by the decline of liberalism and rise of dictatorships. George Orwell passionately defended liberty and the common man, and his last book, *1984*, written after the war, was a warning, a terrible vision of the totalitarian State. Rex Warner's allegories, *The Aerodrome* and *The Professor*, exposed the potential weakness of liberalism in conflict with extremists, and in *Mr Norris Changes Trains* and *Goodbye to Berlin* Christopher Isherwood portrayed the decline of German liberalism which prepared the way for Hitler.

Isherwood was a friend of Auden, and in 1935–6 they collaborated in writing two plays, *The Dog beneath the Skin* and *The Ascent of F6*, the first little more than a charade, the other more serious, both of them political, topical, and satirical, important mainly because they were attempts to revive the poetic drama, virtually dead since the seventeenth century. The nearest approach that was at the same time good theatre had been the lyrical prose of Synge's Irish peasants, though there was an element of poetry in the speech of Sean O'Casey's back-street Dublin characters in *Juno and the Paycock* and *The Plough and the Stars*. Then in 1935 came Eliot's *Murder in the Cathedral*, the dialogue of which, recalling that of the old morality play *Everyman*, formed a contrast to the expansive poetry of the Chorus of Canterbury women. During this decade Shaw was writing his last plays, and was eighty-two when *Geneva* was produced in 1938. Mussolini and Hitler appeared as the harmlessly inflated Bombardone and sentimental Battler, and within a year the Second World War had begun.

Another friend of Auden's was the young composer Benjamin Britten, who wrote incidental music for his plays, and in 1934 when only twenty-one attracted attention with *A Boy Was Born*, a setting of carols for unaccompanied voices. It was well that a new star had risen when the old ones were setting, for 1934 was a year of great loss for British music, Elgar, Delius, and Holst all dying within a few months of one another. This was also the year of the first festival of opera at Glyndebourne in Sussex, and musically the decade was remarkable for its opera and ballet. It began with the Camargo Society's production of Vaughan Williams's *Job*, and formation of the first British ballet company, the Ballet Rambert. The old Sadler's Wells Theatre was restored, and became the home of ballet and of opera sung in English – not in Italian or German. At Covent Garden the orchestra for the summer season of opera was the London Philharmonic, formed out of the Royal Philharmonic Society by the indefatigable Beecham, while Lord Berners, Walton, and Lambert all wrote music for the ballet, and in 1937 came the international success of Bliss's *Checkmate*. These pre-war years were also those of Edmund Rubbra's first two symphonies, and of Michael Tippett's first memorable work, the polyphonic *Concerto for Double String Orchestra*, performed at Morley College in 1940 shortly before its destruction by a bomb.

Checkmate, a ballet of 1937 with music by Arthur Bliss and choreography by Ninette de Valois. Two costumes by E. McKnight Kauffer: Black King and Black Knight.

The war years were no time for building, but merely of saving as much as possible – Queen's Hall went in 1941 – and again, as in 1914–18, war artists discovered a strange beauty in destruction. For Paul Nash, crashed German bombers became a Dead Sea, a metallic glacier, John Piper painted dramatic grey and gold backcloths of the ruins of Georgian Bath, and Henry Moore drew disquieting perspectives of reclining figures in London Tube shelters. Writers had little chance for major work, but Cyril Connolly's review *Horizon* gave them the chance to express themselves briefly both in verse and prose. For Connolly the departure of Auden and Isherwood for America was a symptom of the failure of social realism as an aesthetic doctrine, and he looked for a return to literature as an art in which politics were irrelevant. Day Lewis, Spender, and MacNeice were already abandoning political themes, Edith

All Saints Chapel, Bath, by John Piper, 1942. Piper was employed as an official war artist, and his gouaches proved a splendid medium for recording the dramatic and lurid scenes of the bombing of Bath.

Group of Figures in Underground Shelter, by Henry Moore, 1941. Moore's shelter drawings are the drawings of a sculptor, concerned not with facial expression but with the solid forms of human bodies, sometimes nobly, sometimes grotesquely, grouped or huddled inside a London 'tube'.

Sitwell writing majestically in terms of gold and green and elemental imagery, the young men George Barker and David Gascoyne, influenced by Surrealism, discovered the freedom of a new Romanticism, and in 1944 Dylan Thomas wrote ecstatically of his 'thirtieth year to heaven'. The greatest event of the war years in poetry, however, was Eliot's *Four Quartets*, Anglican meditations on time and eternity. In music the most memorable events were Tippett's *A Child of Our Time*, an oratorio based on a Jewish boy's shooting of a Nazi official, and Britten's opera *Peter Grimes*, a dramatic version of a poem by George Crabbe. It was produced at Sadler's Wells in June 1945, shortly before the dropping of the first atomic bomb. A new age had begun.

It was also an age of television, of the long-playing gramophone record, and in Britain of Government patronage of the arts through the Arts Council, incorporated in 1946 as part of the Welfare State. The Government, and public authorities such as the London County Council, were also responsible for the urgently needed buildings, particularly houses and schools, to replace those destroyed during the war. Shortage of materials meant standardization and prefabrication, yet the Roehampton Estate built by Leslie Martin and Robert H. Matthew for the L.C.C., blocks of flats and maisonettes in open country near Richmond Park, is a notable example of what can be done by imaginative planning. Then there are the new towns, not merely dormitories, but planned for living, each with the essentials of its own community life, as at Harlow and Stevenage near London, and Cumbernauld near Glasgow; and England's new schools, light and functional, pioneered by C. H. Aslin in Hertfordshire, have set a standard for the rest of the world.

To implement the Education Act of 1944, many new schools were urgently needed, and this primary school at Pentley Park, Welwyn Garden City, is an example of the simple buildings that could be quickly erected from standardized prefabricated parts, and arranged in various ways.

Then, after the early post-war austerities came a time to relax and celebrate the centenary of the Great Exhibition of 1851. Many distinguished architects made their contributions to this Festival of Britain, among them Maxwell Fry, Jane Drew, and Basil Spence, and the whole was directed by Hugh Casson, who was able to introduce the public to the new art of 'townscape', the aesthetically satisfying disposition of buildings, in much the same way as landscape was planned in the eighteenth century. The one permanent building was the Royal Festival Hall, designed by the L.C.C. architects Robert Matthew and Leslie Martin, a great rectangular concert hall insulated within an outer shell, the long horizontal windows of which reveal the spaciousness of its surrounding public rooms and promenades, a splendid memorial to the first modern building, the Crystal Palace.

Whatever Prince Albert and Ruskin might have thought of the Festival Hall had they seen it, they would have been, to put it moderately, surprised

The Royal Festival Hall on the South Bank of the Thames, designed by Leslie Martin and Robert Matthew for the Festival of Britain, 1951. This view of the riverside terrace shows how the glass wall increases the spaciousness of the interior.

New materials and new forms of the 1950s. (*Left*) *Box*, 1952, by Reg Butler, architect, engineer and wartime blacksmith. In his later work he has turned to the female figure, often in movement in space.

by the sculpture, so very different from that of 1851. There was the monumental work of Moore and Barbara Hepworth, but younger men in the new Expressionist idiom were beginning to make their names: F.E. McWilliam, a sculptor of rare imagination and wide sympathies; Reg Butler, who applied his knowledge of architecture and engineering to sculpture in wrought and welded iron; Lynn Chadwick, whose insecure spindly-legged creatures were also the

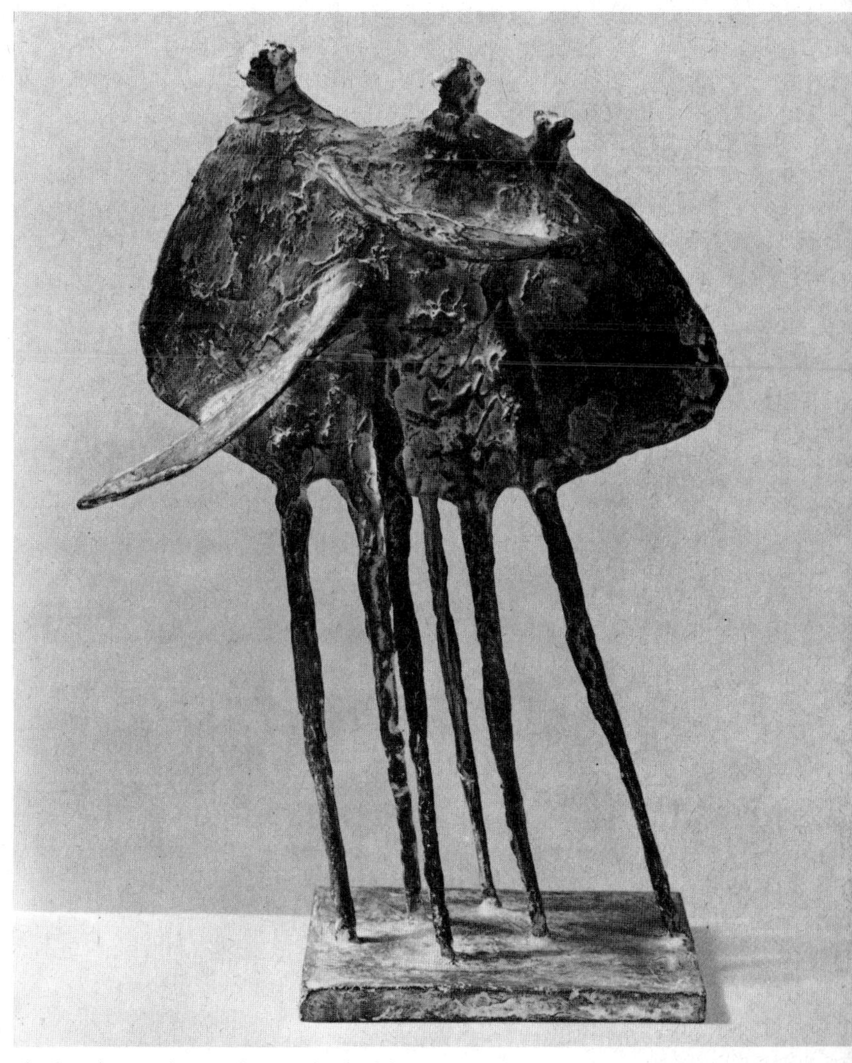

(*Centre*) *Encounter IV*, 1956, by Lynn Chadwick, another sculptor who had been trained as an engineer.
(*Right*) *Walking Group*, 1951, an early work by Kenneth Armitage.

work of an engineer; Kenneth Armitage, whose human figures suggested man's helplessness and kinship with the insects. Even more disquieting expressions of the age of anxiety and guilt, of the Bomb, Cold War, and Belsen, were the paintings of Francis Bacon, the magnificent and violent colour of which powerfully emphasized the horror of the distorted, screaming faces.

Henrietta Moraes, by Francis Bacon, 1966.

The Expressionism of Bacon is very close to Surrealism and the world of nightmare, and there was something of Surrealism, though without the horror, in the poetry of Dylan Thomas, the most significant new work of the post-war years. Reacting against the flat statement and satire of the pre-war poets and giving rein to his Celtic imagination, he encouraged image to beget image in rich profusion, a process that sometimes produced obscure rhetoric, though generally poetry, as in *Fern Hill*:

Dylan Thomas in 1938, aged twenty-four.

> Now as I was young and easy under the apple boughs
> About the lilting house and happy as the grass was green,
> The night above the dingle starry,
> Time let me hail and climb
> Golden in the heydays of his eyes,
> And honoured among wagons I was prince of the apple towns
> And once below a time I lordly had the trees and leaves
> Trail with daisies and barley
> Down the rivers of the windfall night.

His last work was *Under Milk Wood*, first presented as a reading in New York, shortly before his death in 1953. The public-house humour and pathos of this 'Play for Voices' was very different from the dry *Cocktail Party* verse of Eliot, and the witty, self-conscious poetry of Christopher Fry's comedies, *A Phoenix too Frequent*, *The Lady's Not for Burning*, and *Venus Observed*, which in the late 1940s brought a welcome though brief revival of the poetic drama.

There was a parallel movement to revive English opera. Britten, an admirer of Purcell, composer of the first great English opera, *Dido and Aeneas*, formed his own English Opera Group, who performed his *Rape of Lucretia* at Glyndebourne in 1946, and the Wilde-like *Albert Herring* in the following year. Words, particularly English poetry, inspire Britten, and in 1951 came *Billy Budd* with libretto by E.M. Forster and Eric Crozier, and in 1953 *Gloriana*, an opera of Elizabeth I celebrating the accession of Elizabeth II with words by William Plomer. Tippett prefers to be his own librettist, for the words must exactly express his meaning, as in the symbolism, too obscure for popular appreciation, of *The Midsummer Marriage*, produced at Covent Garden in 1955. The post-war decade had been a good time for music, and saw the formation of annual festivals at Edinburgh, Cheltenham, and Aldeburgh, the little town on the Suffolk coast which Britten had made his home. Barbara Hepworth had designed the sets for *The Midsummer Marriage*, and by this time her abstract sculpture had at last received international recognition, as had the painting of Ben Nicholson, now joined in the exploration of abstraction by Merlyn Evans, Victor Pasmore, and William Scott.

Relief painting in white, black, ochre and maroon, by Victor Pasmore, 1956–66. After winning fame as a landscape painter, Pasmore turned to abstraction in 1948.

With few exceptions, Conrad's for example, English novels had been about England, but the war and air travel brought an extension of place. Thus, the scene of Graham Greene's *The Heart of the Matter* was West Africa, of his *The Quiet American* Indo-China; in his Guy Crouchback trilogy, beginning with *Men at Arms* in 1952, Evelyn Waugh made use of his war experiences in Crete; the poet Lawrence Durrell wrote about other Mediterranean islands, and in *Justine*, first of a series of four novels in unfashionably decorative prose, about Alexandria. The Proustian novel in several volumes had become fashionable, and somewhat Proustian in manner as well was the first instalment of Anthony Powell's long sequence *The Music of Time*. More functional in style, no doubt because the work of a scientist, was C.P. Snow's sequence *Strangers and Brothers*, of which *The Masters*, a struggle for power in a Cambridge college, is the most memorable. Most of these novels had an upper-class background of public school, Oxford or Cambridge, but in the middle 1950s there was a dramatic change. In 1954 came William Golding's *Lord of the Flies*, an allegory of the collapse of civilization after the dropping of atomic bombs, played by a gang of prep school boys who murder their social inferior. This was a warning, and so up to a point was Samuel Beckett's macabre play *Waiting for Godot*, though it was primarily an exposure of the futility of many people's lives. Meanwhile Kingsley Amis had published *Lucky Jim*, a satirical novel about life at a Redbrick university, and John Osborne's *Look Back in Anger*, produced at the Royal Court Theatre in 1956, was the tragi-comedy of Jimmy Porter, graduate of a 'not even red brick, but white tile' university and a neurotic misfit who revenged himself on society by humiliating his socially superior wife. The young Oxford poets of the poverty-stricken 1930s had felt guiltily over-privileged and therefore angry, the young Redbrick dramatists of the affluent 1950s were angry because they felt that their generation, first products of the Education Act of 1944, remained underprivileged outsiders in a class-ridden society. Arnold Wesker gave further reasons for his indignation in his play *Roots*: '"We know where the money lie," they say, "hell we do! The workers 've got it so let's give them what they want. If they want slop songs and film idols we'll give 'em that then. If they want words of one syllable, we'll give 'em that then. If they want the third rate, *blust*! we'll give 'em *that* then. Anything's good enough for them 'cos they don't ask for no more!" The whole stinkin' commercial world insults us and we don't care a damn.'

Twentieth-century culture is more complex, more varied, and at its extremities thinner than ever before. The culture of Anglo-Norman times was essentially that of the Church; in the thirteenth and fourteenth centuries it became more courtly and aristocratic, though still dominated by French fashions, but by the fifteenth century, with the breakdown of feudalism, rise of a middle class and enfranchisement of the serfs, a vigorous native folk-culture flourished, that of miracle play, folk-song, and ballad. The Reformation at the beginning of the sixteenth century inevitably meant the secularization of culture, which was disseminated by the printing-press, and the Elizabethan drama was so vigorous because it appealed to all classes of society. The impact of the European Renaissance in the seventeenth century produced a split between aristocratic and popular culture, between, for example, the Restoration theatre and the art of Bunyan, and the culture of the eighteenth century remained predominantly classical and aristocratic. The Industrial Revolution and enfranchisement of a new wealthy middle class led to a lowering of standards and the complacent insularity of Victorian times, while the spread of elementary education and rudimentary literacy created a demand for more entertaining forms of art, a demand greatly intensified in our own day, despite our rediscovery of the European tradition and a more serious interest in the arts.

Clearly there is something wrong, but then there always has been something wrong. For the great majority of people, the England of 1966 is a far better place to live in than that of 1066 or any of the ninety intervening decades, and it is no fault of the young that they have few responsibilities and more leisure and money than ever before, and only partly their fault that, instead of creating a culture comparable to that of the folk-song and ballad of their forefathers, they buy the fashionable ready-made entertainment of pop art and slop song so eagerly offered by their exploiters. These are the mischief-makers, but as the standard of education rises, the demand for this dispensable sub-culture will fall, and something better will take its place. And when children are taught a belief in man, an appreciation of his creative achievements, and a realization of his potentialities, there will be a lightening of the load of disillusion and uncertainty, anxiety and despair that so oppresses us and our culture.

Look Back in Anger, by John Osborne, 1956. 'I said she's an old bitch, and should be dead!' Jimmy Porter attacks his wife Alison, by insulting her mother.

Yet the malaise is not peculiar to this country, and in spite of all, in spite of ignorance and philistinism, it may be that English culture and its art *as a whole* have never stood higher than now, as we approach the last quarter of the century. Of course there have been periods that far exceeded the present in one or more forms of art, the age of Shakespeare and Byrd, for example, yet even in that wonderful era there was little English painting of importance, and even less sculpture, and in the eighteenth and nineteenth centuries, with very few exceptions, there was neither music nor drama nor sculpture that counted. It is true that today there is no outstanding literary figure, but there is much good verse and good prose, and the National Theatre, to mention only the most important of the new playhouses and companies, and the work of John Osborne, Harold Pinter, Robert Bolt, and others are evidence of the vigour of the drama. Again, although we cannot boast of modern buildings that rival the best of those in Europe and America, and there is an unwelcome proliferation of box-like houses and unimaginative blocks of city offices, we have the architects, and the new universities that they are building – Denys Lasdun's University of East Anglia is a fine example – may well lead to another cultural revolution.

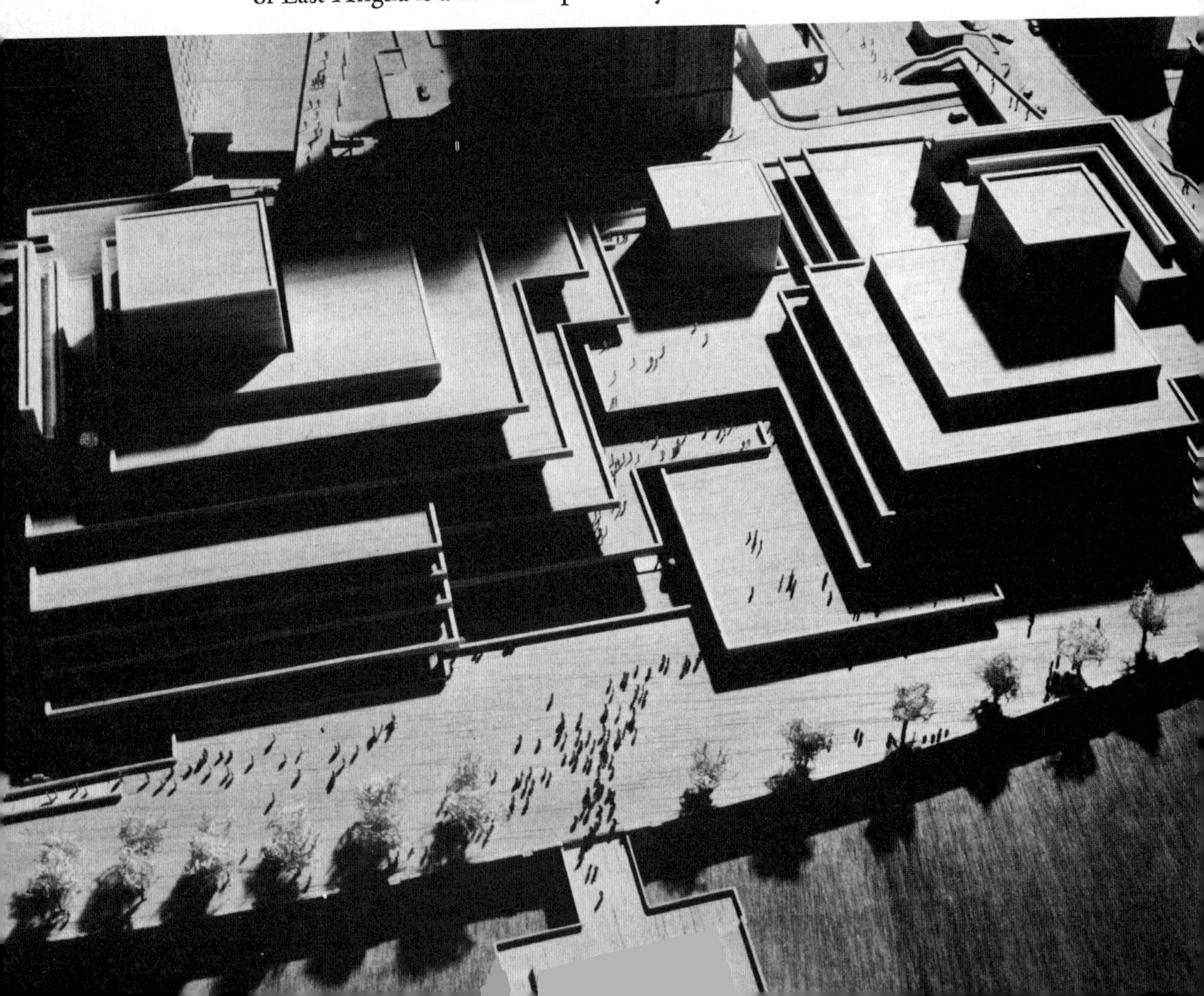

Contrapuntal, 1953,
by Ben Nicholson.
'Harmony and counterpoint
made visible, a concord of
colour, plane and line.'

Stoneware covered pot, 1965,
by Bernard Leach.

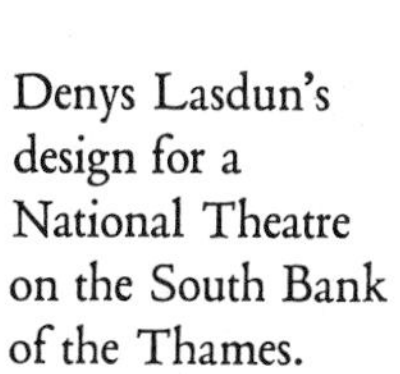

Denys Lasdun's
design for a
National Theatre
on the South Bank
of the Thames.

King and Queen, 1952–3, Henry Moore.

The quality of English architecture has almost always been high, and England's greatest glory is its literature, but only once has it been famous for its music, once only for its painting, and never for its sculpture. Yet today we have composers who are the equals of those in any other country – one thinks particularly of Britten's recent *War Requiem* and Tippett's *St Augustine* – women as well as men, Priaulx Rainier and Elisabeth Lutyens being among the most distinguished, painters who receive international acclaim, in Bernard Leach the master potter of the western world, and for the first time in our history sculptors who have led the world in the creation of new forms. It is sometimes complained that there has been a break with tradition, yet a carving by Henry Moore or Barbara Hepworth has much in common with the monumental forms of Neolithic tombs and Stonehenge, a painting by Ben Nicholson by its quality of line goes back to Nicholas Hilliard and the Middle Ages, and beyond that to the bone carvings of palaeolithic man in the caves of Derbyshire, with which the cultural history of England began.

List of Illustrations

The publishers wish to thank all authorities, museums, galleries and libraries by whose courtesy works are reproduced in this book, and the Syndics of the Fitzwilliam Museum, Cambridge; the Trustees of the Chatsworth Settlement; the Trustees of the British Museum; the Trustees of Sir John Soane's Museum; the Trustees of the Tate Gallery, London; the Visitors of the Ashmolean Museum, Oxford.

Chapter 1

Chapter 2

Chapter 3

Chapter 4

Chapter 5

Chapter 6

Chapter 7

Chapter 8

Chapter 9

Chapter 10

Chapter 11

Chapter 12

Chapter 13

Chapter 14

Index

Numbers in italics refer to illustrations